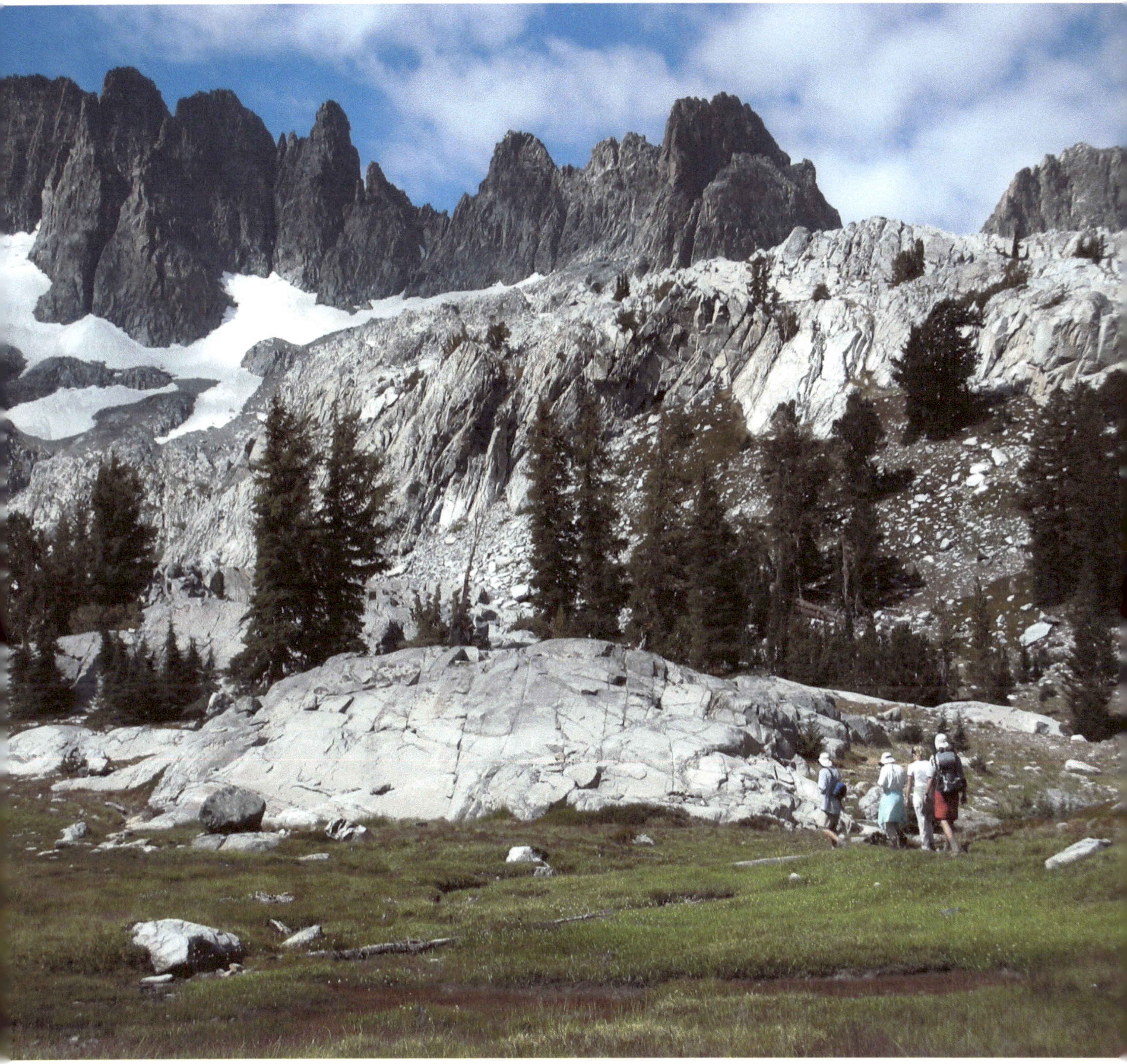

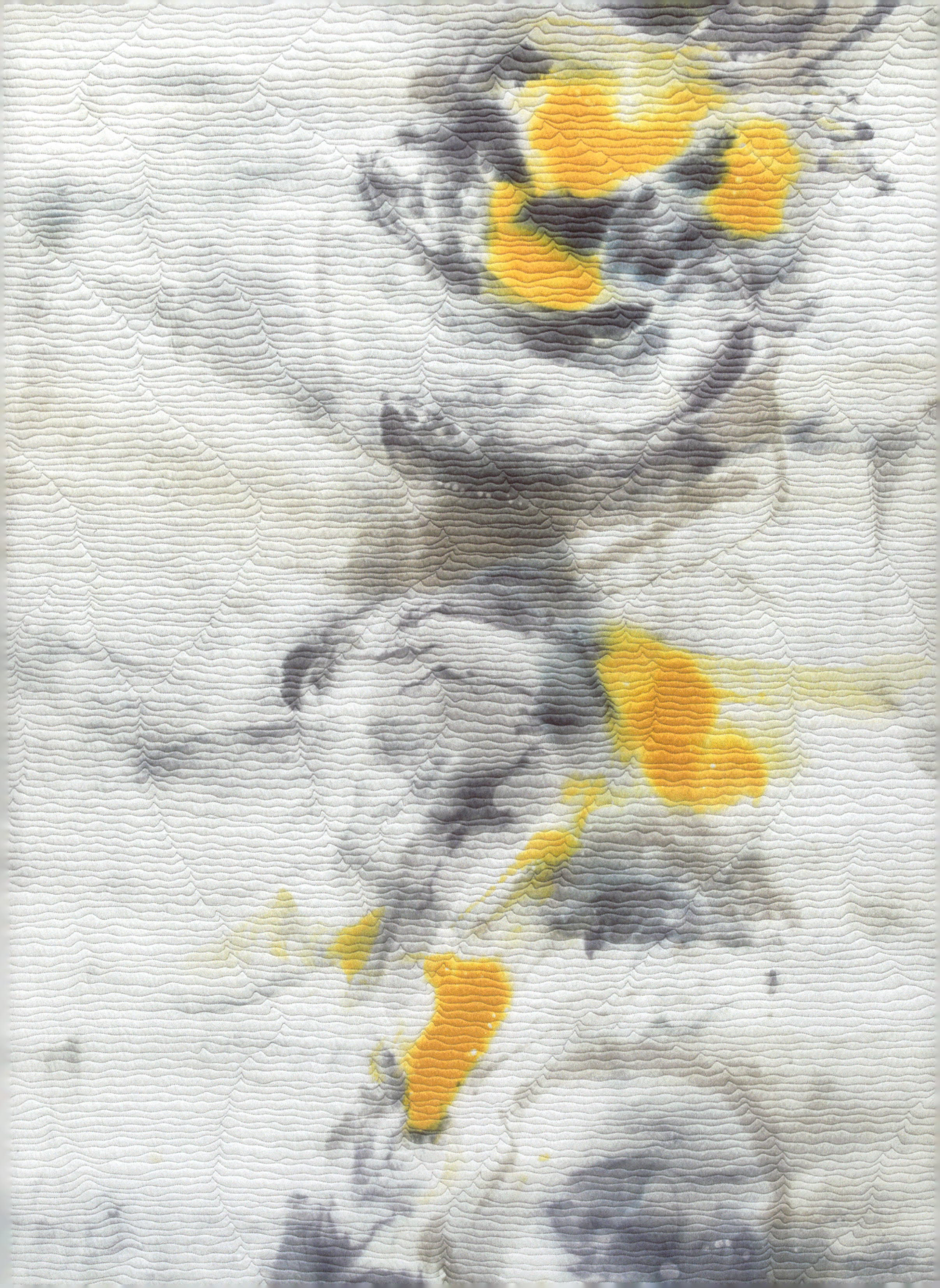

The Contact: Sierra Nevada, Dyed & Stitched

Ann Johnston

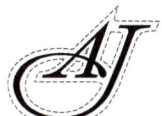

ANN JOHNSTON, PUBLISHER
LAKE OSWEGO, OREGON
USA

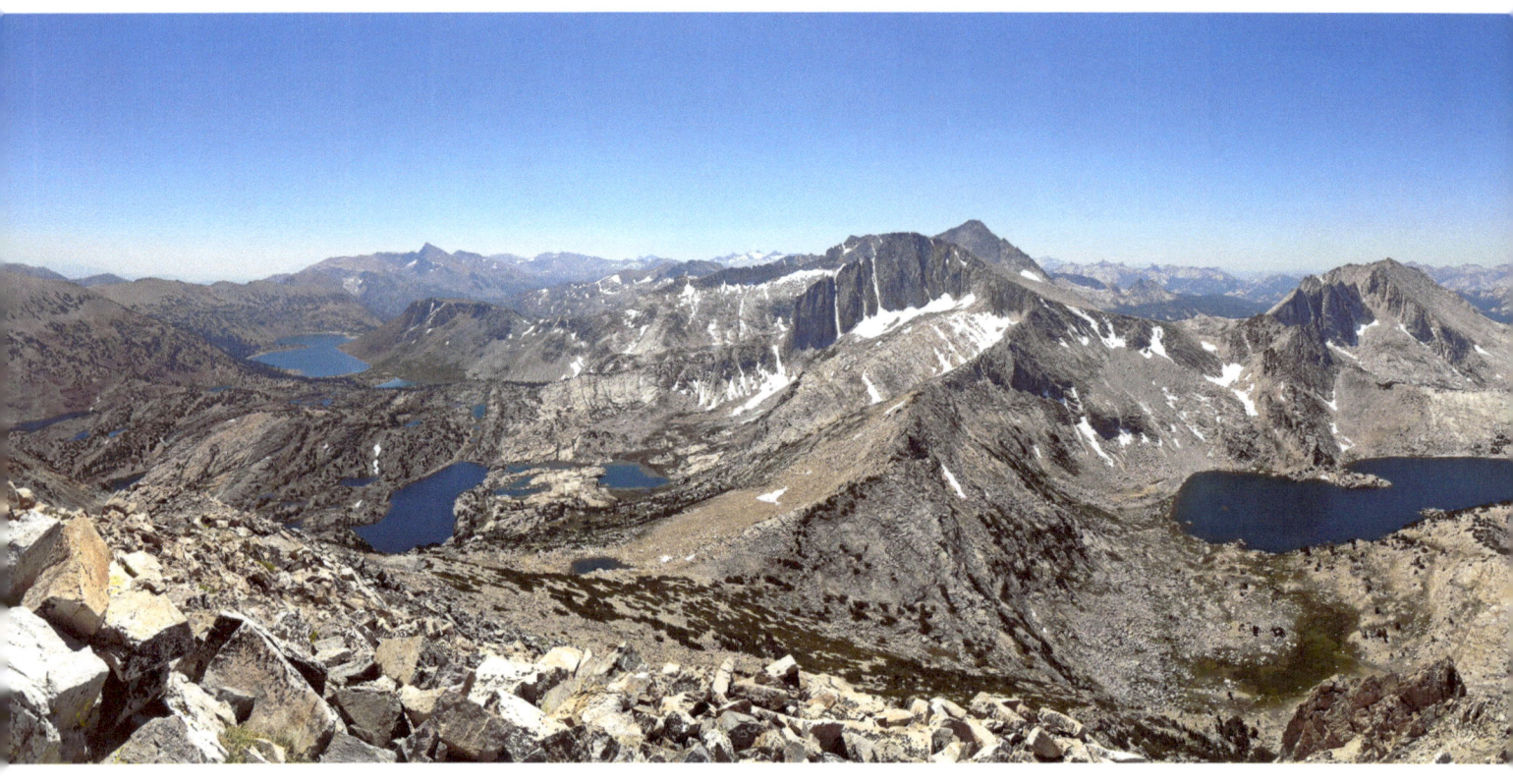

The Contact: Sierra Nevada, Dyed and Stitched
© 2017 Ann Johnston

ISBN 978-0-9656776-6-0

Library of Congress Control Number: 2017900695

QUILT PHOTOGRAPHY
Bill Bachhuber
Dan Kvitka

OTHER PHOTOGRAPHS
Jim, Scott, Elena, Tod, Molly, and Ann Johnston

DESIGN
Ann Marra

Front cover: "Eureka Chimney" detail. • Back cover: "Cross Polarized Granite" back detail. • Frontispiece: "Deep Blue Lead" detail.

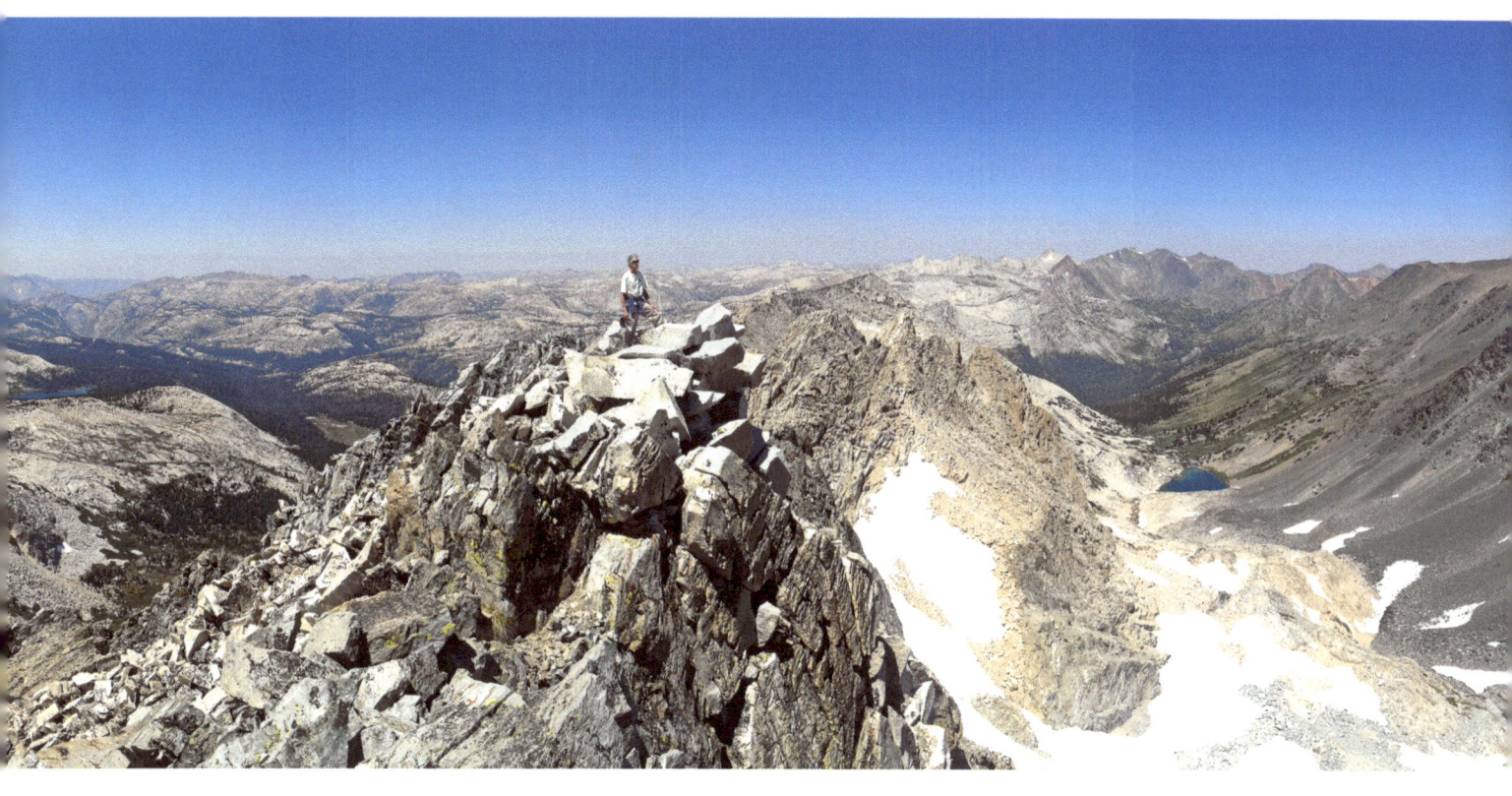

for Jim

THE CONTACT: CONTENTS

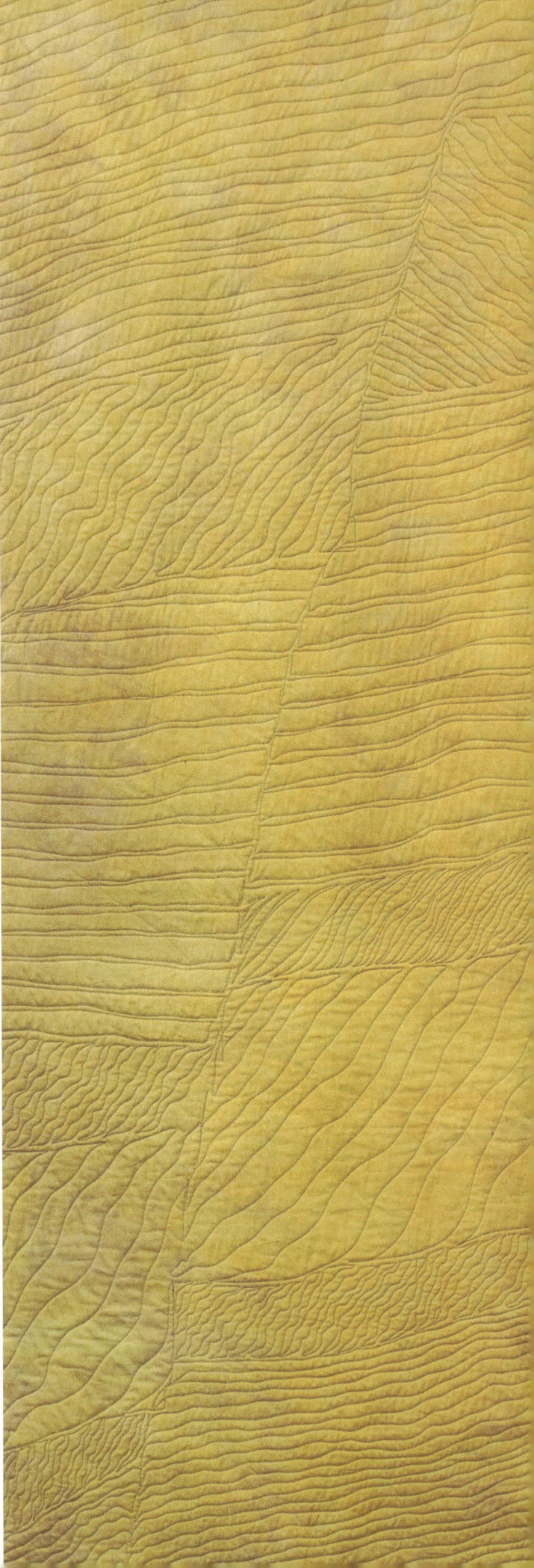

INTRODUCTION	8
GALLERY	12
GOLD FEVER 110 MA	14
NEVADAN OROGENY	16
CROSS POLARIZED GABBRO	18, 20
CROSS POLARIZED GRANITE	19, 21
INSIDE GRANITE	22
PRESSURE SENSITIVE	24
SHEETED INTRUSION	28
TUOLUMNE INTRUSIVE SUITE	30
CRACKED AND COOKED	32
BLACK AND WHITE	34
SPLIT	36
AFTER THE ICE	38
VIGIL	40
VERTICAL JOINTS	44
CIRQUE 1	46, 48
CIRQUE 2	47, 49
DEEP BLUE LEAD	50
EUREKA CHIMNEY	52
SKYLINE	54
SHEEPHERDER'S LEDGE	58
HEADWATERS	64
STAMP MILL	66
07.25.2012; 19:55	68, 70
07.25.2012; 20:13	69, 71
NEW NAILS	72
SOUPTIME	74
DRY LAKE	76
TALUS	78
SMOKE AT SUNSET	82
CLIMAX FOREST	84
SIERRA HONEYMOON	86

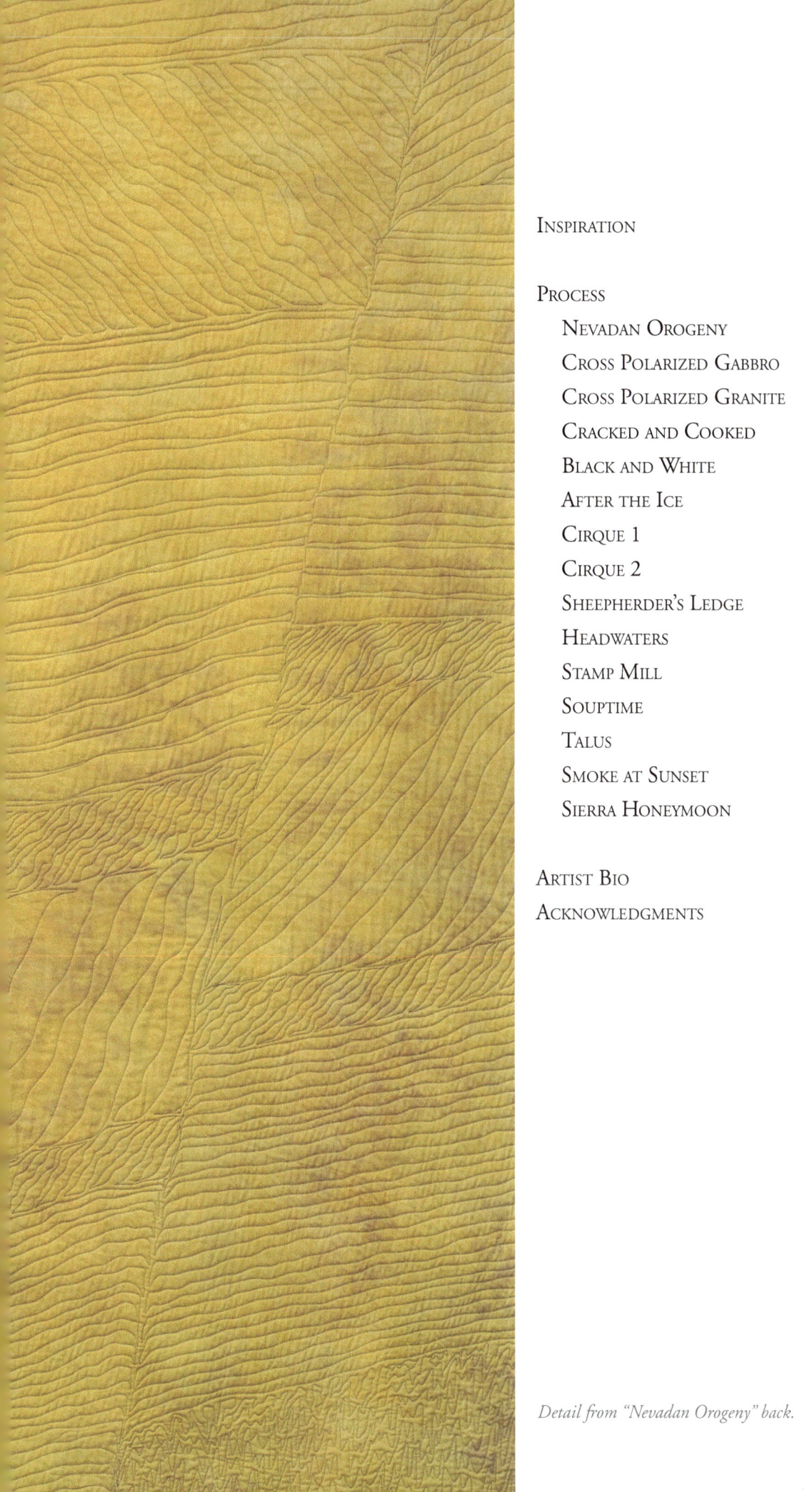

INSPIRATION   90

PROCESS   102

    NEVADAN OROGENY   106

    CROSS POLARIZED GABBRO   108

    CROSS POLARIZED GRANITE   112

    CRACKED AND COOKED   114

    BLACK AND WHITE   116

    AFTER THE ICE   118

    CIRQUE 1   120

    CIRQUE 2   121

    SHEEPHERDER'S LEDGE   124

    HEADWATERS   126

    STAMP MILL   128

    SOUPTIME   130

    TALUS   132

    SMOKE AT SUNSET   136

    SIERRA HONEYMOON   138

ARTIST BIO   143

ACKNOWLEDGMENTS   144

Detail from "Nevadan Orogeny" back.

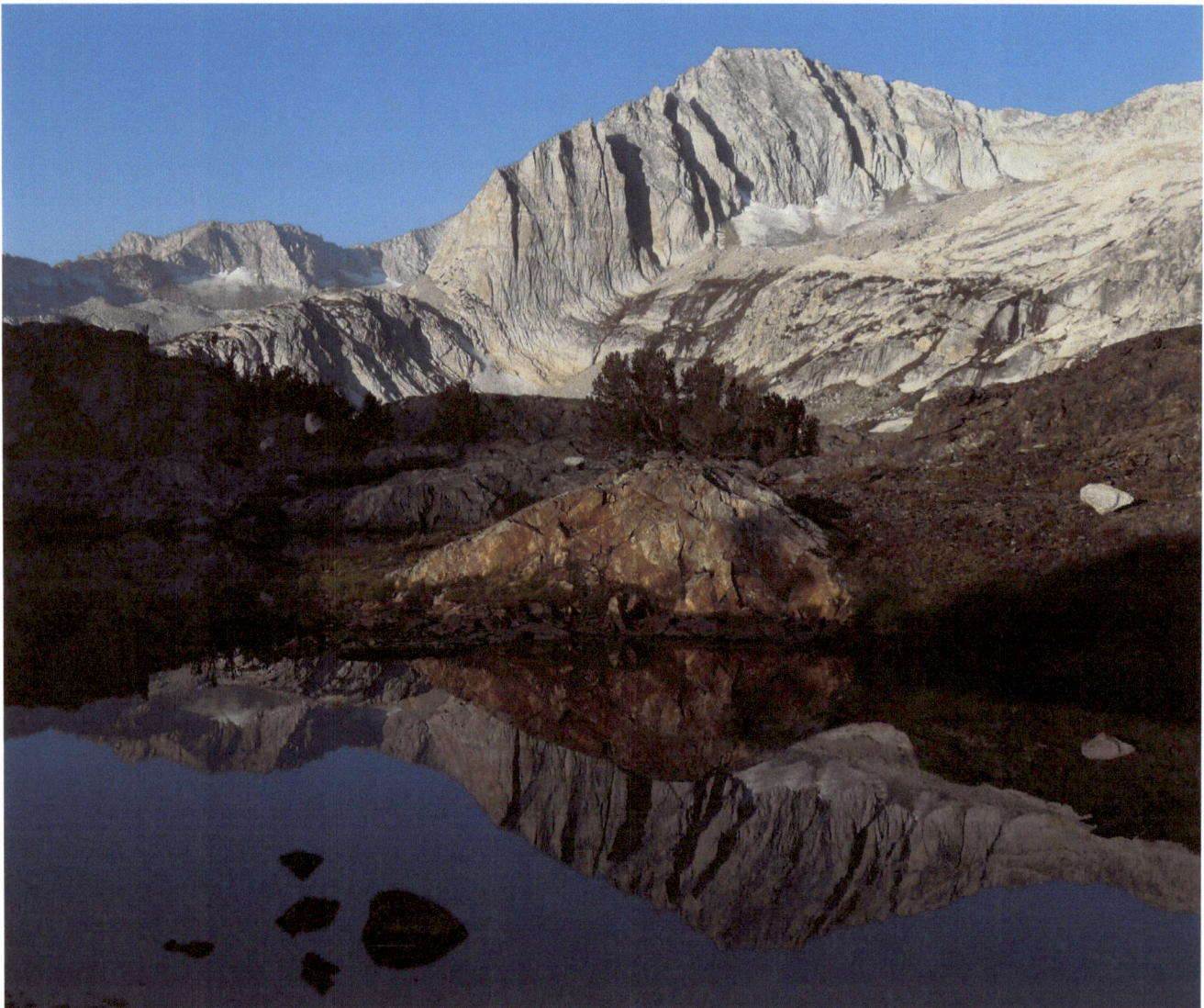

The word "contact" refers to a place where geologic units touch each other. A mining claim at 11,000 feet, near Tioga Pass, California, has been in my family since before it was patented in a deed dated 1881. It is a place where you can see bands of colors in the earth, mineral-rich rock layers that have been squeezed and heated between intrusions of light granites on the west and the dark meta-sedimentary and meta-volcanic rocks on the east. The word "contact" also conjures a human influence on the landscape. The forests, the rivers, and even the mountains themselves have been shaped forever by people seeking their fortunes.

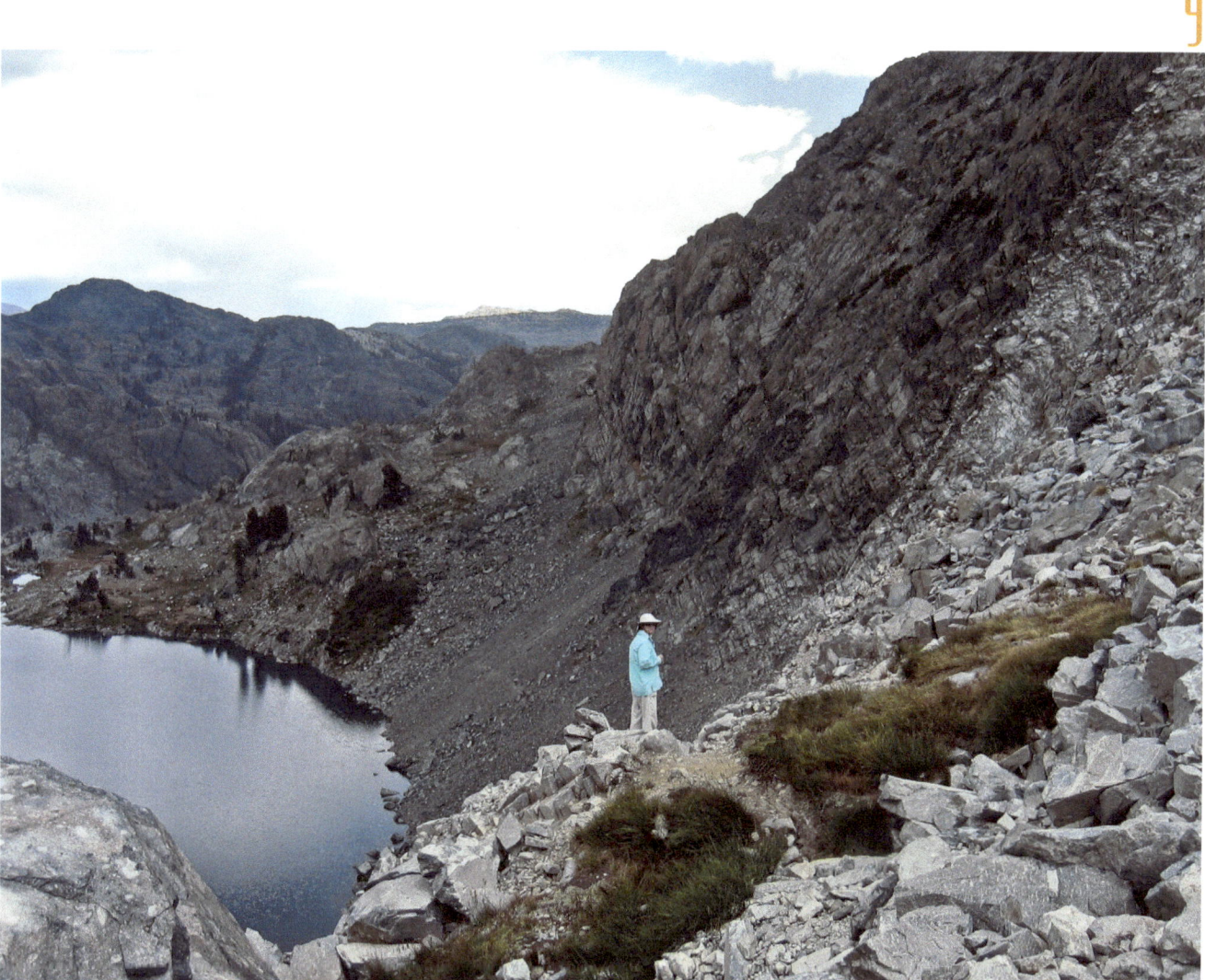

The Contact comprises 31 works so far, most of them seven feet tall—a scale in keeping with the very vertical subject matter of the Sierra Nevada. This project has required me to study the history and geology of California, as well as the documents and stories passed on from my parents. It has also required me to develop more surface design techniques and precision color mixing as I dye many very large pieces of fabric. In addition to hand-manipulated low-water immersion dyeing, I use thickened dyes with brushes, sponges, rollers, scrapers, silk screens, and water-soluble resists for smooth gradations of colors and layers of visual texture. My creative process has involved both looking at what is there on the land at present, as well as trying to imagine events unseen.

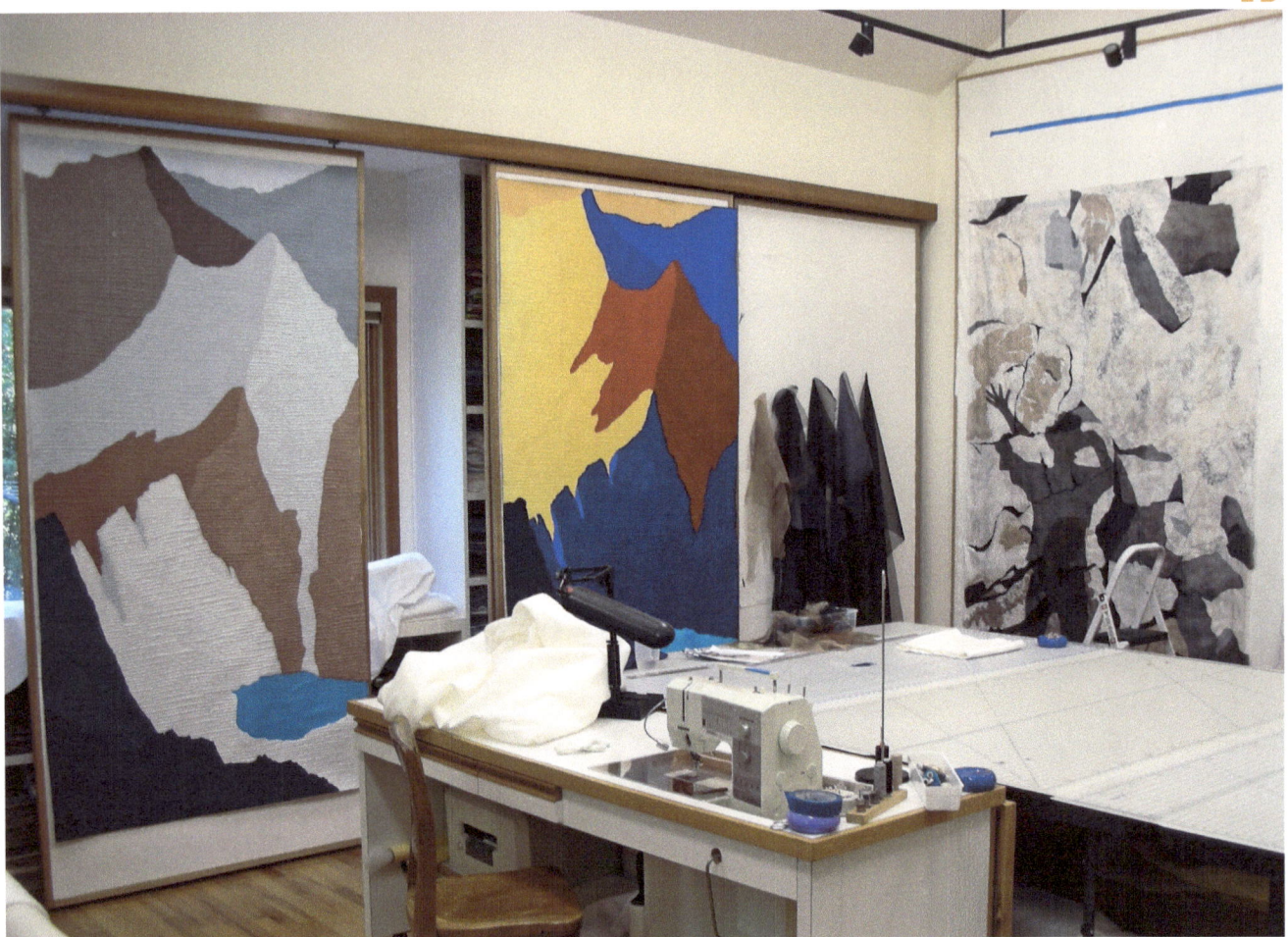

Each design required different construction techniques: some are whole cloth and some are many parts, pieced and appliquéd. Each work represents multiple transitions in idea and design—from the 7-inch to the 7-foot drawings, from pure white cloth to yards of complex dyed colors and patterns, and from the flat assembled fabric compositions to the dimensional surface created by machine and hand stitching through the fiber layers.

I use a broad array of literal, abstract, and purely imaginative imagery and envision them viewed all at once, as one body of work. I started working on the concept in 2011 after I had been invited to do a solo exhibit of 14 pieces by the Martin Museum of Art. Since then, I have been able to exhibit the growing series in several other places. When you ask, I will tell you that I am not finished yet!

ANN JOHNSTON
January, 2017

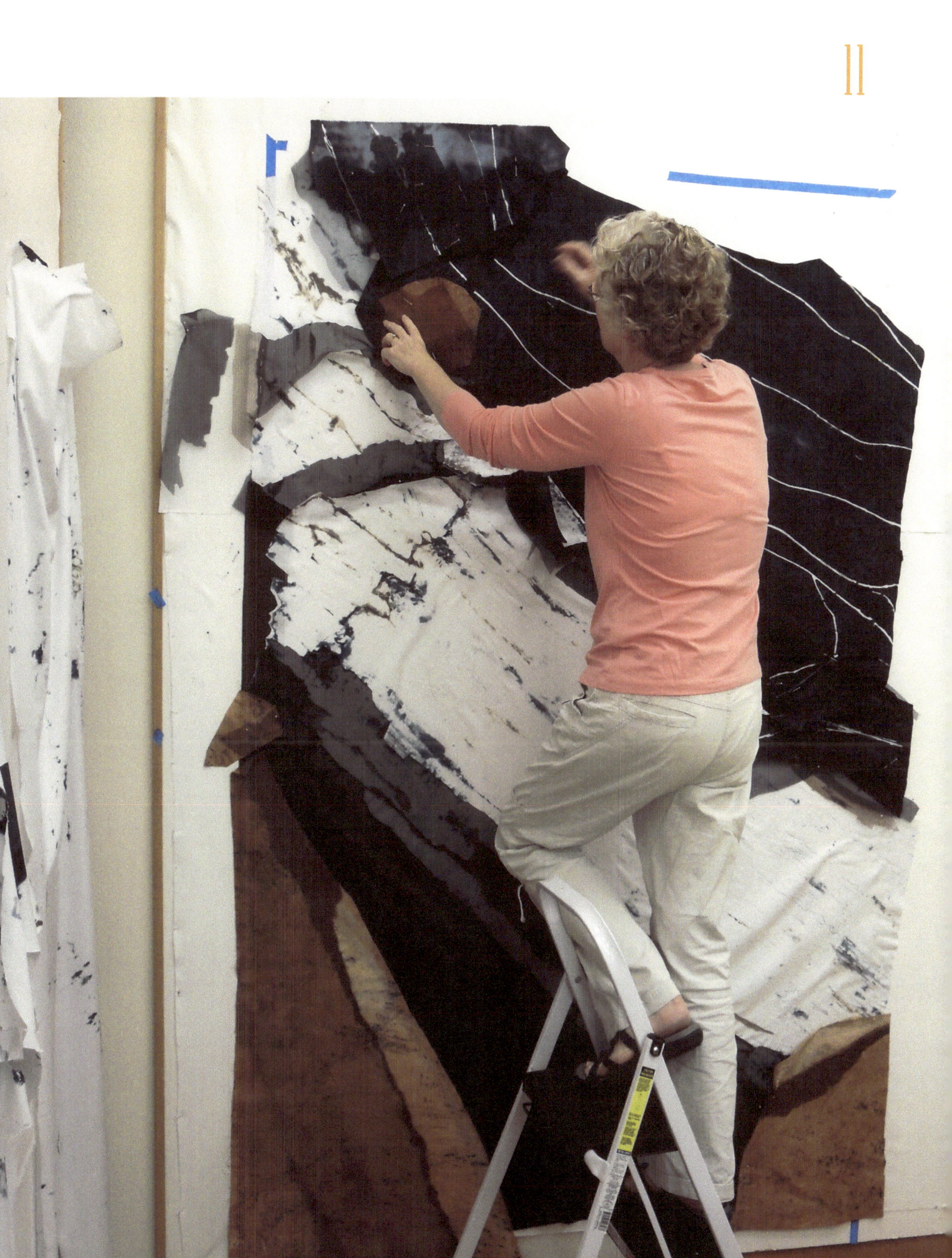

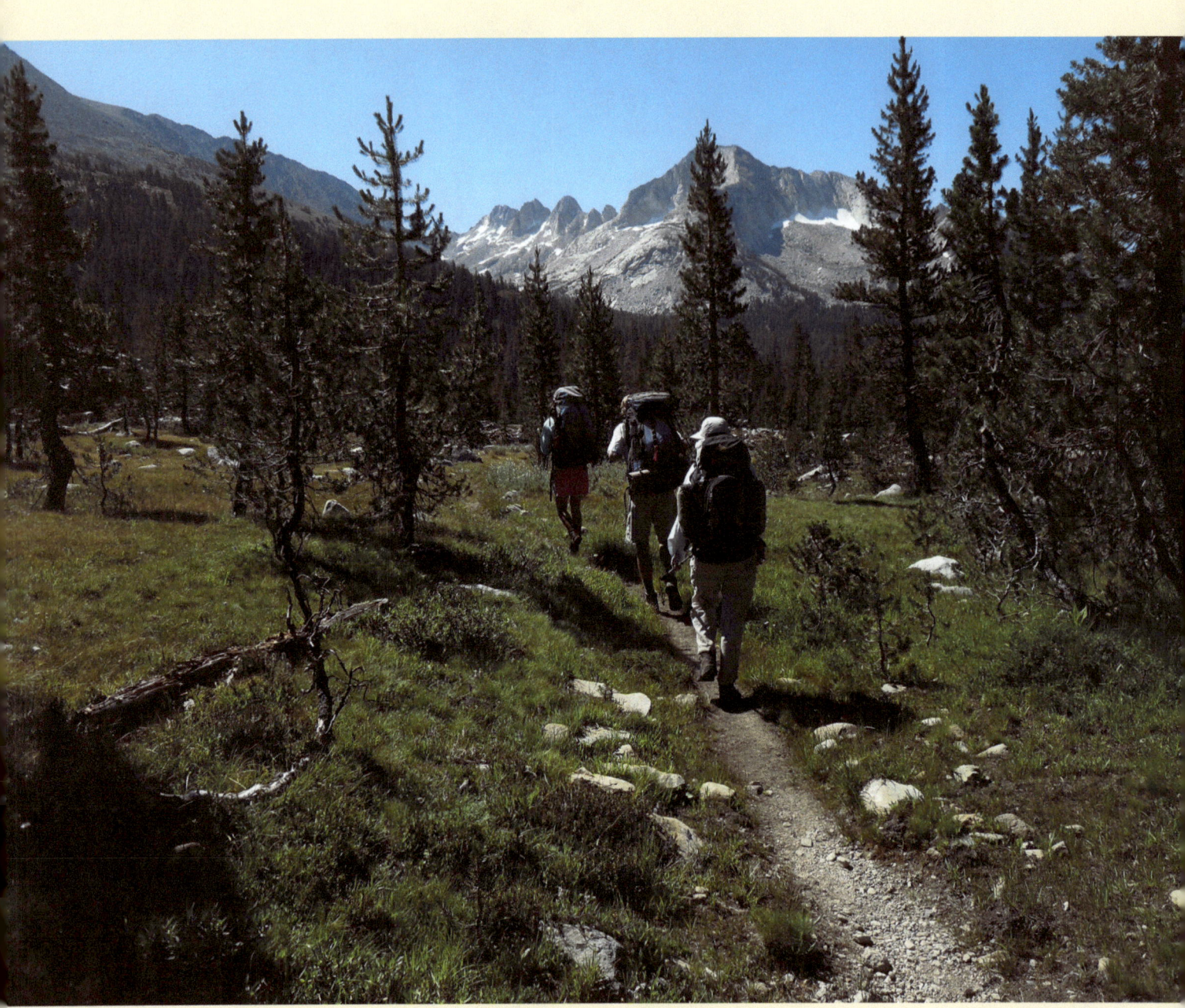

Gallery

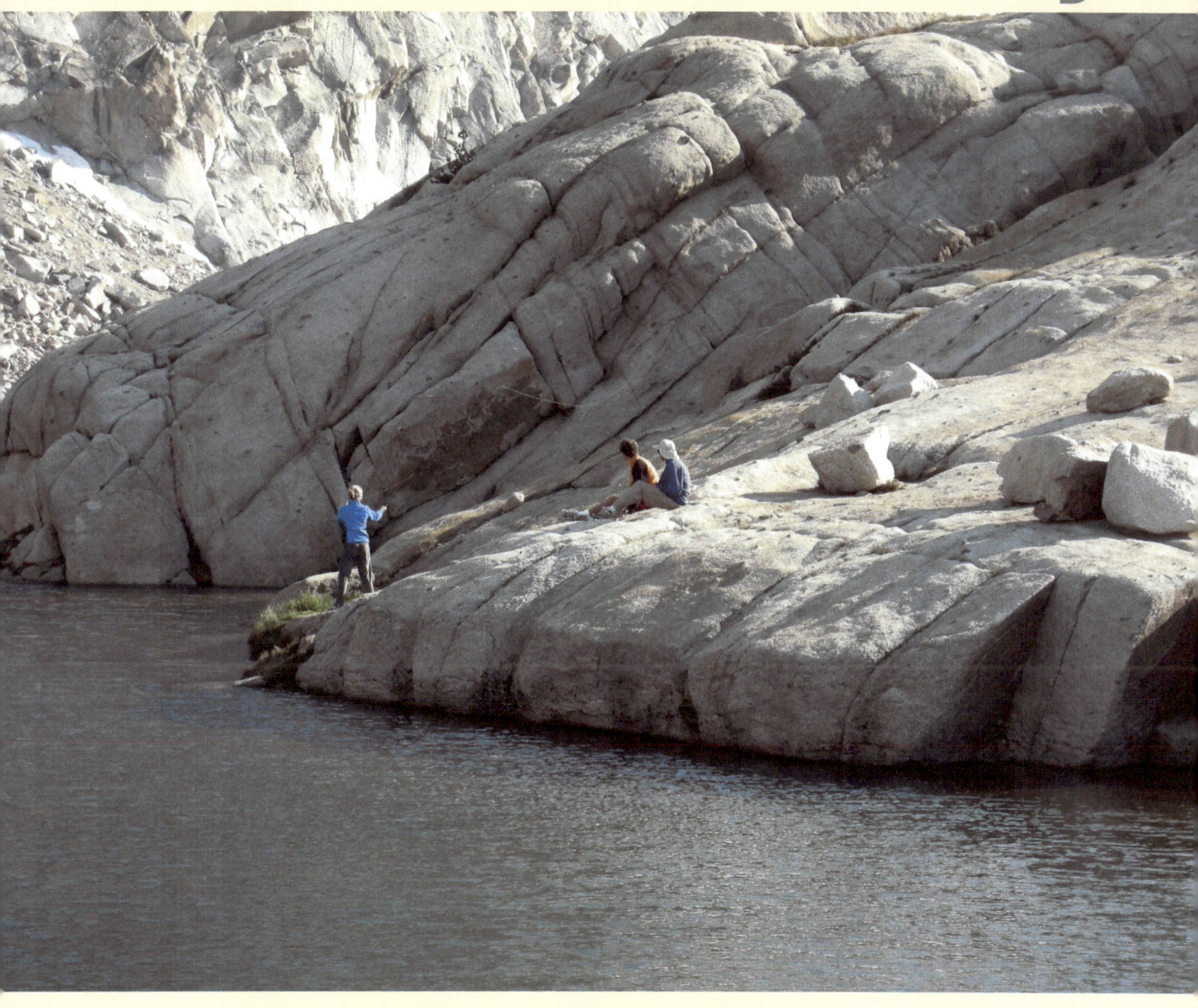

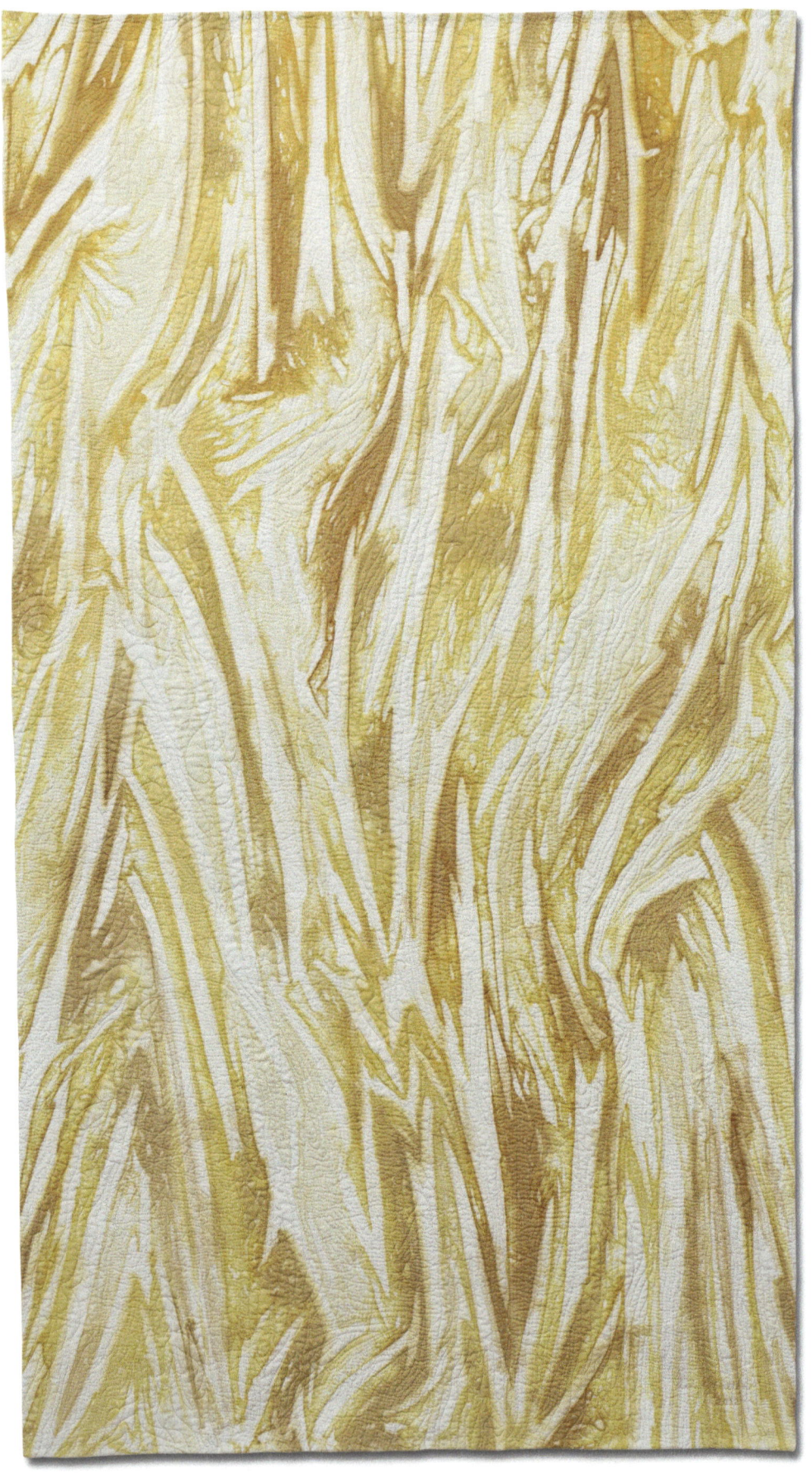

84" x 47" • Cotton sateen, hand painted with dye, machine stitched. 2012

About 200 million years ago (200 Ma), the sea floor was spewing elements dissolved in superheated water; about 160 Ma, ridges of minerals accreted onto the existing edges of our continent. At about 110 Ma, in another magmatic flare-up, gold was remobilized from the country rock into the quartz veins where we find it today. In California in 1849, miners used the same fire assay techniques of ancient Troy, in which quartz was returned to liquid, mixed with fluxes, and processed to determine the weight of gold it contained.

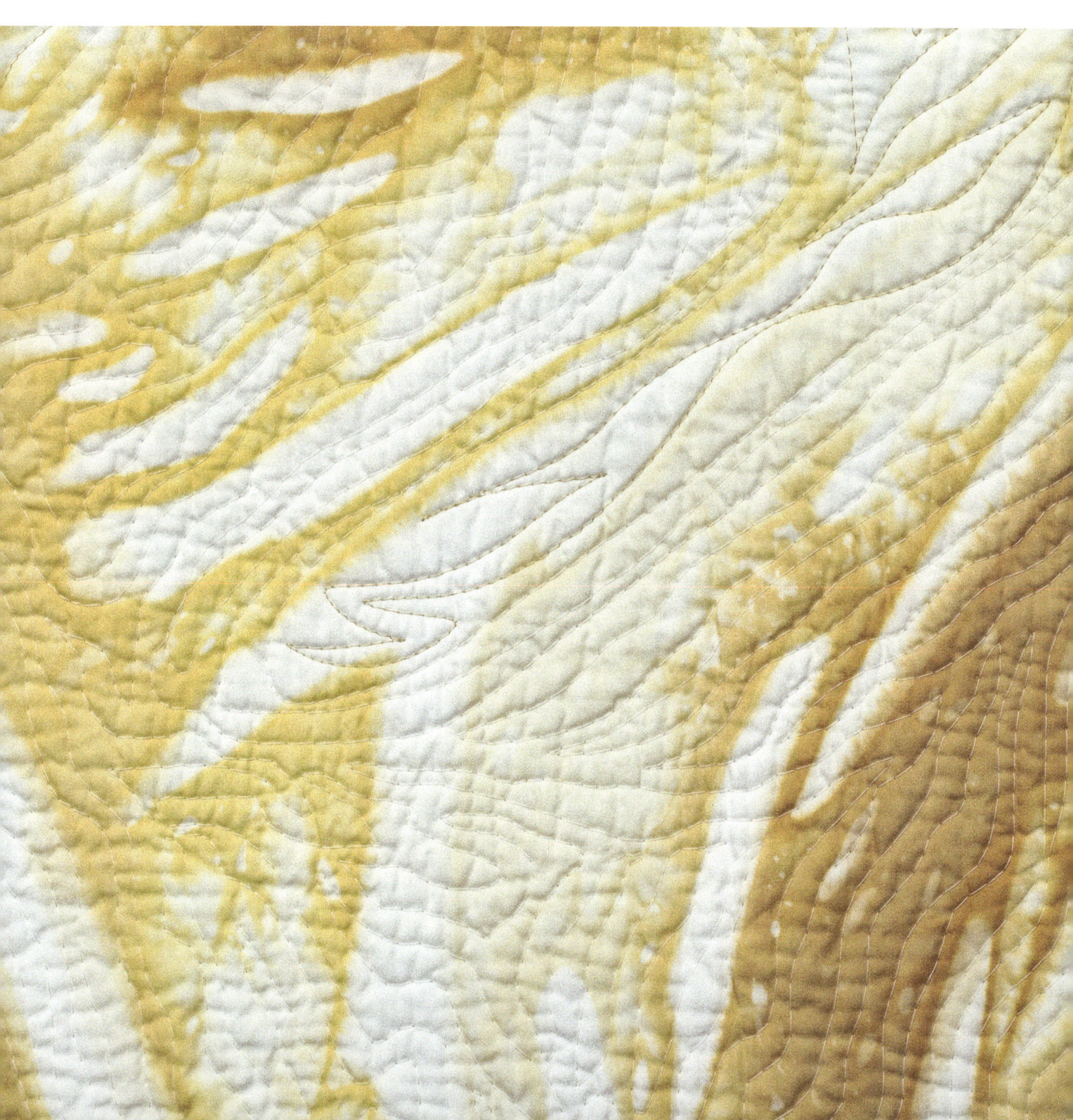

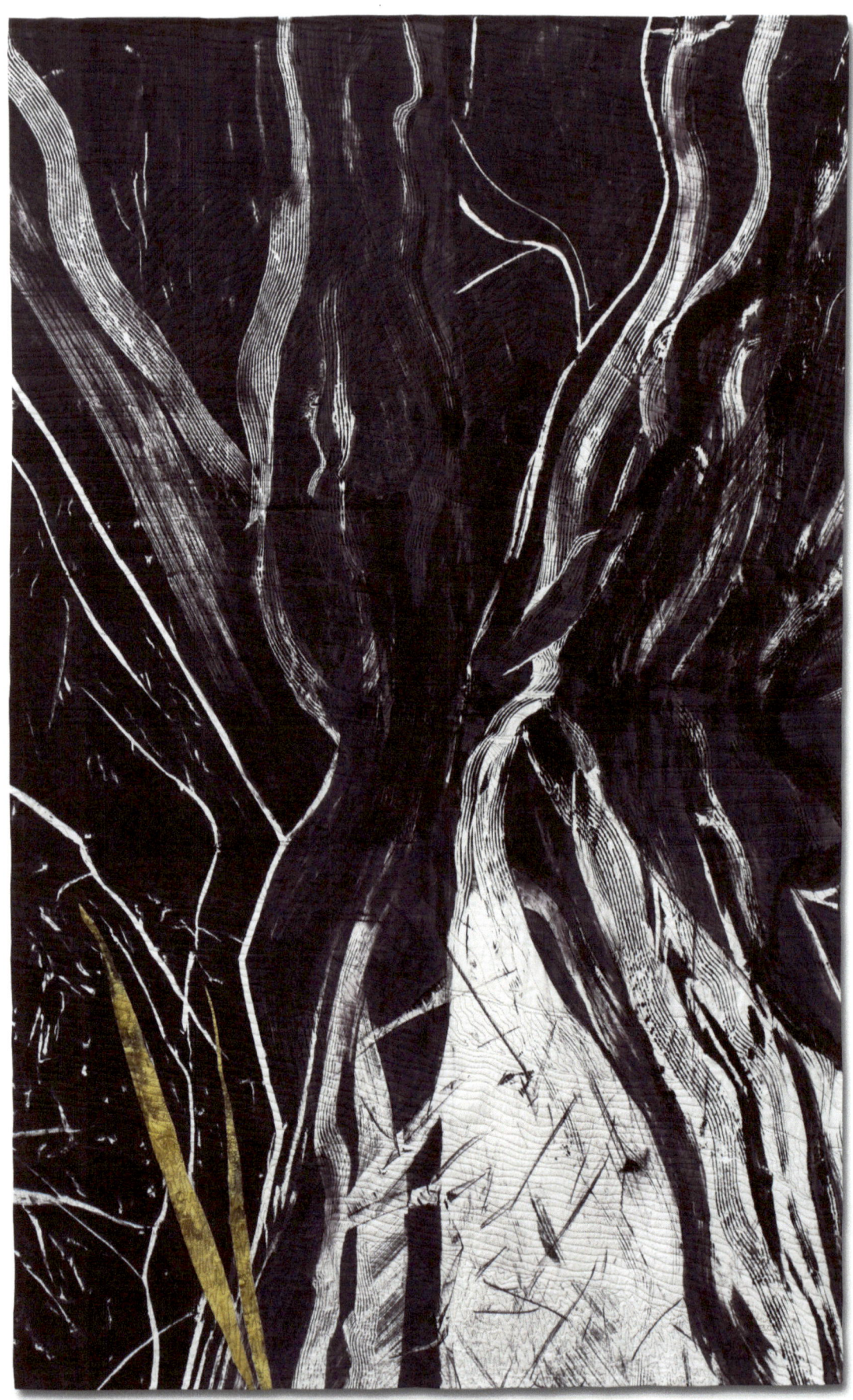

84" x 53" • Cotton sateen, hand printed and painted with dye, machine stitched. 2011

Nevadan Orogeny is sometimes used to designate an era of folding and/or stretching—
a massive deformation of the earth's crust that was one of the stages in the growth and creation
of the western part of what is now North America—thought to have occurred between 160 and
150 million years ago.

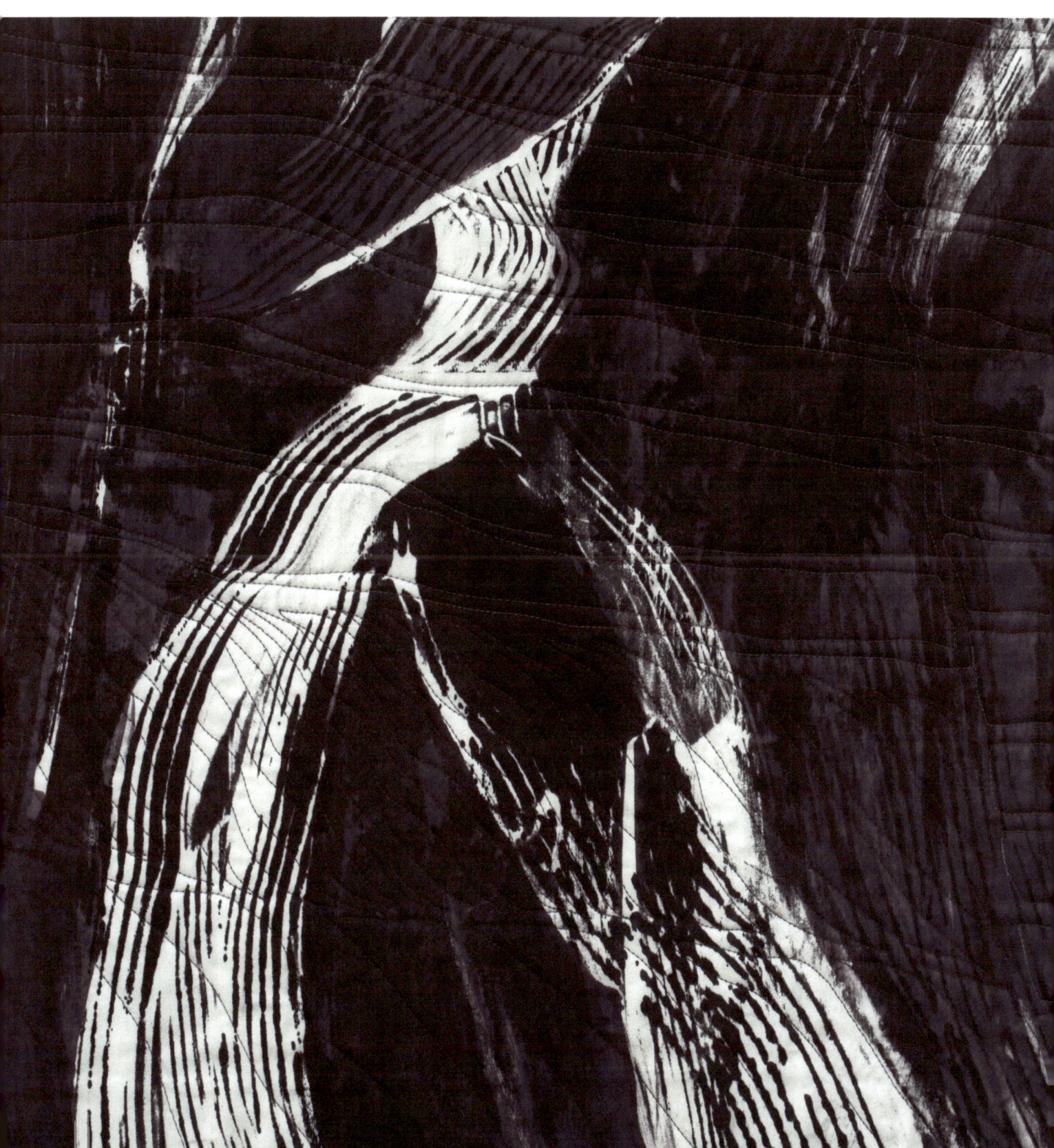

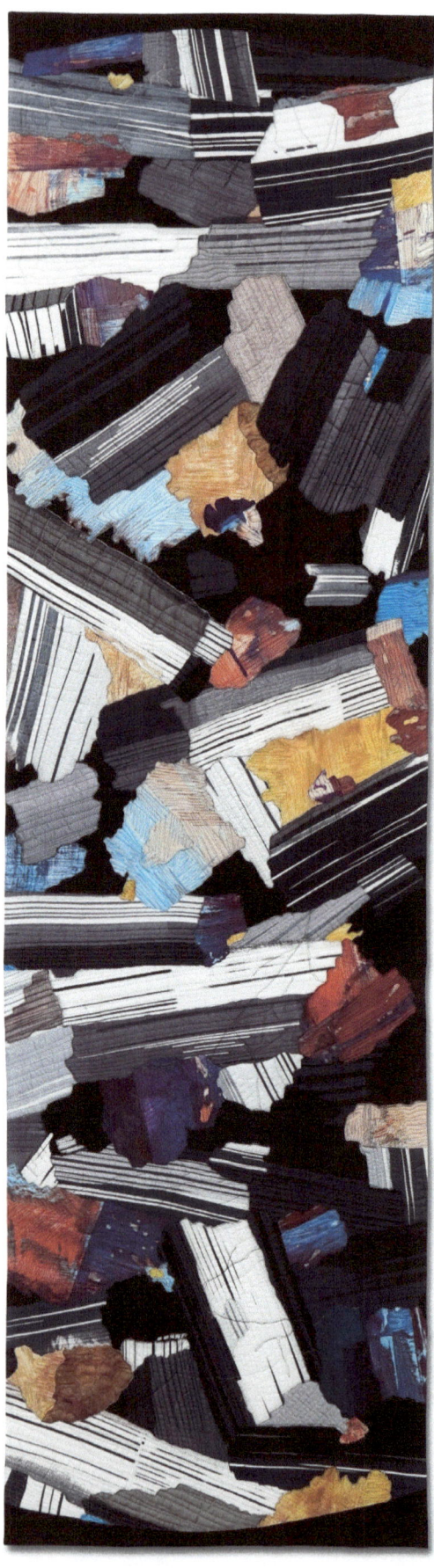

85″ x 25″ • Cotton sateen and silk organza, low-water immersion dyed, hand painted
and printed with dye, hand and machine stitched. 2014

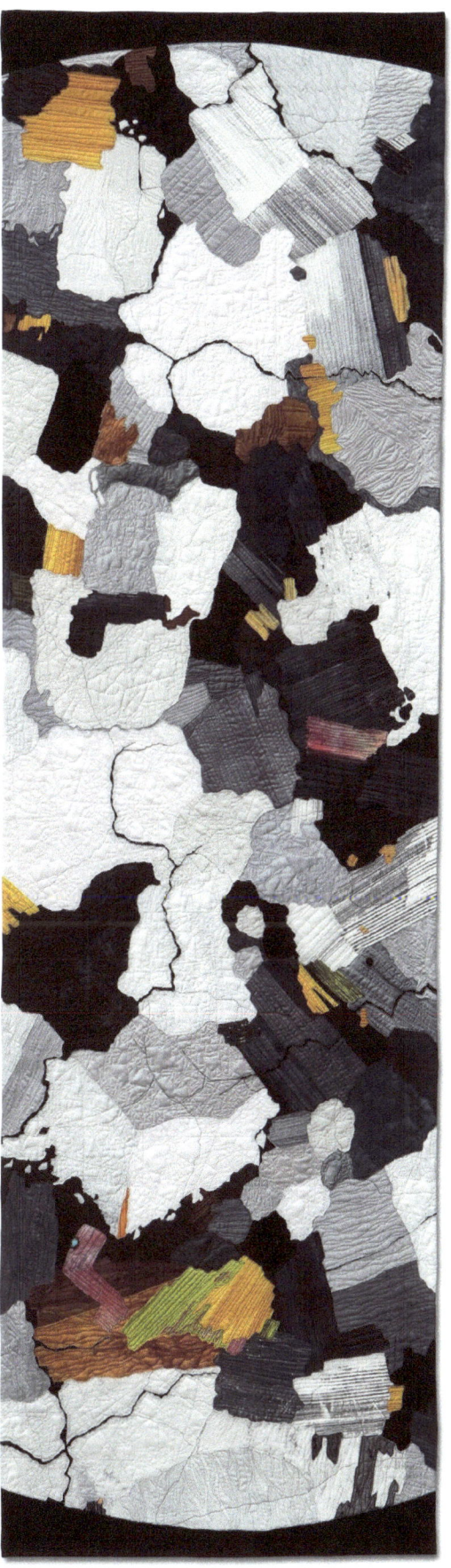

*85" x 25" • Cotton sateen and silk organza, low-water immersion dyed, hand painted
and printed with dye, hand and machine stitched. 2015*

THE CONTACT: CROSS POLARIZED GABBRO | *detail*

Gabbro is a dark intrusive rock that is sometimes associated with gold-bearing quartz veins. It is monotonous and plain to the naked eye, but polarized light passing through a 30-micron thin section reveals an infinite variety of sharply contrasting crystal twins of feldspar intergrown with colorful pyroxene.

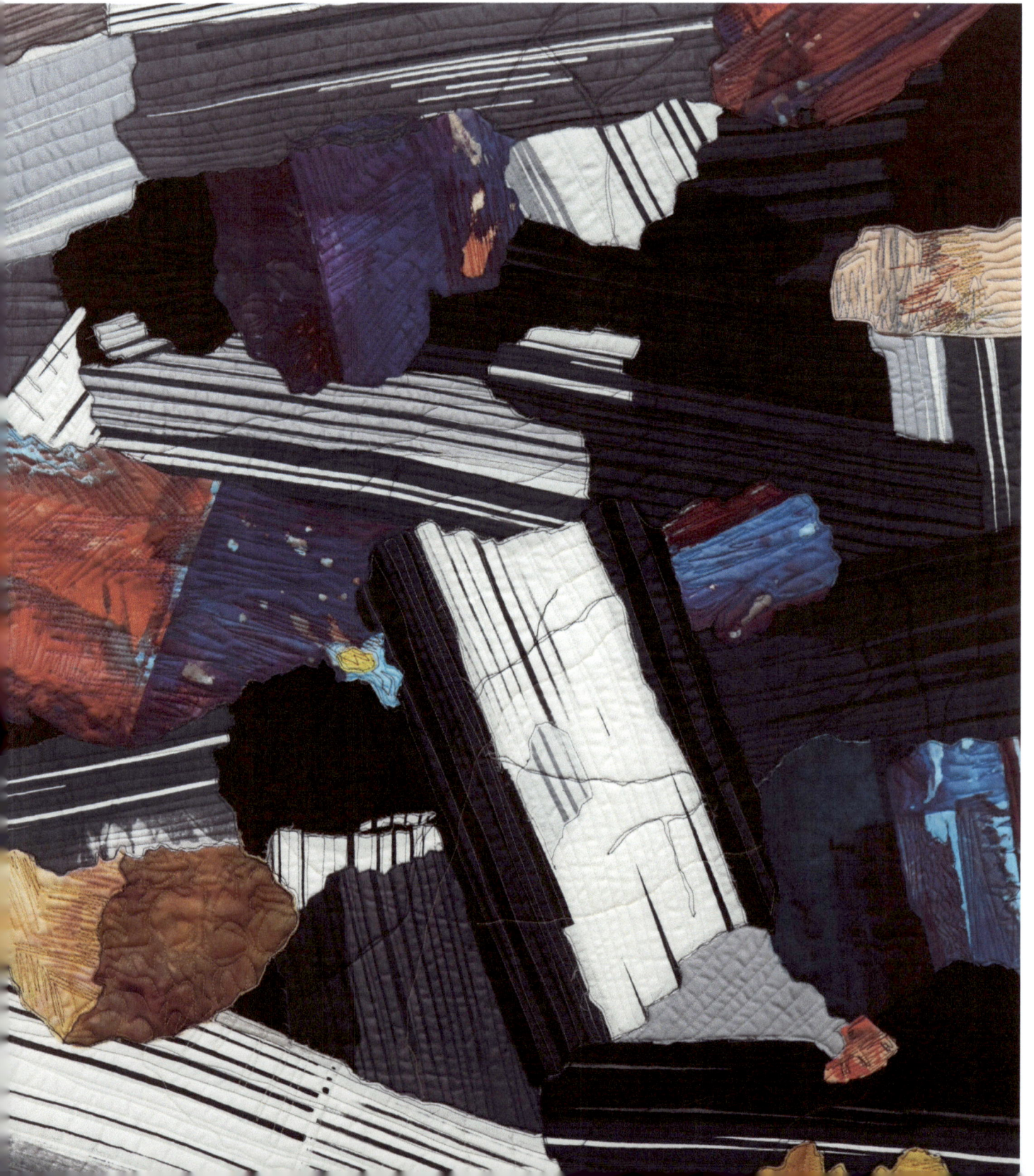

THE CONTACT: CROSS POLARIZED GRANITE | *detail*

Looking at a thin section of granite through a microscope using cross polarized light reveals two different kinds of feldspars and subtly shaded quartz crystals. The bright colors are produced by biotite and hornblende, dark looking to the naked eye. Can you find the zircon, which can be used to date the age of the rock?

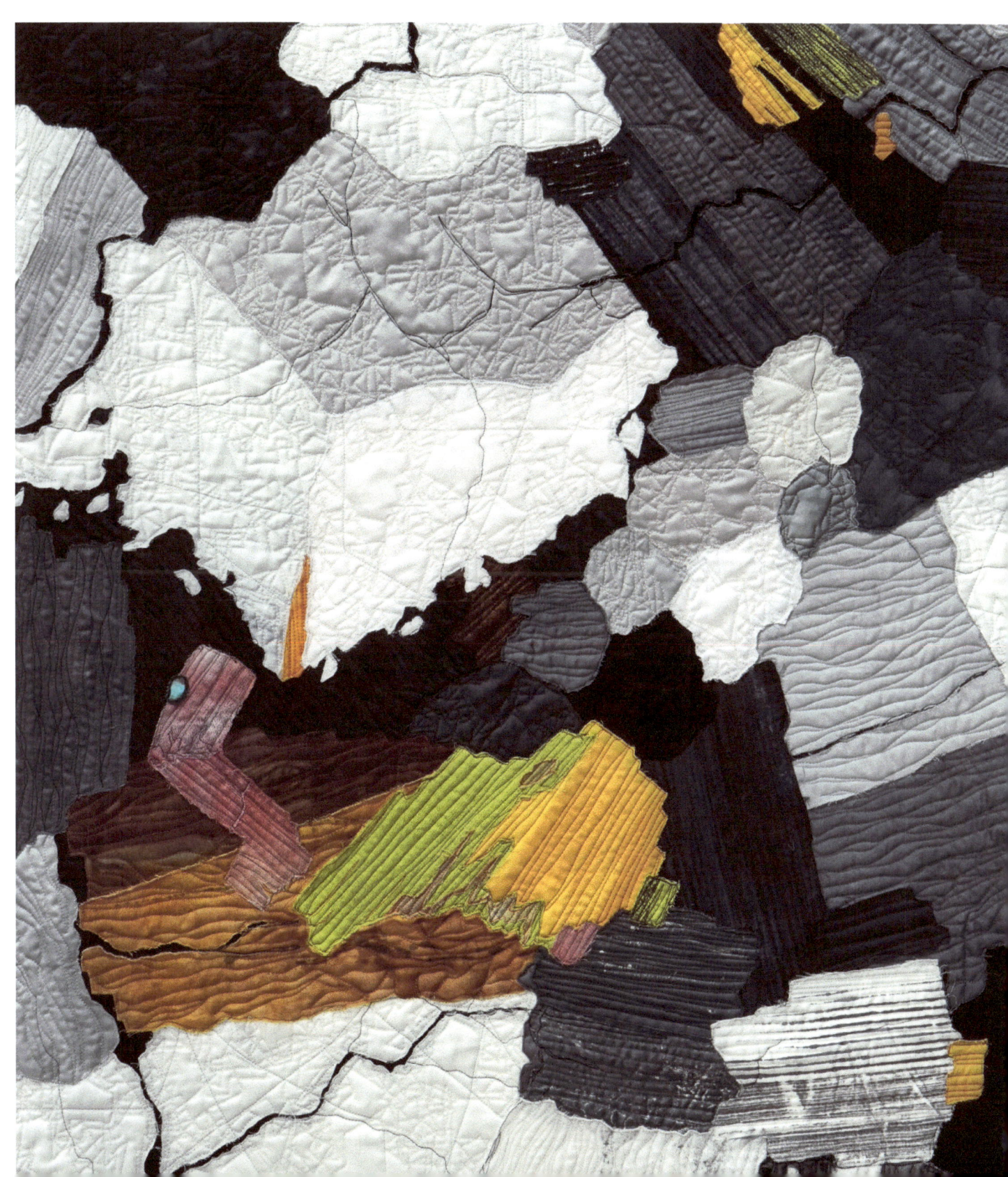

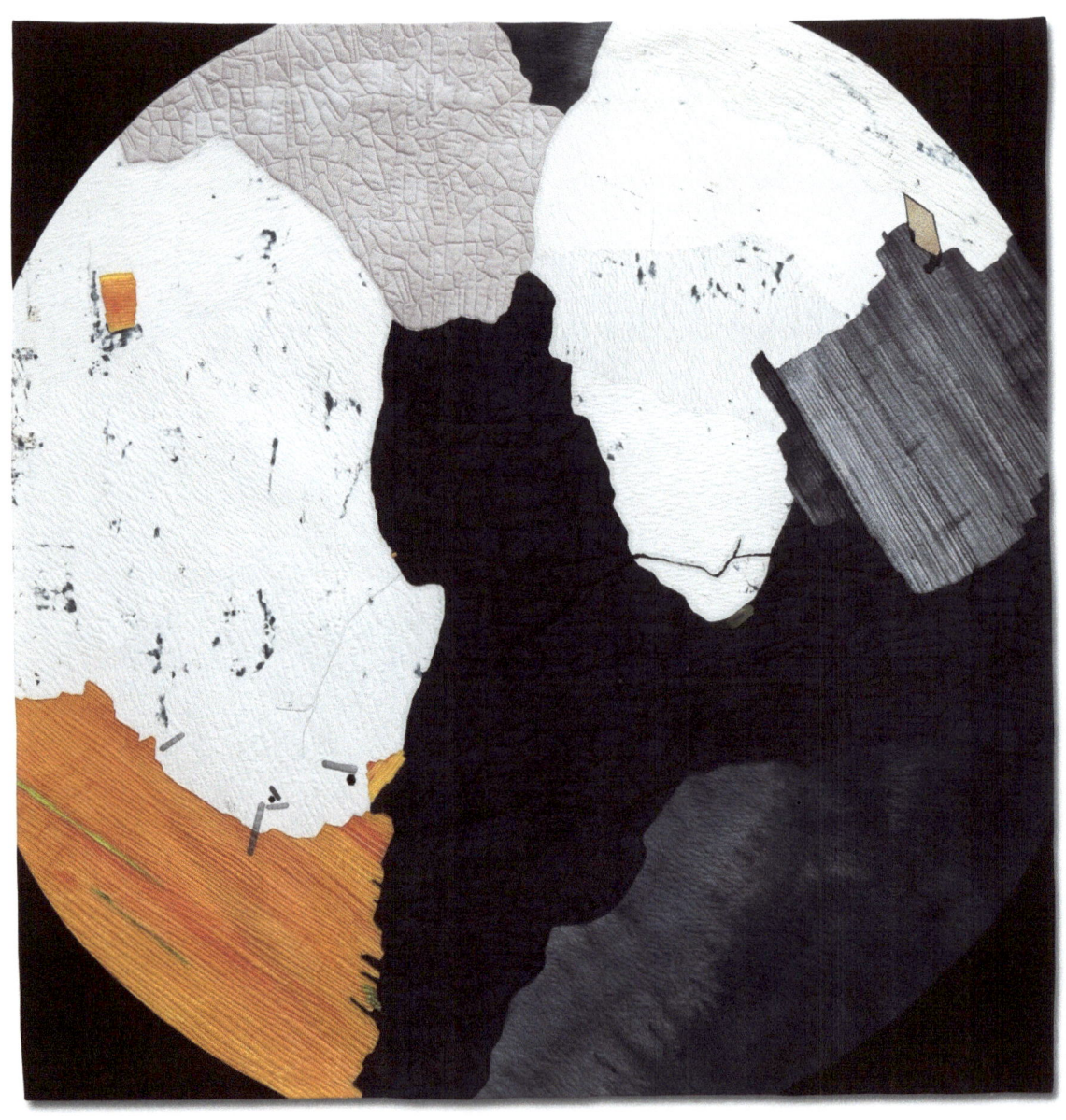

58" x 58" • Cotton and silk organza, low-water immersion dyed, hand painted and printed with dye, machine stitched. 2015

Back detail.

Cross polarized light through a thin section of rock yields false colors—formed as the light passes through solid crystals—that are characteristic of particular minerals. These shapes, textures, and colors identify this sample as granite. This magnification allows observation of accessory minerals including zircon, titanite, and apatite. Here, I see the continents of a whole new world.

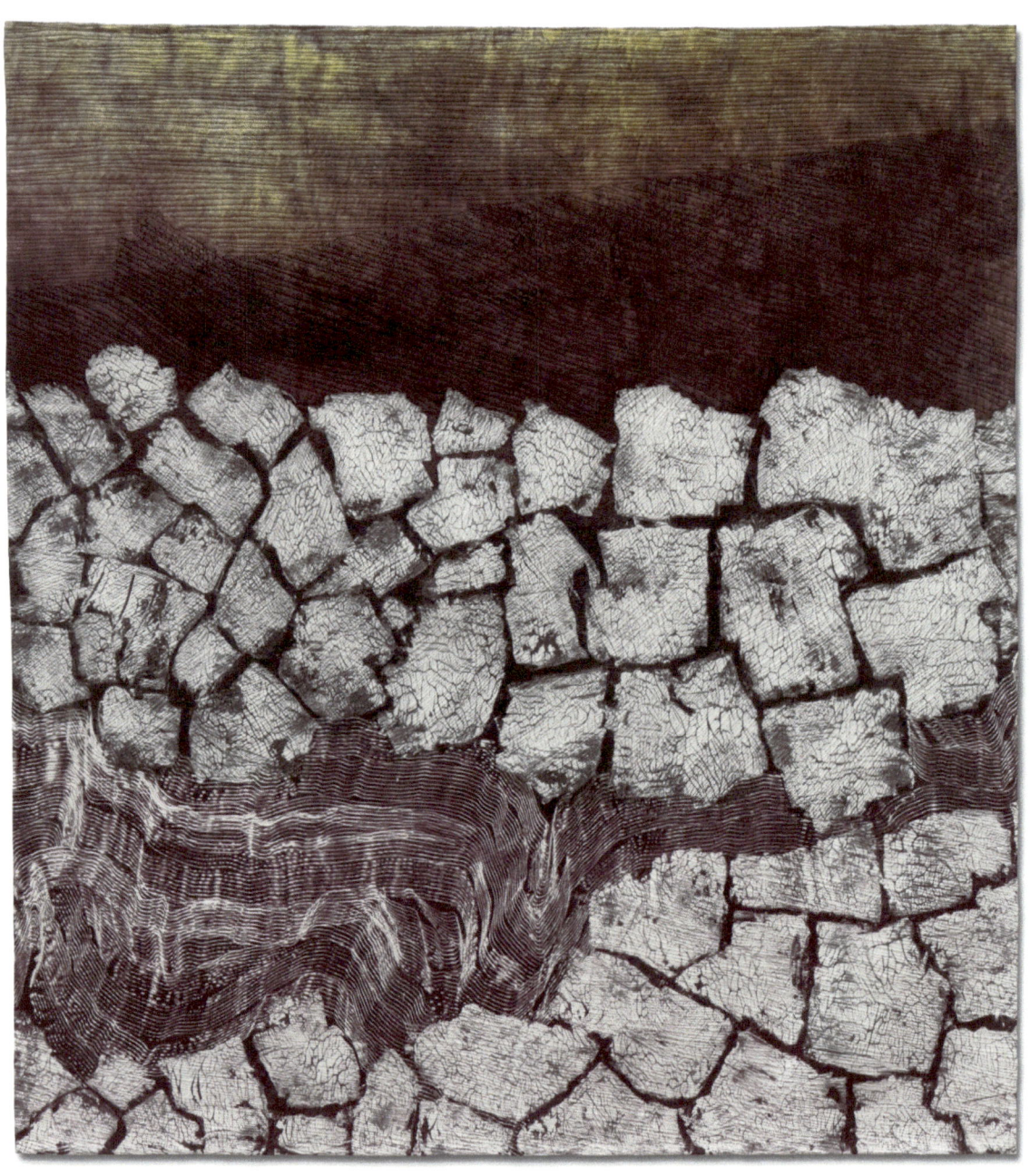

64" x 59" • Cotton sateen, hand painted and printed with dye, machine stitched. 2014

Extreme pressure and high temperatures associated with miles of mountainous overburden and primordial heat over millions of years control the mineralogy and grain shape in the earth. We tiny human beings create another kind of pressure on our sensitive world in a very short time.

Back detail.

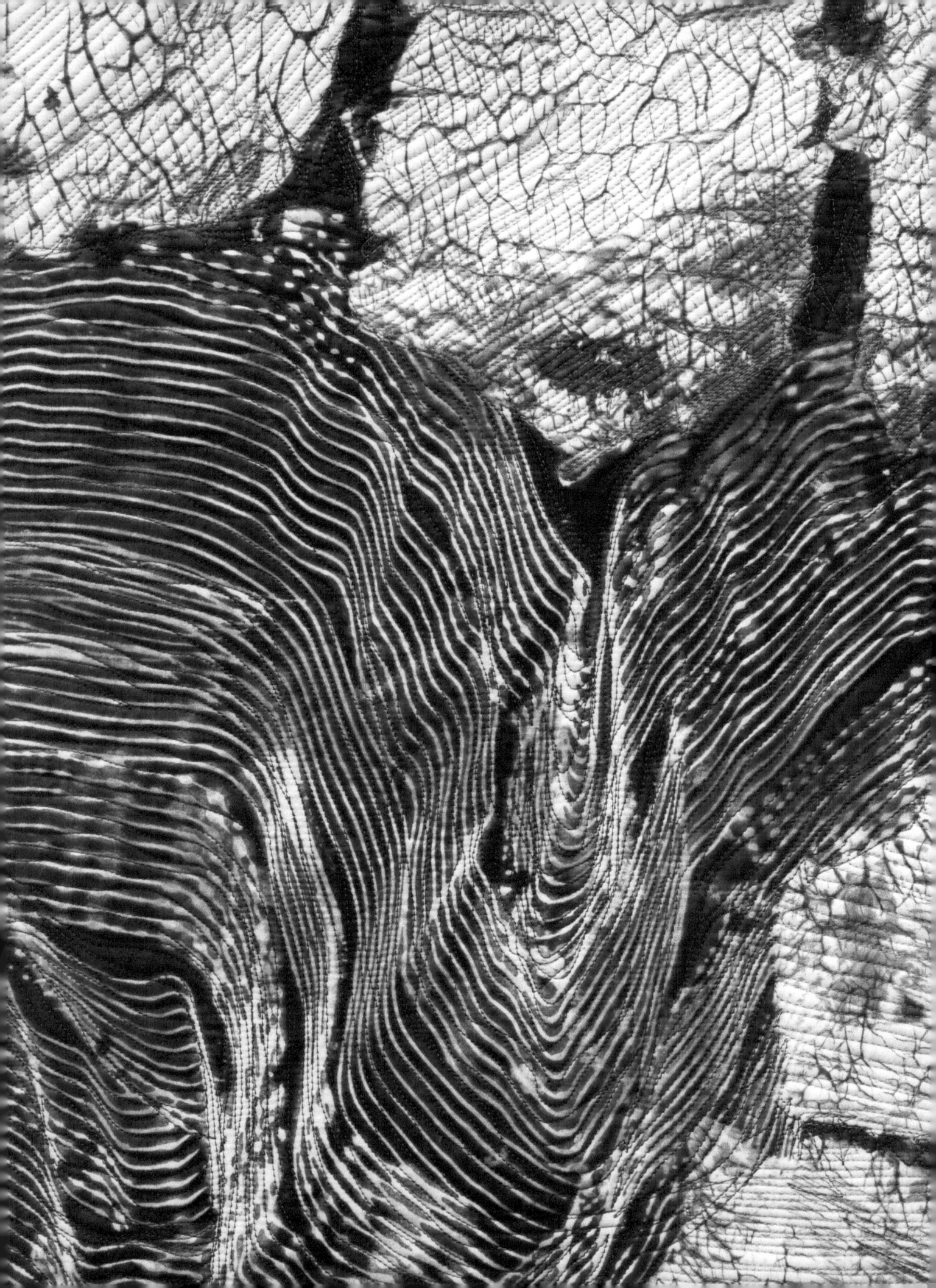

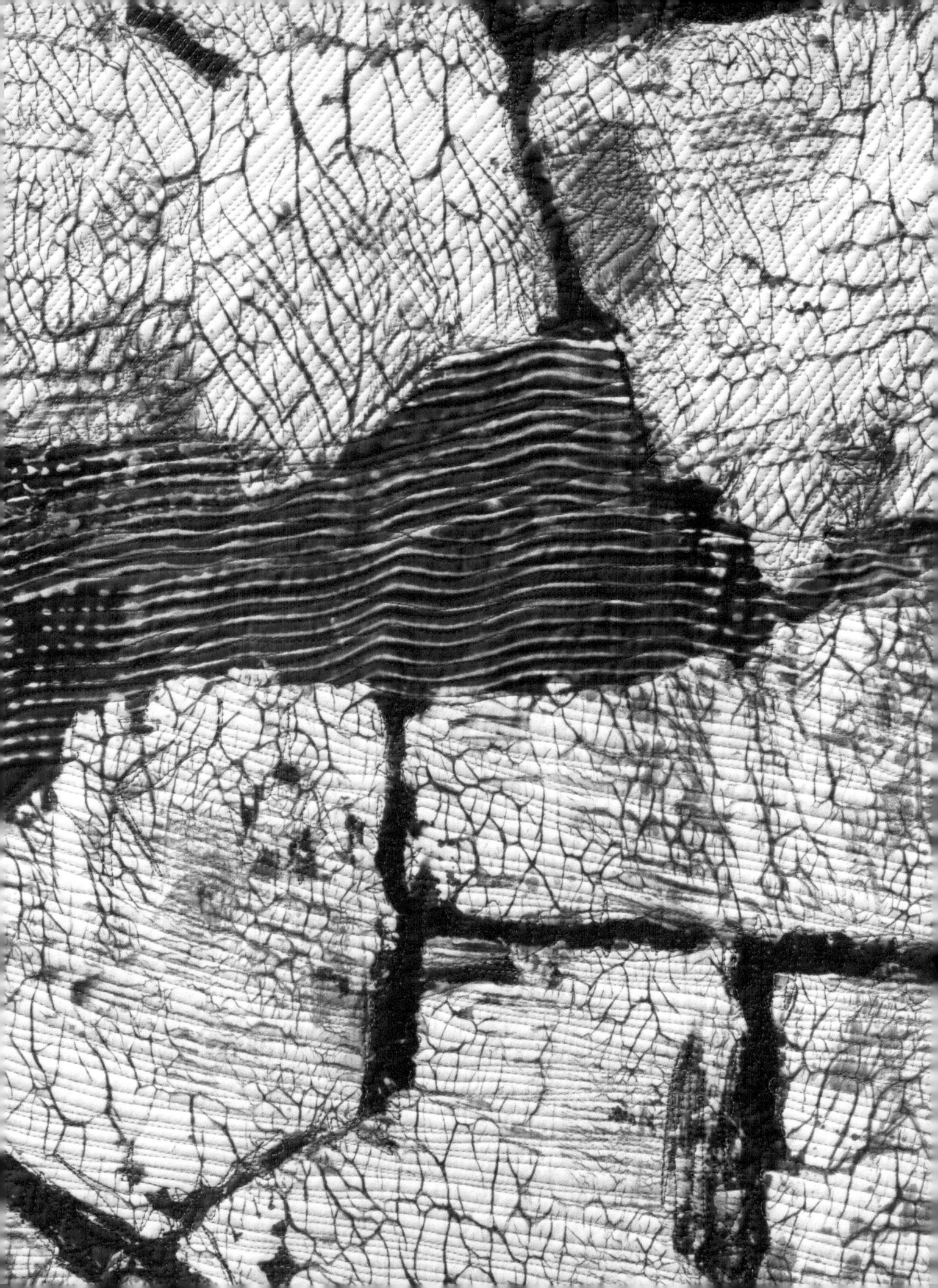

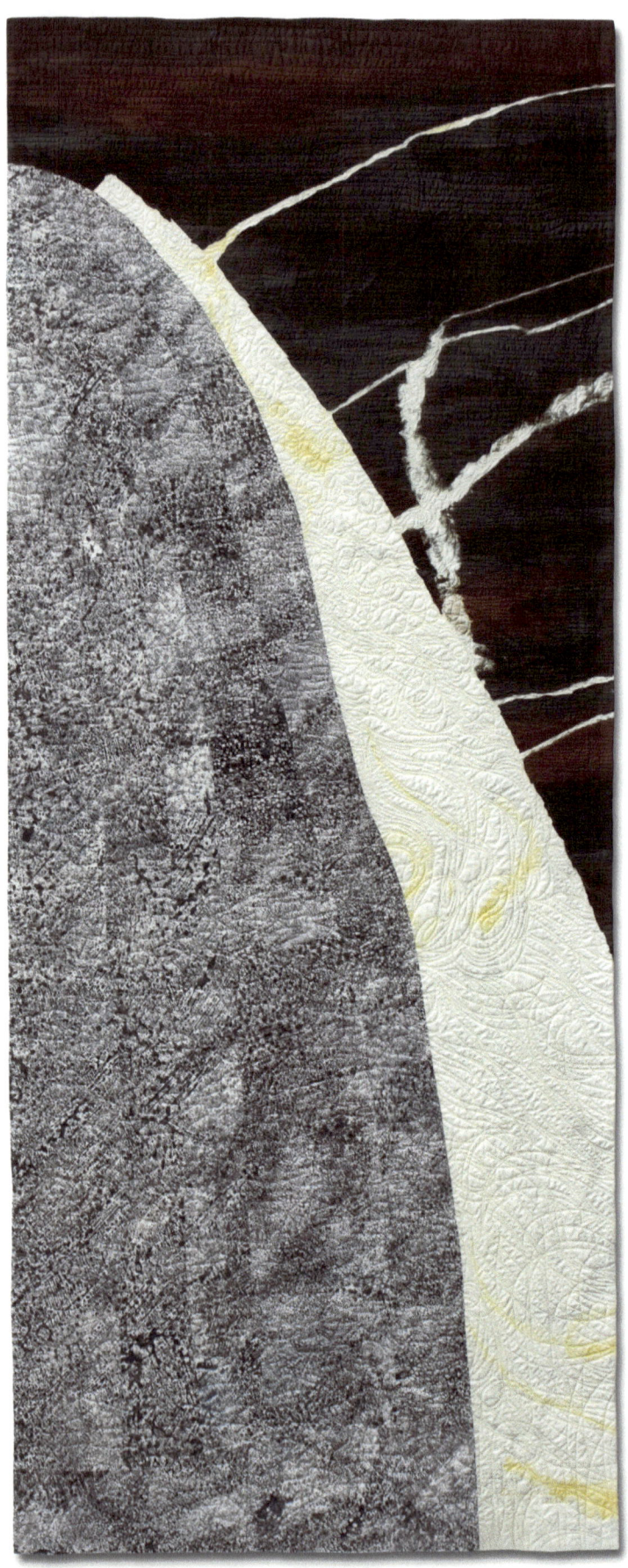

84" x 35" • Cotton sateen, hand printed and painted with dye, machine stitched. 2013

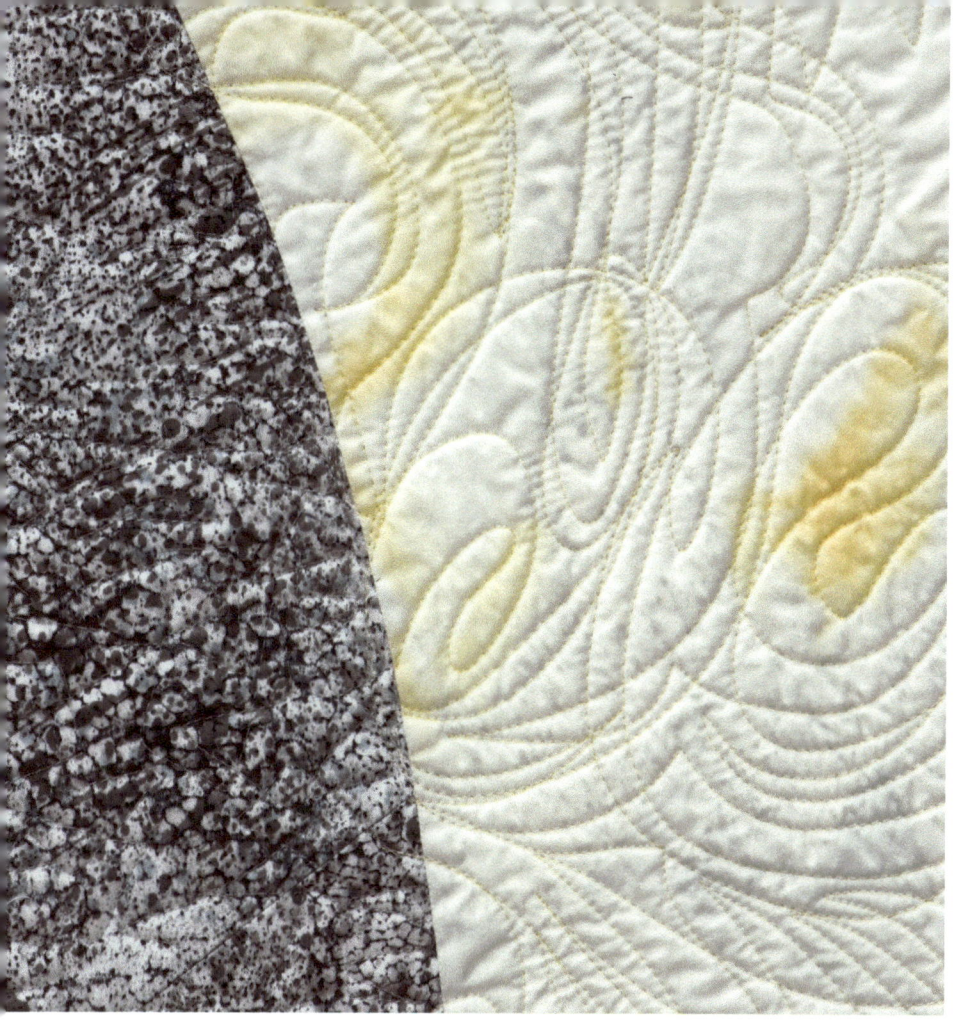

Miles underground, this is the last gasp of a granitic pluton. The lode quartz dissolves in water and, at high pressure, it fractures and invades the country rock to form veins for future gold hunters.

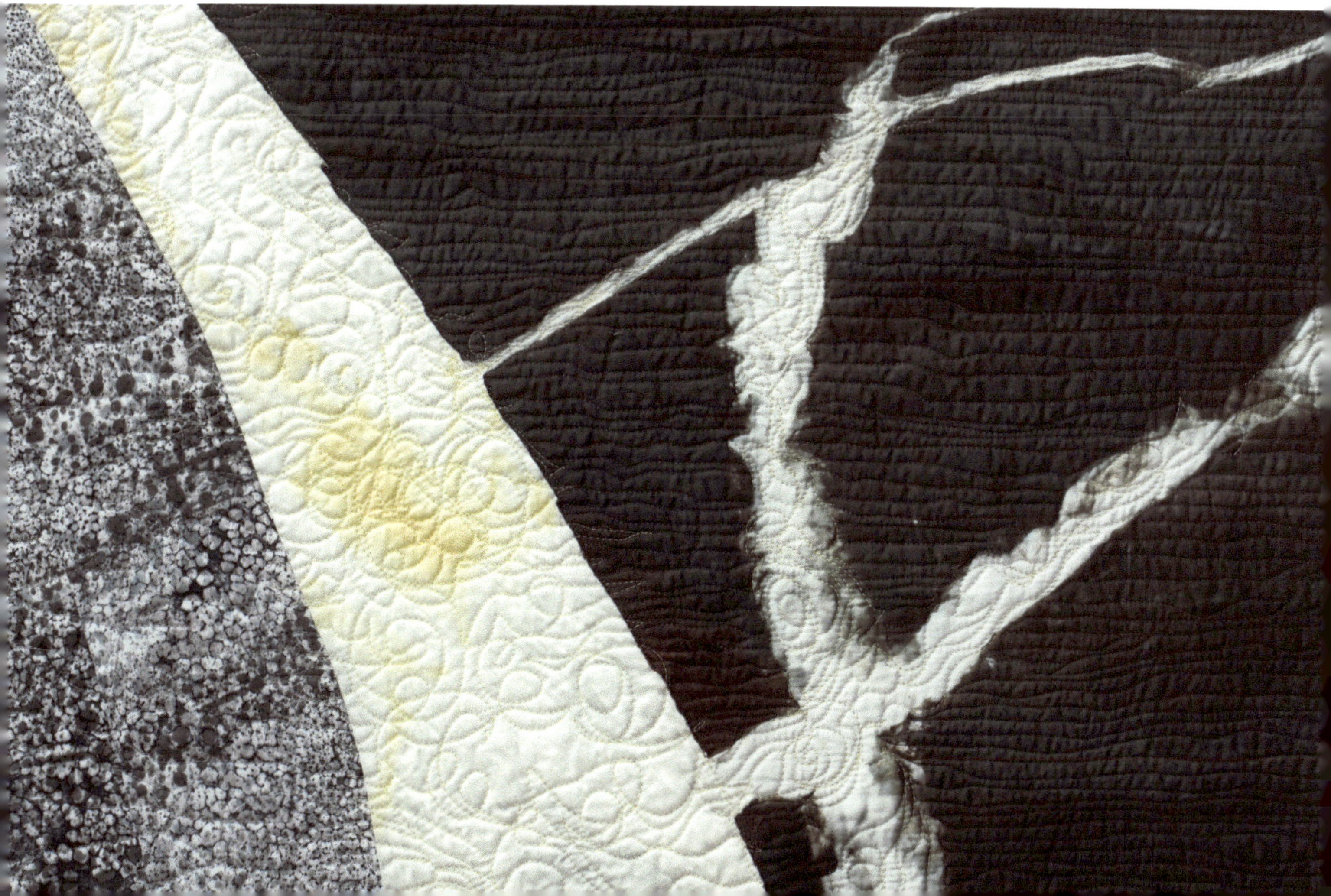

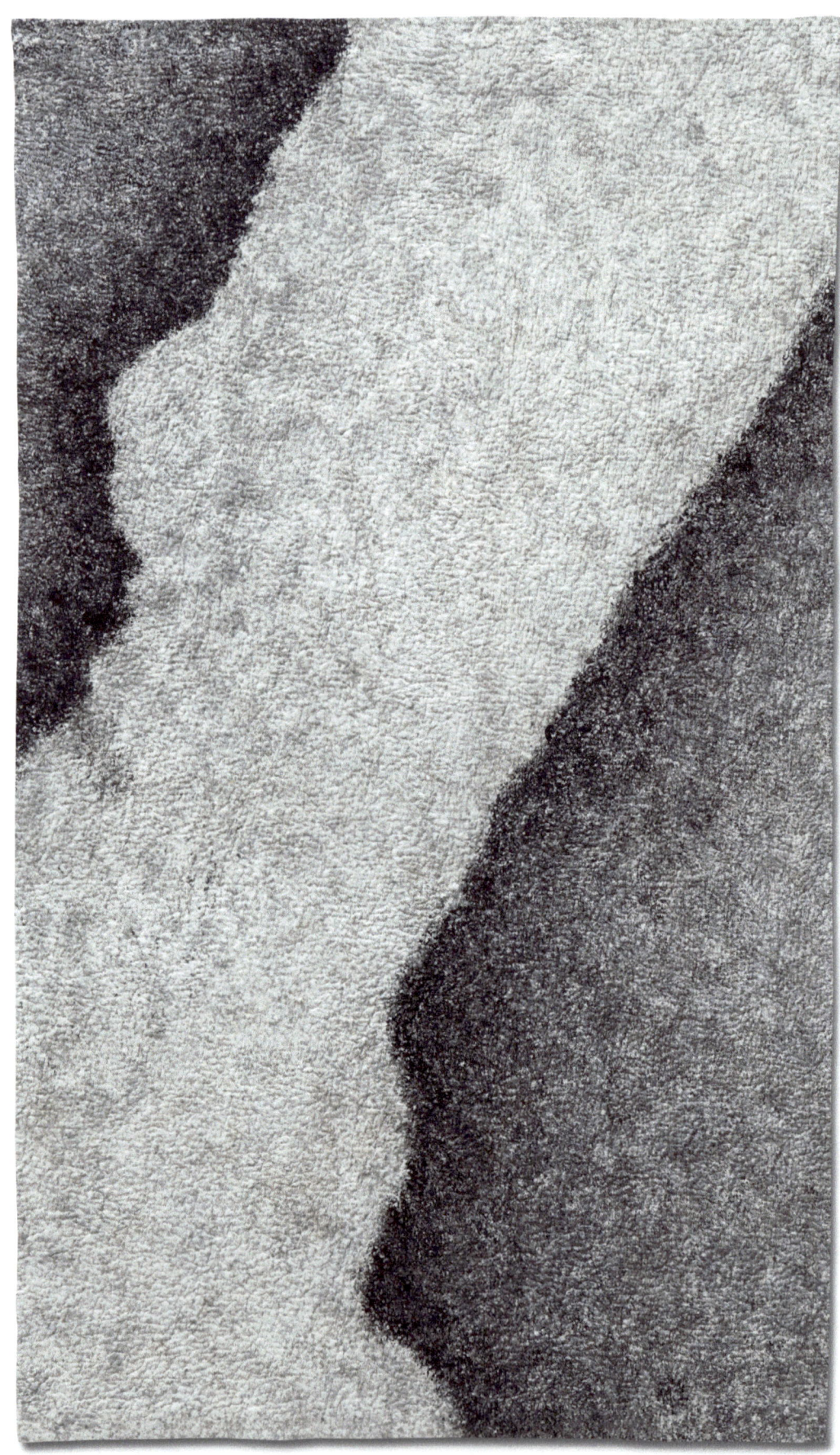

84" x 51" • Cotton sateen, hand printed with dye, hand stitched. 2013

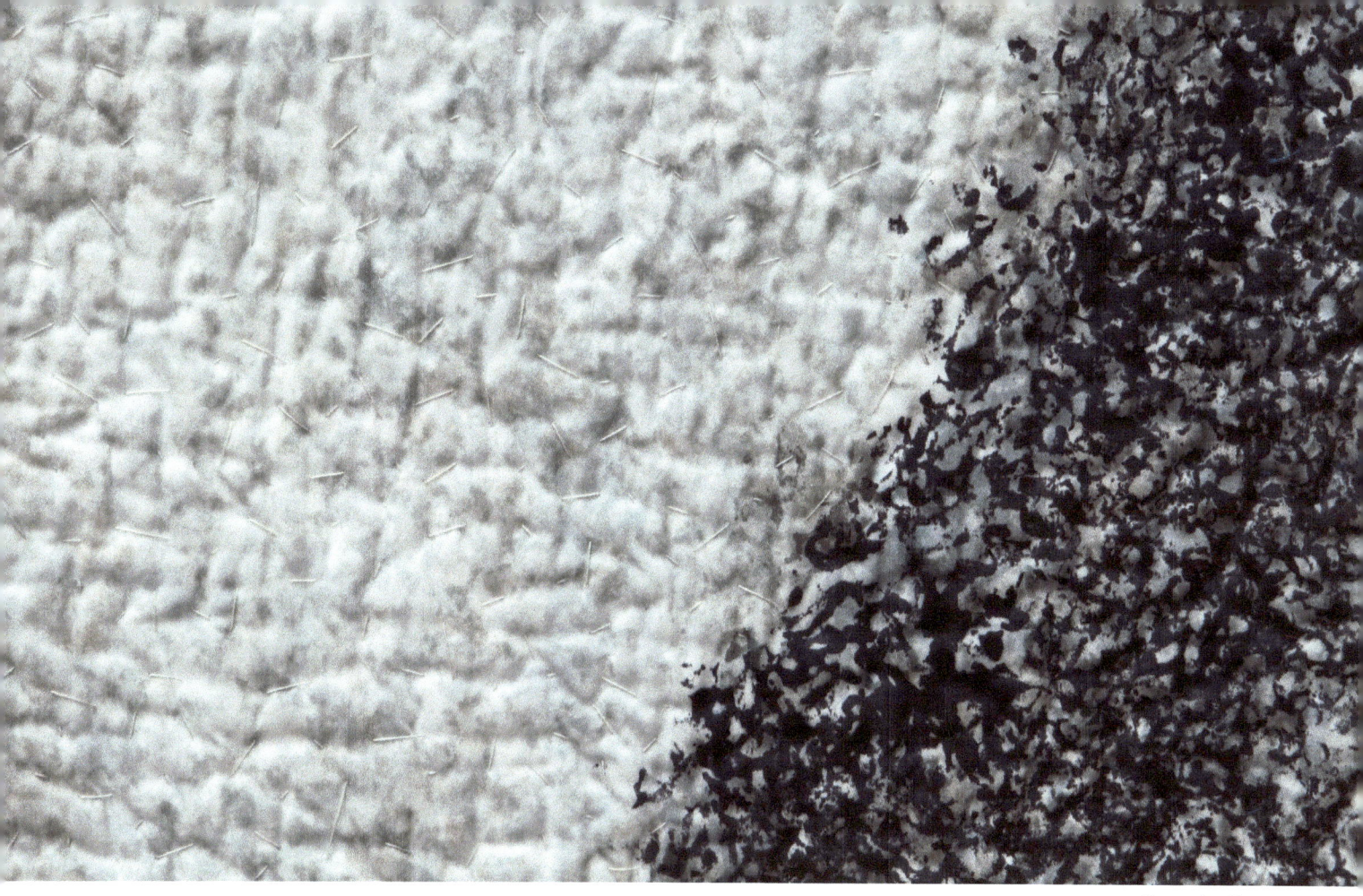

Some kinds of magma don't mix, and where they contact, they react. On the edges,
water from the lighter rocks helps grow larger, darker minerals in the host.

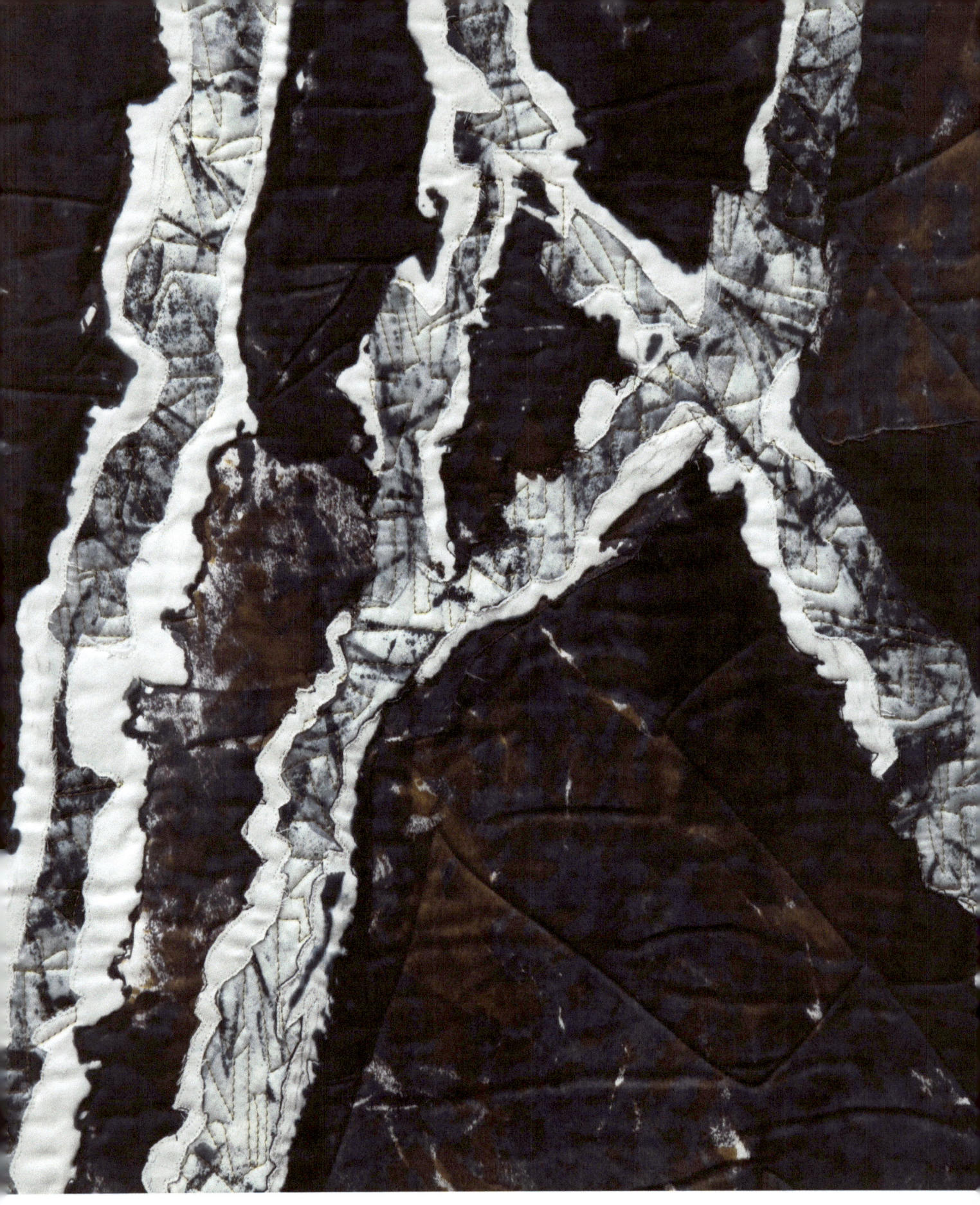

Dark, fine-grained rock cracks under pressure. White-hot quartz-saturated fluids fill the fractures, alter the original rock, and cool to form ragged veins.

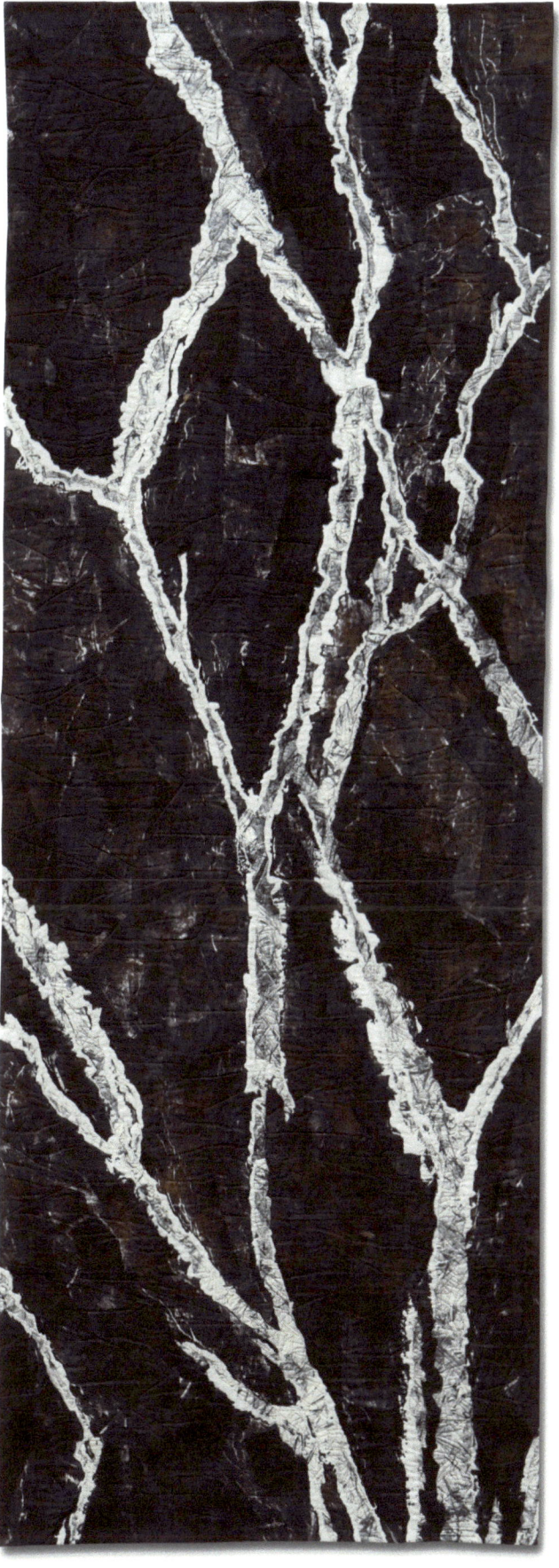

*85" x 31" • Cotton sateen, hand printed and painted with dye,
machine stitched. 2013*

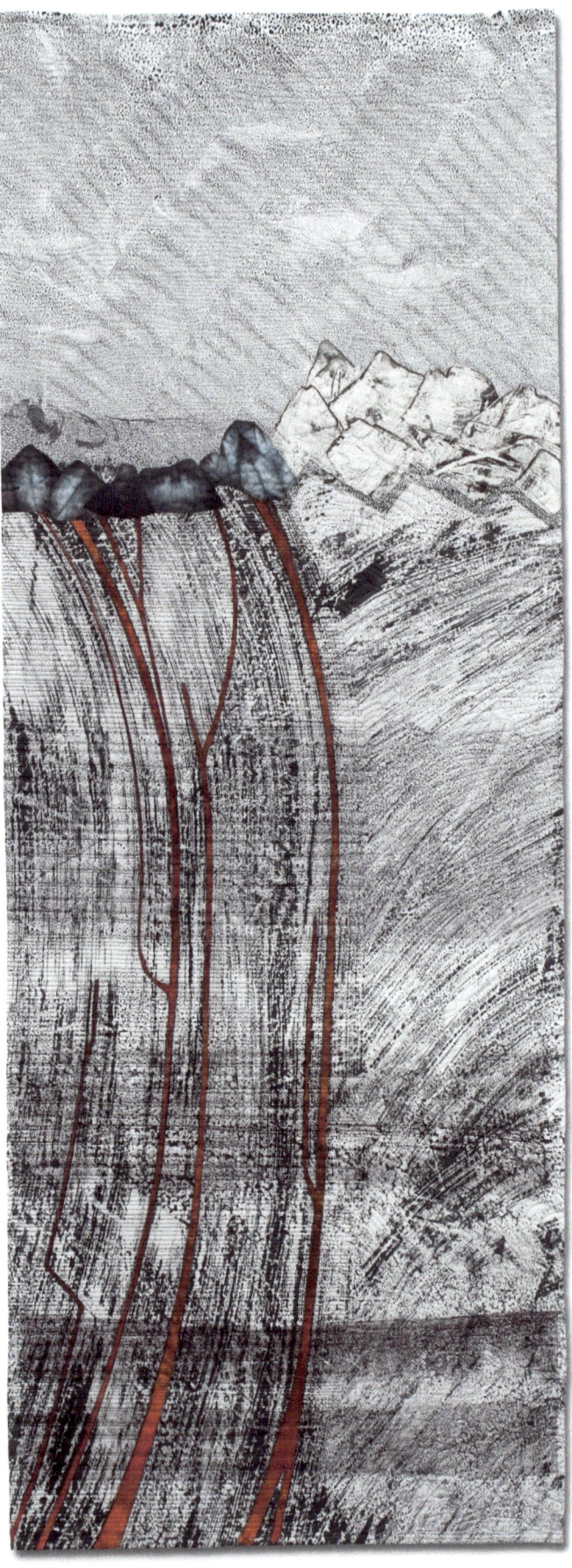

84" x 32" • Cotton sateen, low-water immersion dyed, hand printed
and painted with dye, hand and machine stitched. 2012

The eastern escarpment of the Sierra is one to two miles high, and there are places where you can walk on a contact, between exhumed glacial-cut granites and dark meta-volcanic slopes. Magma tapping the mantle below the continental crust is roughly 18 – 22 miles below the surface.

Back detail.

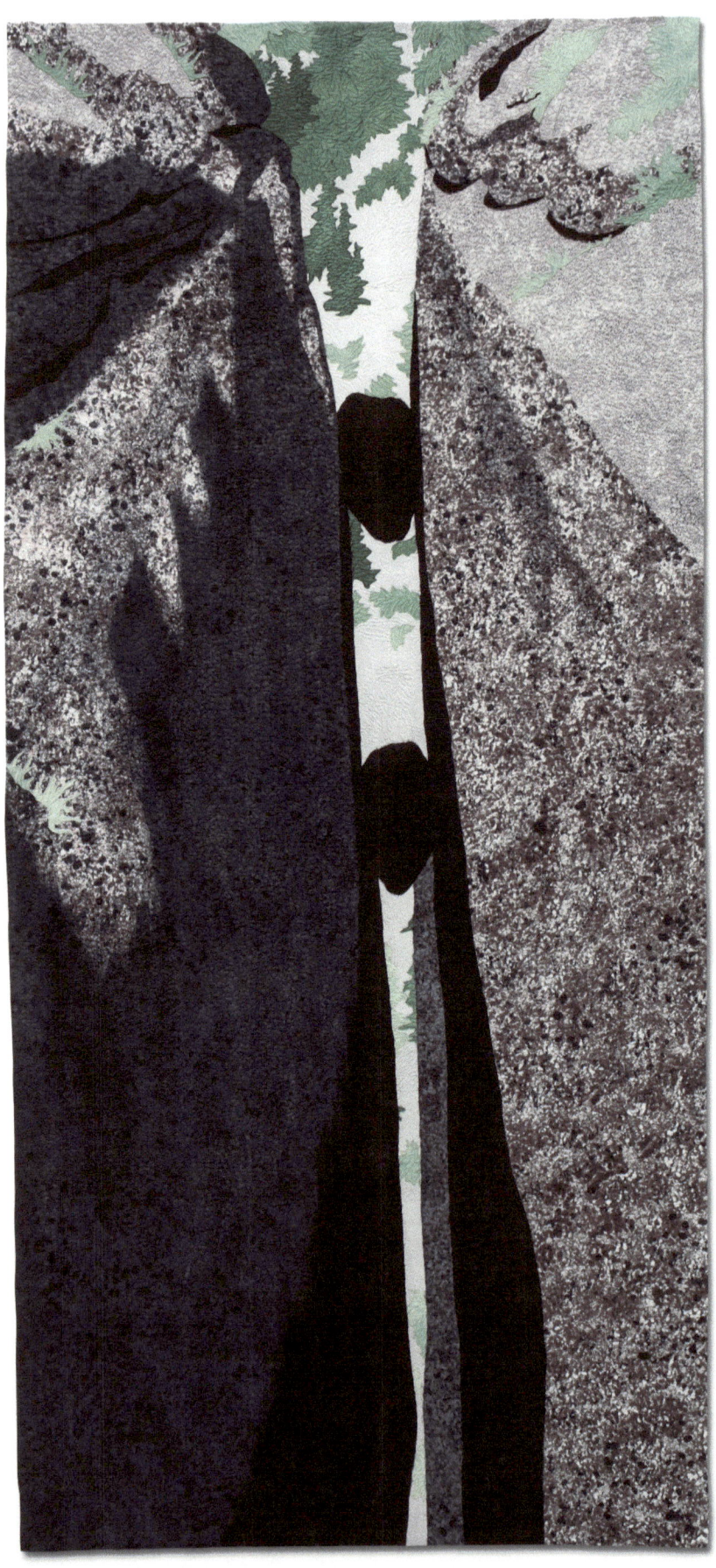

85" x 39" • Cotton sateen and silk organza, low-water immersion dyed, hand printed
and painted with dye, hand and machine stitched. 2016

Vertical joints slowly weather, weakened by mineral dissolution and expanding ice. They widen into fissures that provide a dizzying view—windows through El Capitan Granite to the valley floor 2,500 feet below. The drama of shadows on light stone is impressive; so is the tenacity of the plants finding places to flower.

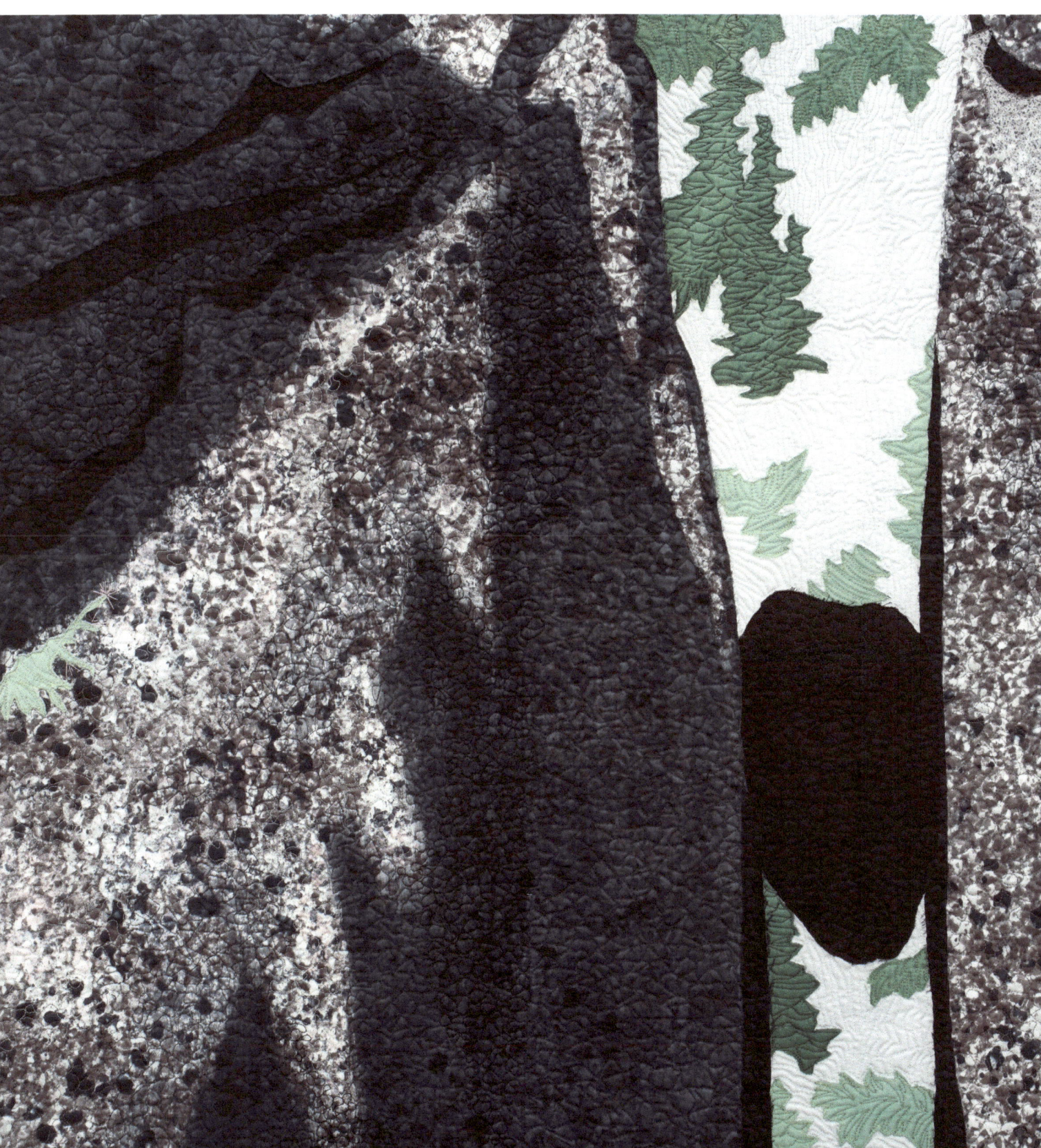

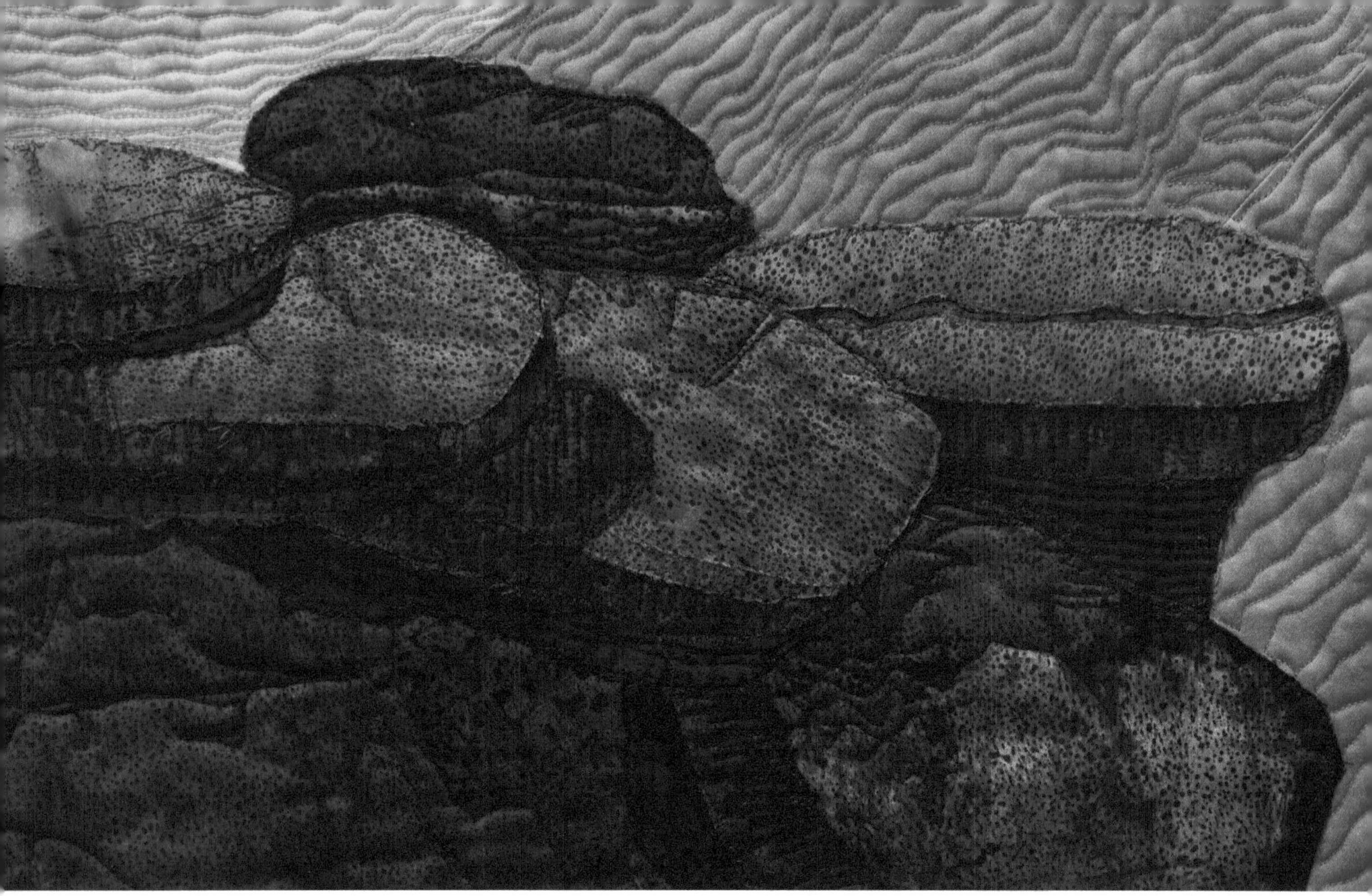

The first people walking in the forest near Taft Point may have been hunting with stones or arrows. I imagine they approached this edge quietly and in wonder. Not so many years later, millions of people come on beaten tracks and look over, also wondering.

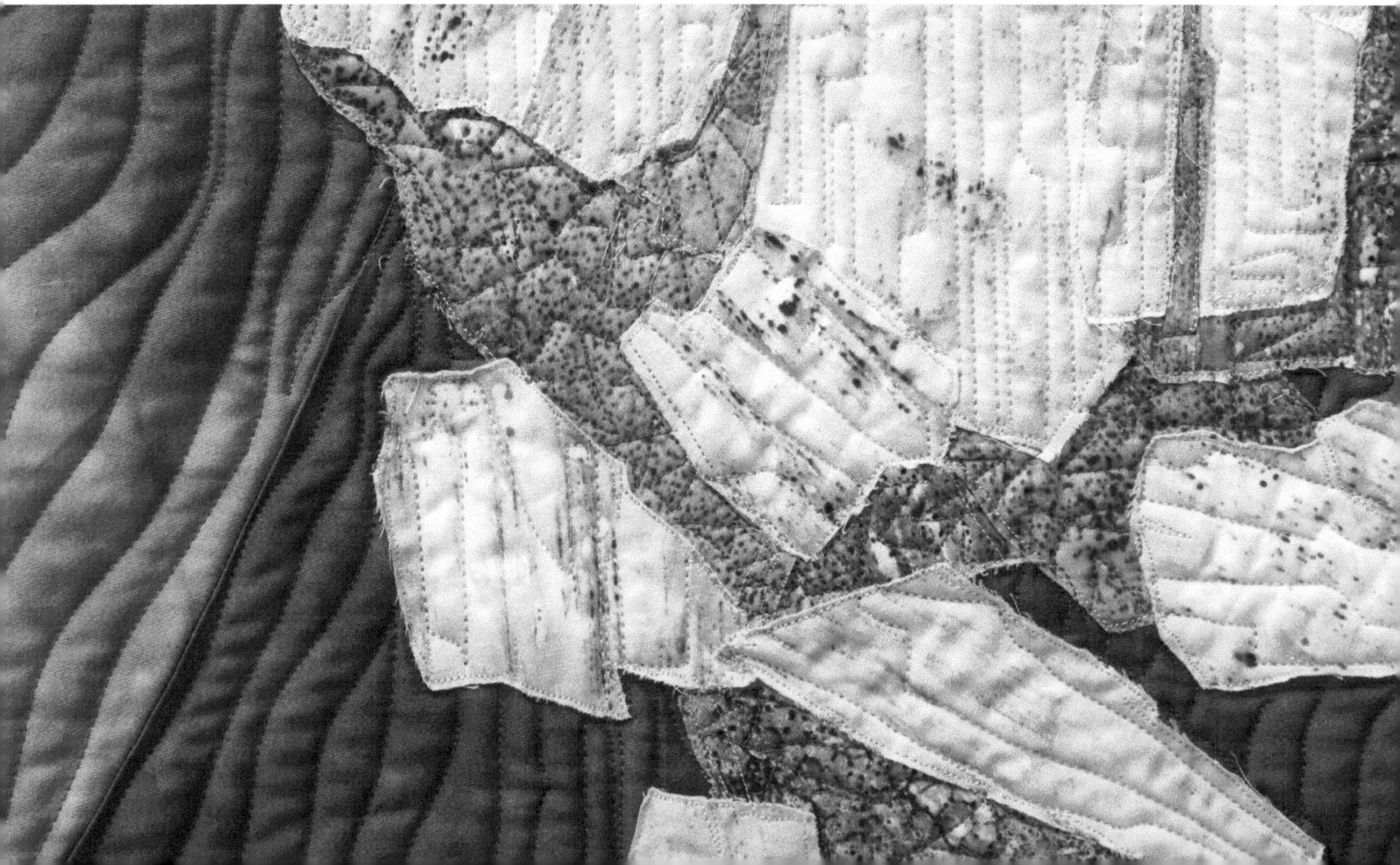

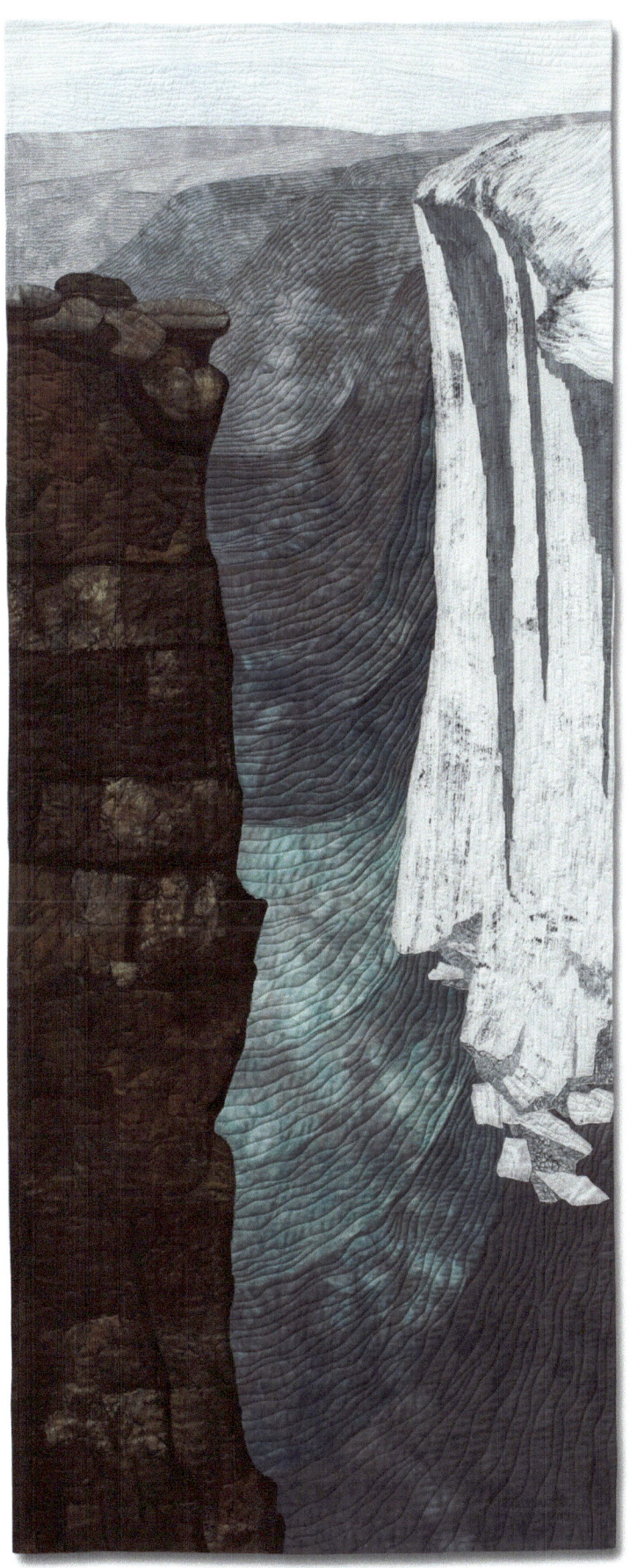

84" x 34" • Cotton sateen, low-water immersion dyed, hand printed
and painted with dye, machine stitched. 2012

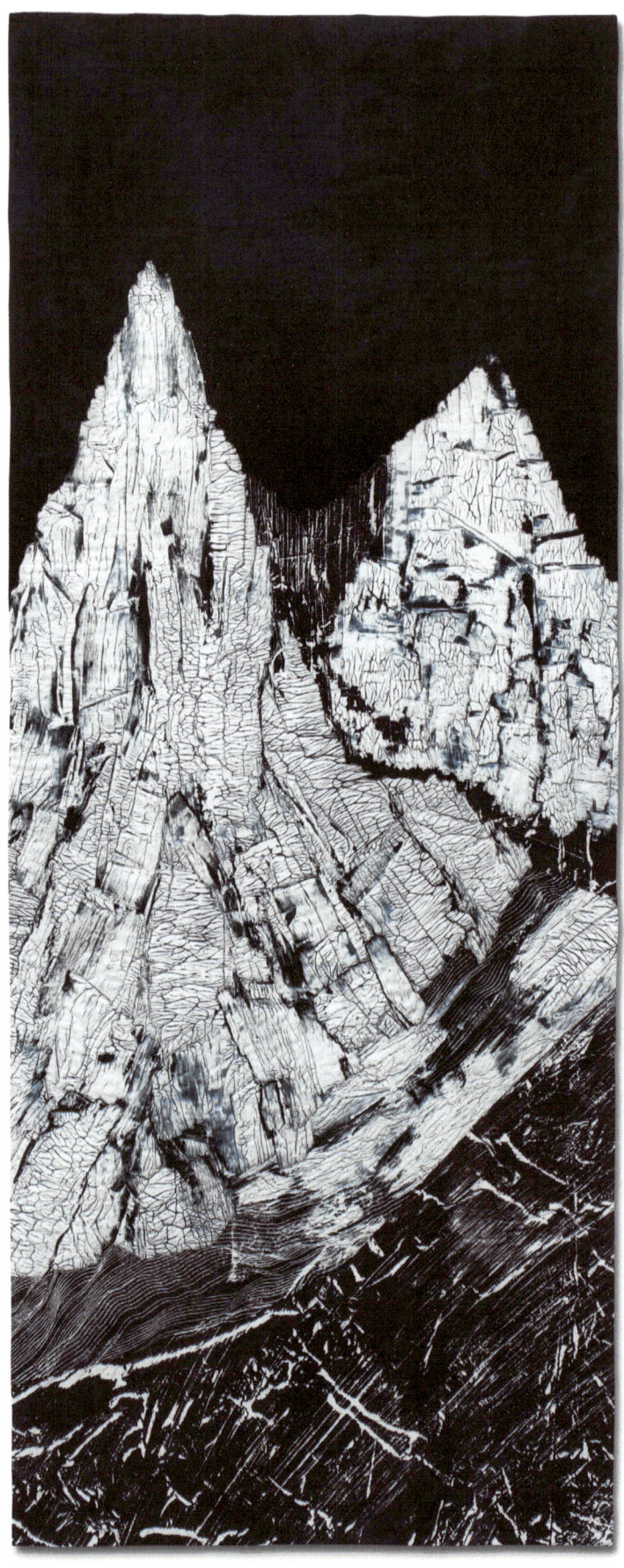

84" x 35" • Cotton sateen, low-water immersion dyed, hand printed
and painted with dye, hand and machine stitched. 2012

During the day I waited for the climbers. During the night I watched the white granitic peak glow with reflected light as the moon and stars cycled through to dawn.

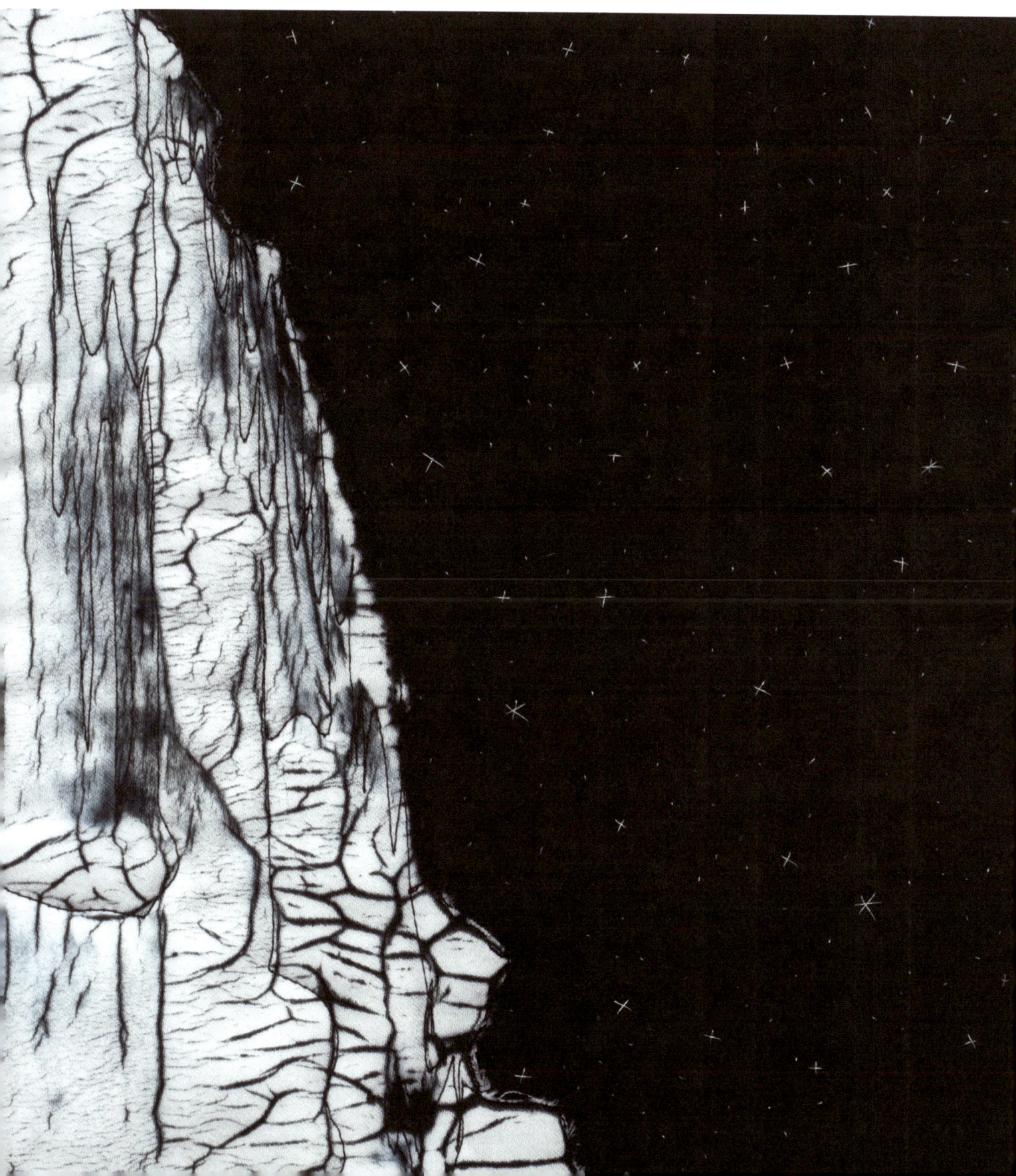

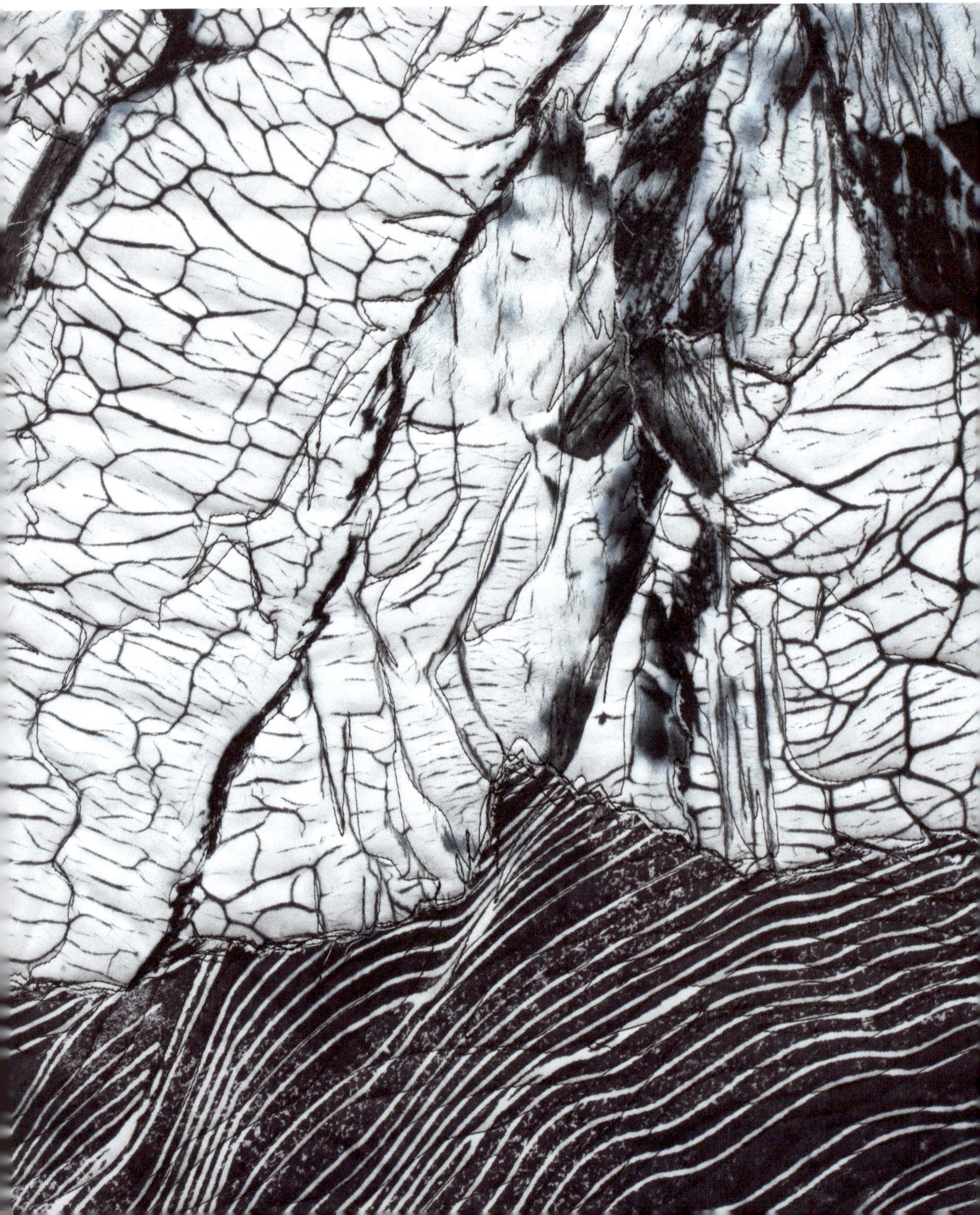

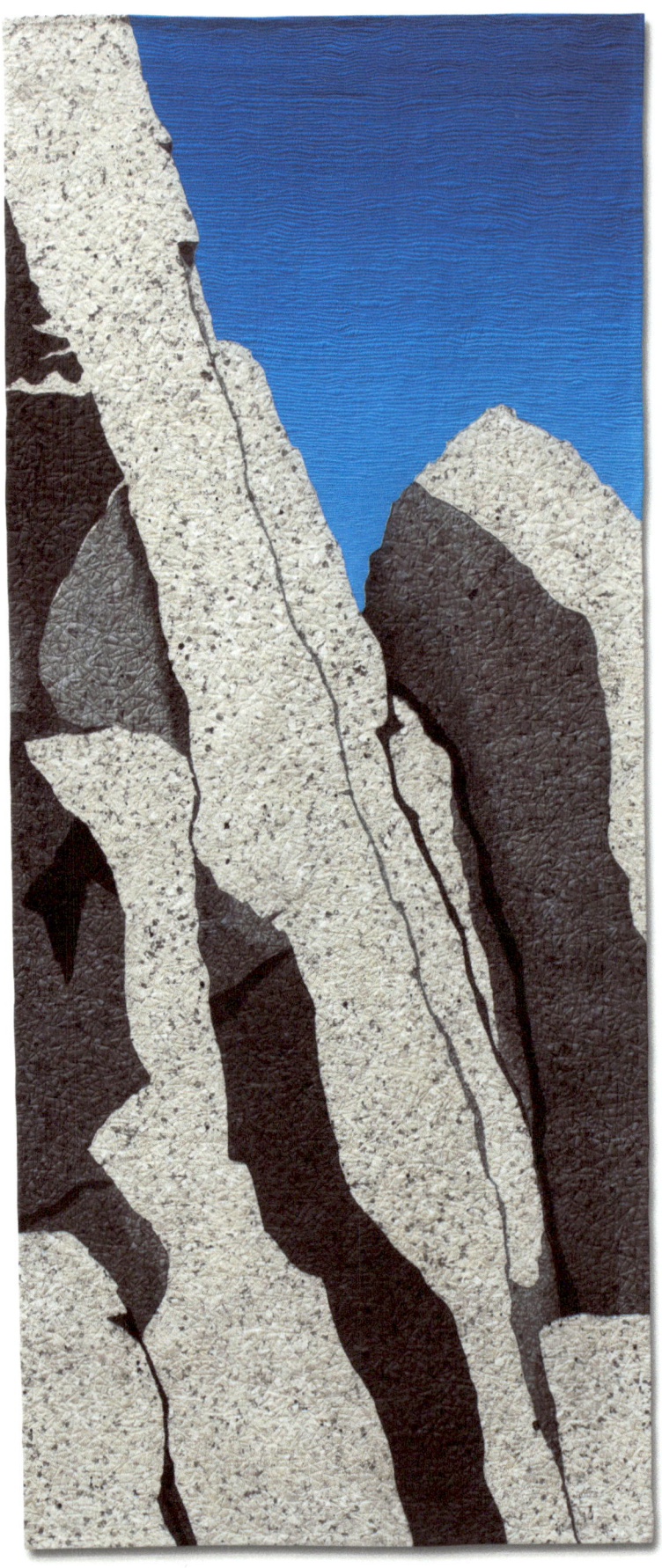

84" x 36" • Cotton sateen and silk organza, low-water immersion dyed,
hand printed with dye, machine stitched. 2013

Bright sunshine and dark shadows fall on rock that has a medium texture with conspicuous large crystals of white potassium feldspar characterizing it as Cathedral Peak Granodiorite. The rock fingers outline the pure blue sky and remind me of the finest views in the Sierra.

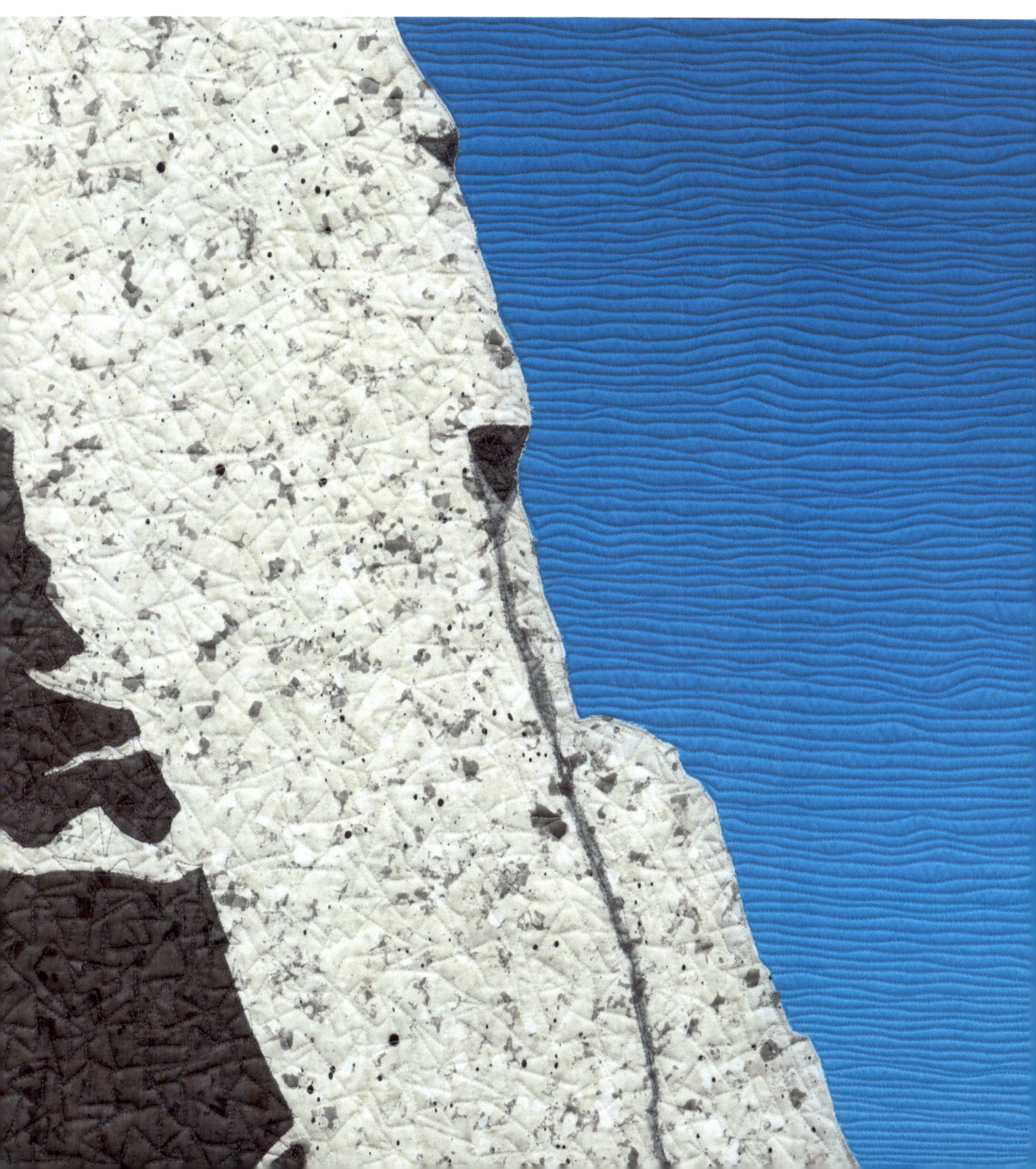

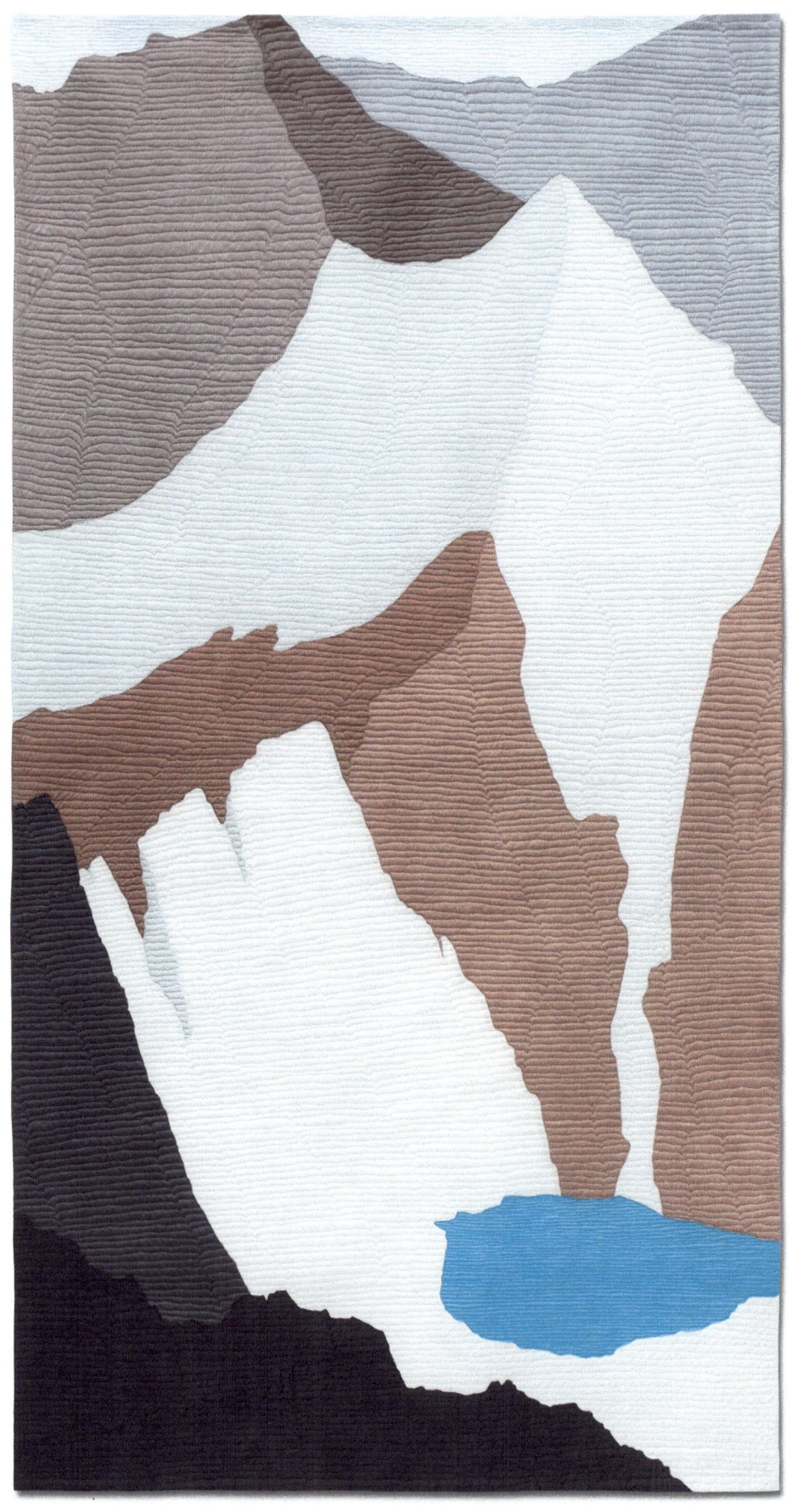

84" x 45" • Cotton sateen, low-water immersion dyed, machine stitched. 2016

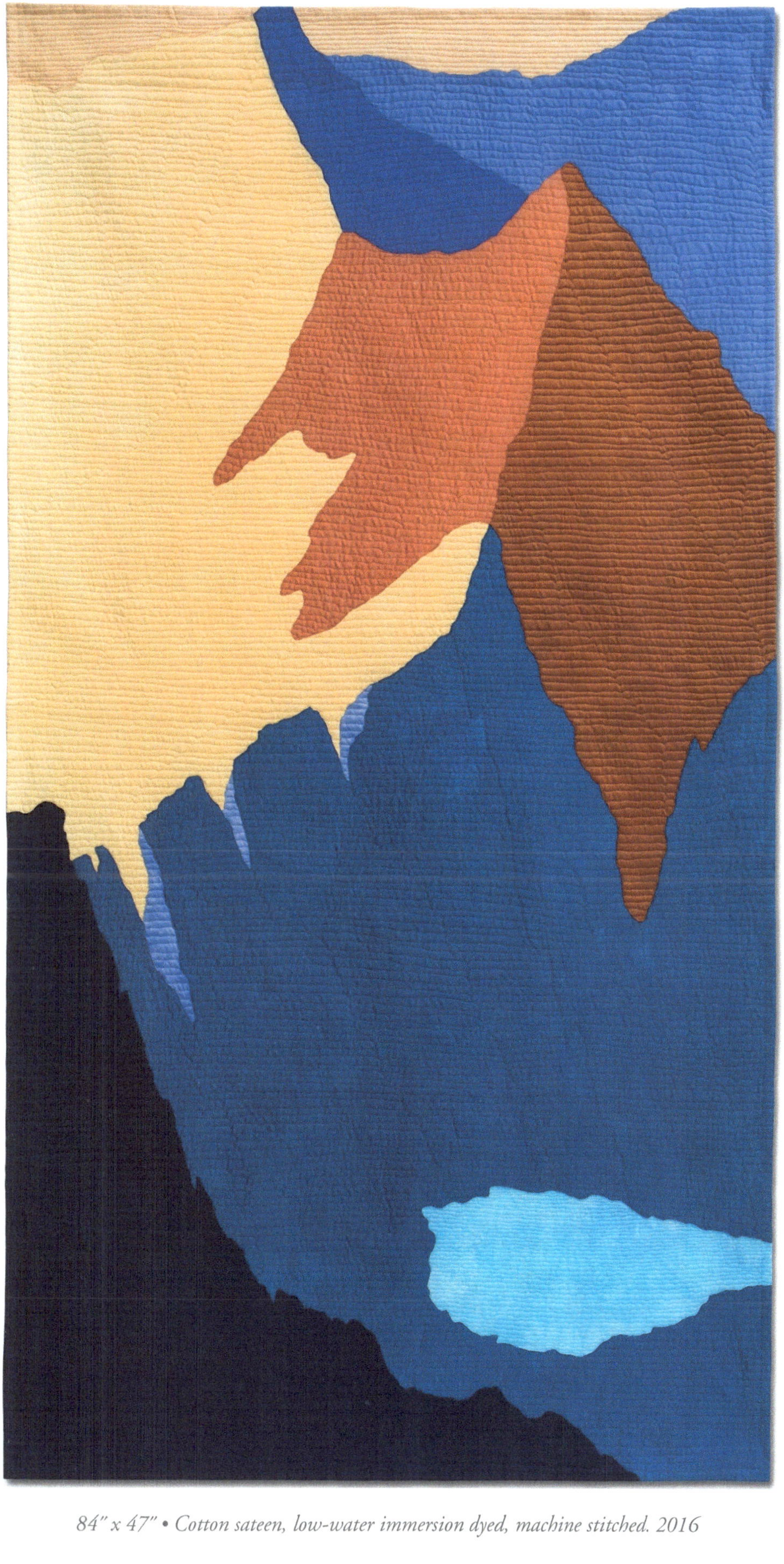

84" x 47" • Cotton sateen, low-water immersion dyed, machine stitched. 2016

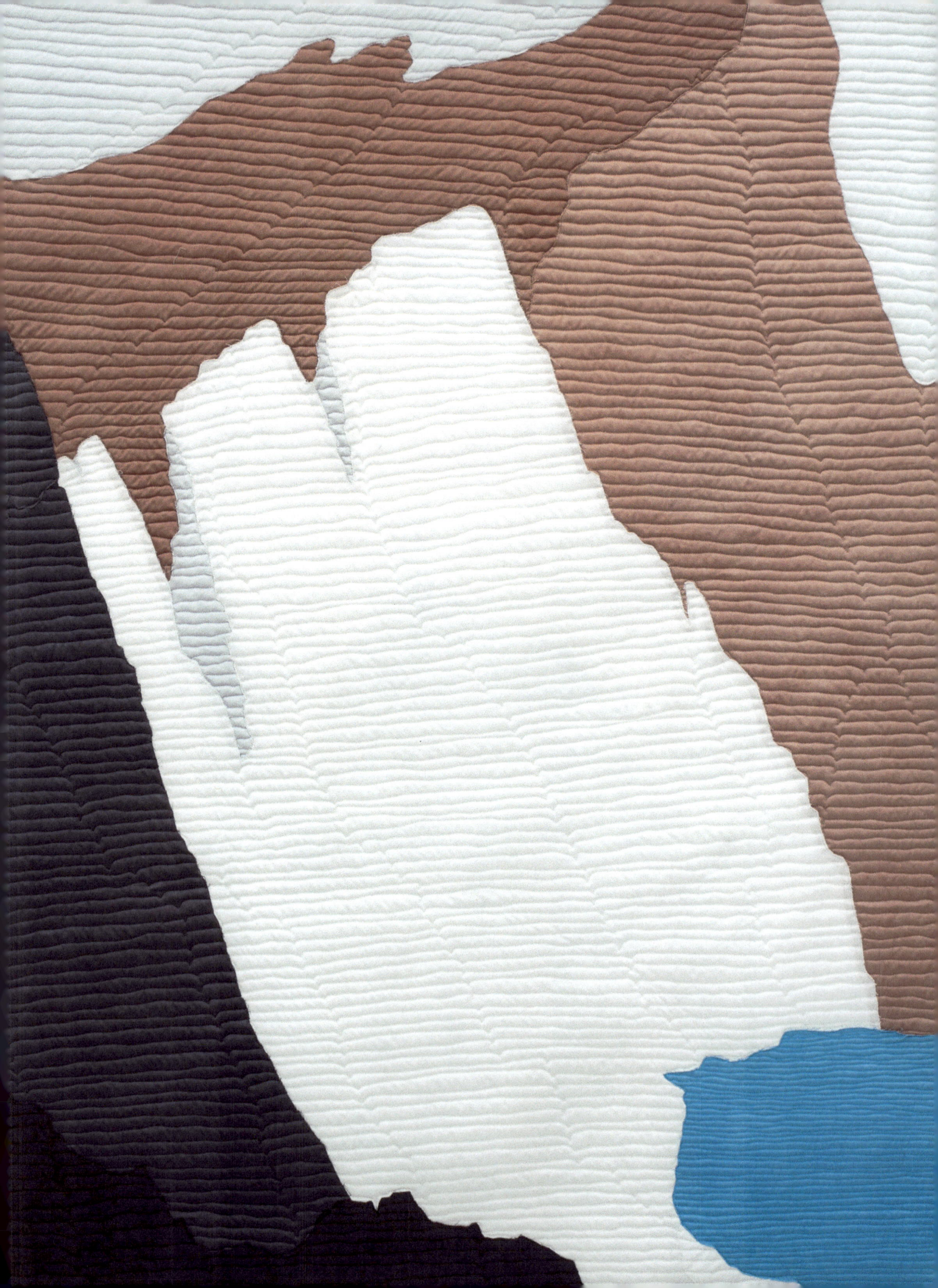

The bowl-shaped recess of a cirque is accentuated by the steepness of its semicircular cliffs. Looking west from a high pass across a glacier carved valley, I am struck by the view of a rust-colored metasedimentary screen that divided the rising granite magma 167 million years ago.

Many of the highest peaks along the crest of the Sierra are sharply steep and bounded by three or more cirques that were carved by glaciers, and now—the glaciers almost gone—they continue to be shaped by rock falls localized by jointed granite. Arêtes that connect the peaks define edges of color at the end of the day.

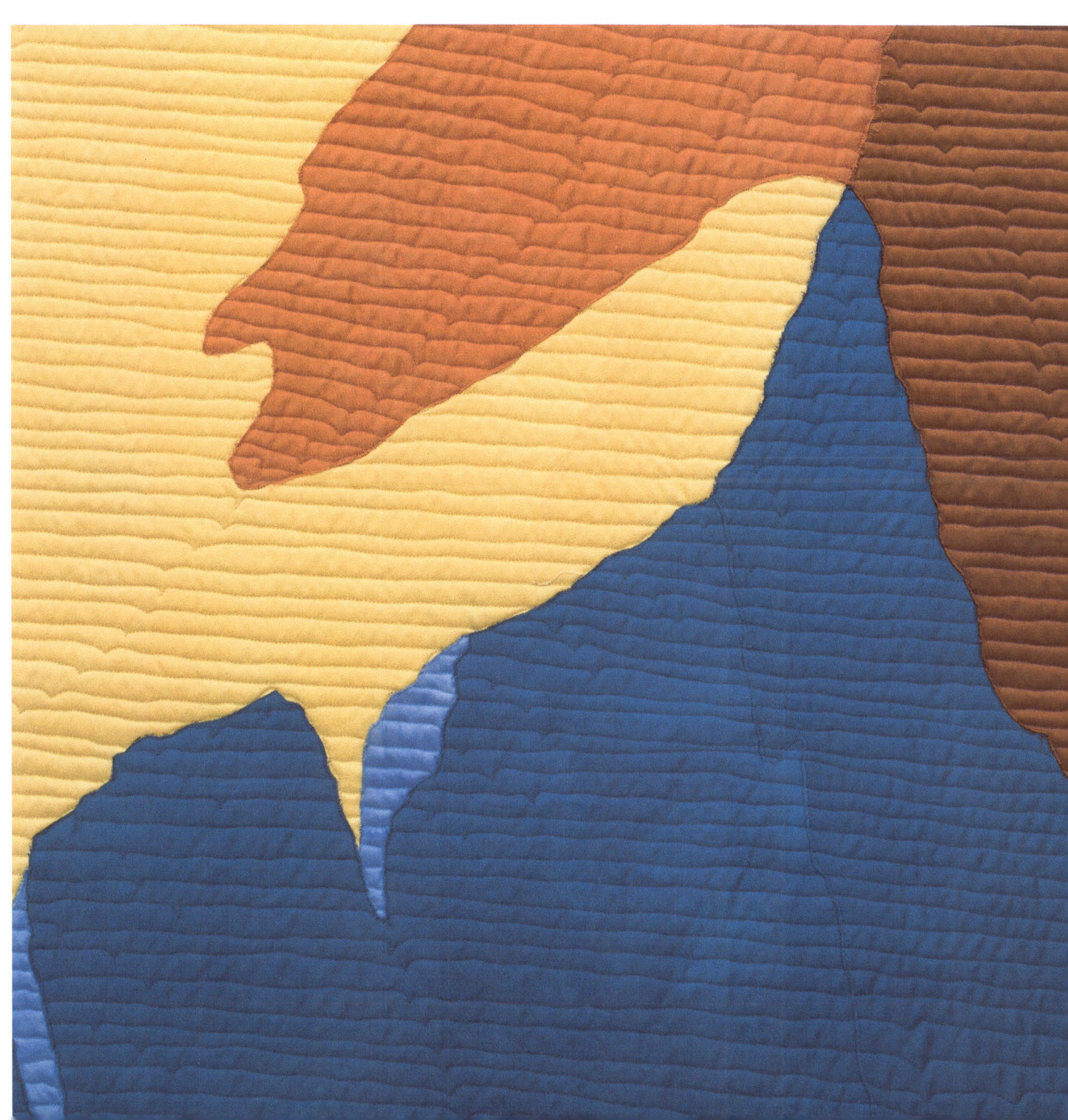

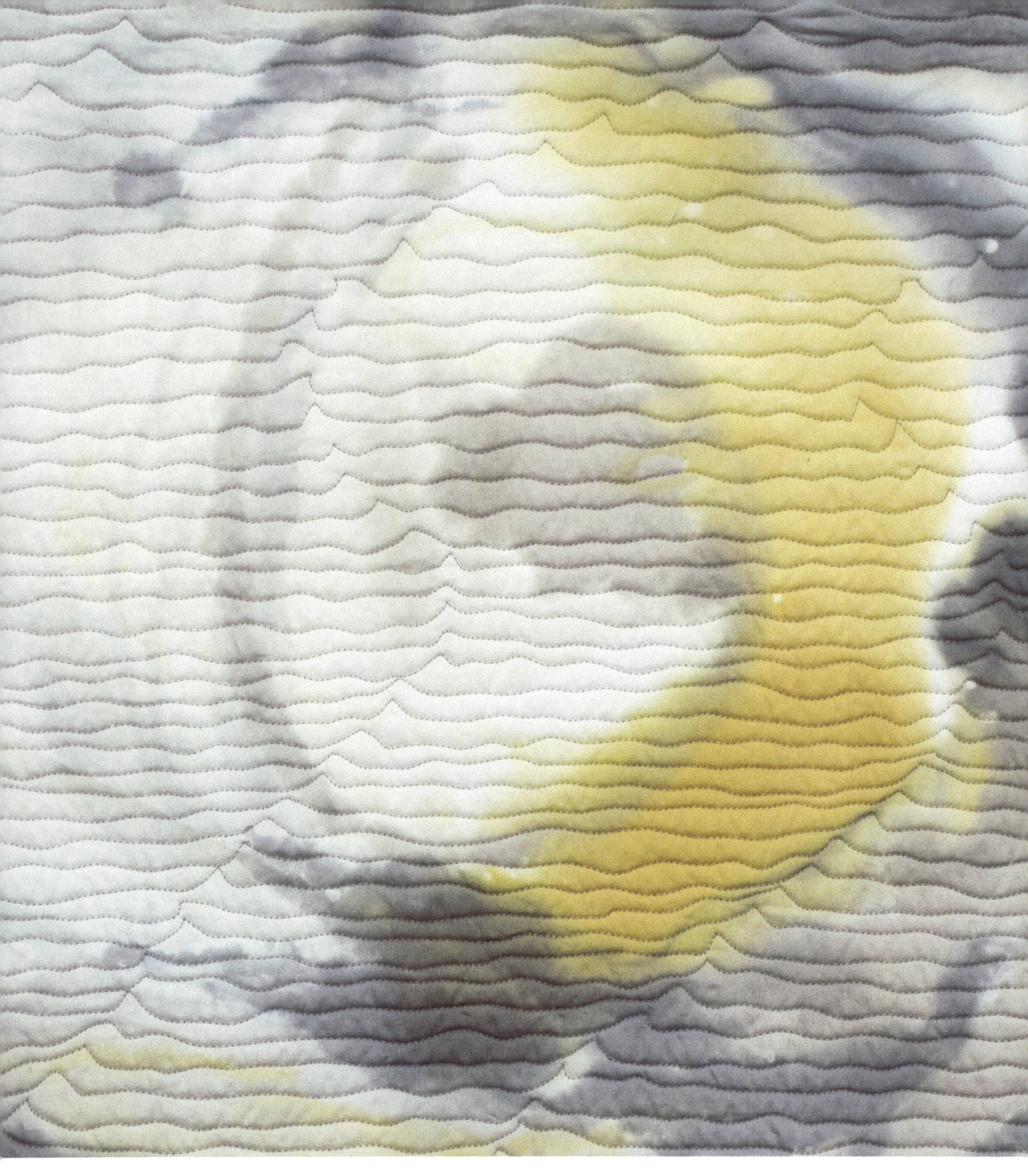

Placer miners in California found ancient riverbeds with rich gold deposits high on Sierra ridges, which they named auriferous gravels. The deepest leads had the most gold and often had bluish-colored gravels. They moved staggering amounts of overlying rock and dirt with water canons to remove the gold. In the 1870s, mud from the sluices filled present-day rivers, covered farmlands in the Central Valley, and reached the ocean at San Francisco Bay.

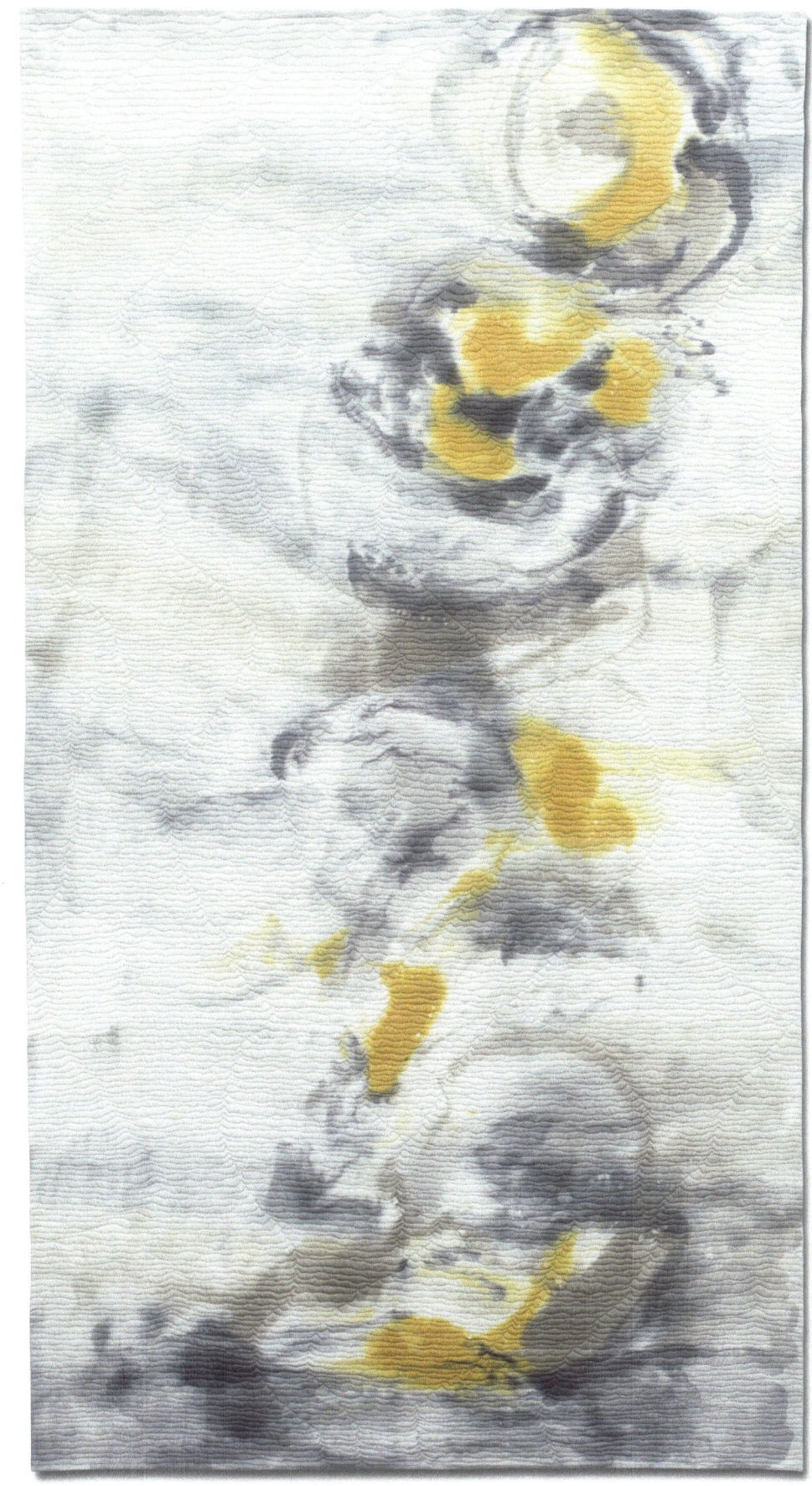

84" x 47" • Cotton sateen, hand printed with dye, machine stitched. 2012

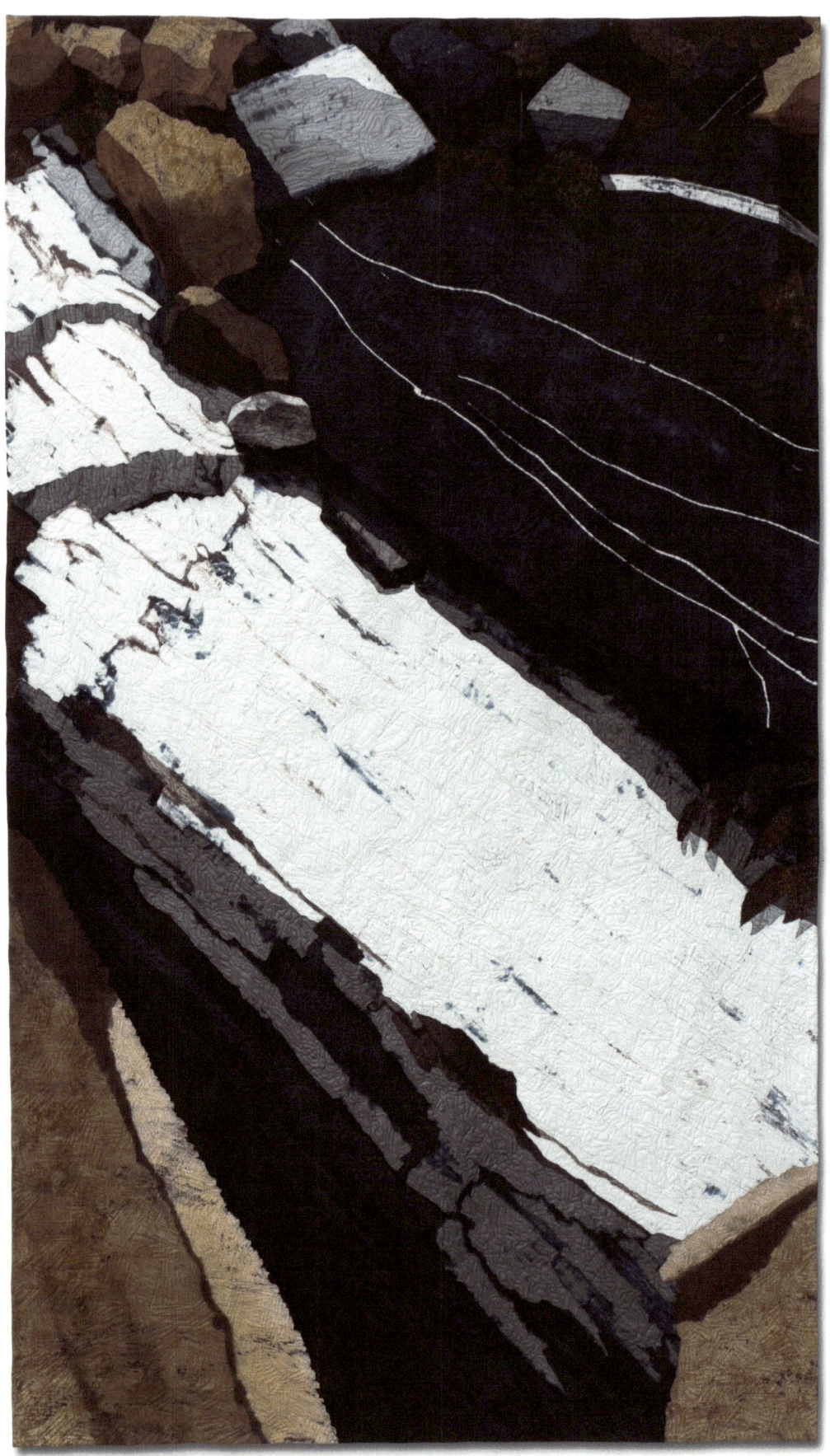

86" x 51" • Cotton sateen and silk organza, hand printed and painted with dye, machine stitched. 2013

When two miners stumbled on it May 21, 1851, the exposed top of the quartz lode was about 20 feet wide, about 400 feet long and stood about four feet above the surrounding dark rock. The stampede began that day; eventually seven tunnels opened up this chimney, and more than 30 miles of holes burrowed into the top 1300 feet of the mountain. Now, blocks of white quartz and black gabbro close the entry to the collapsed tunnels.

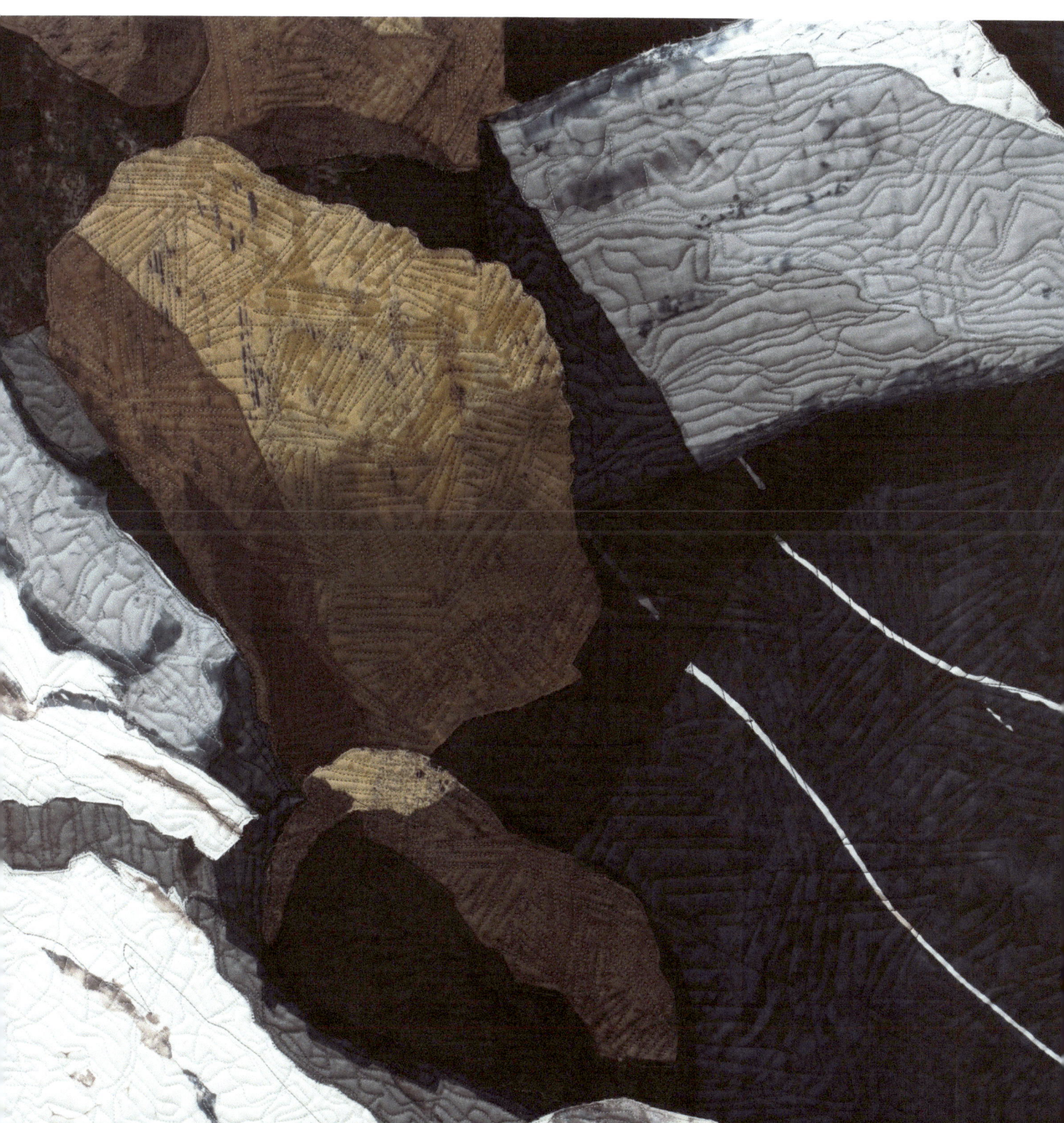

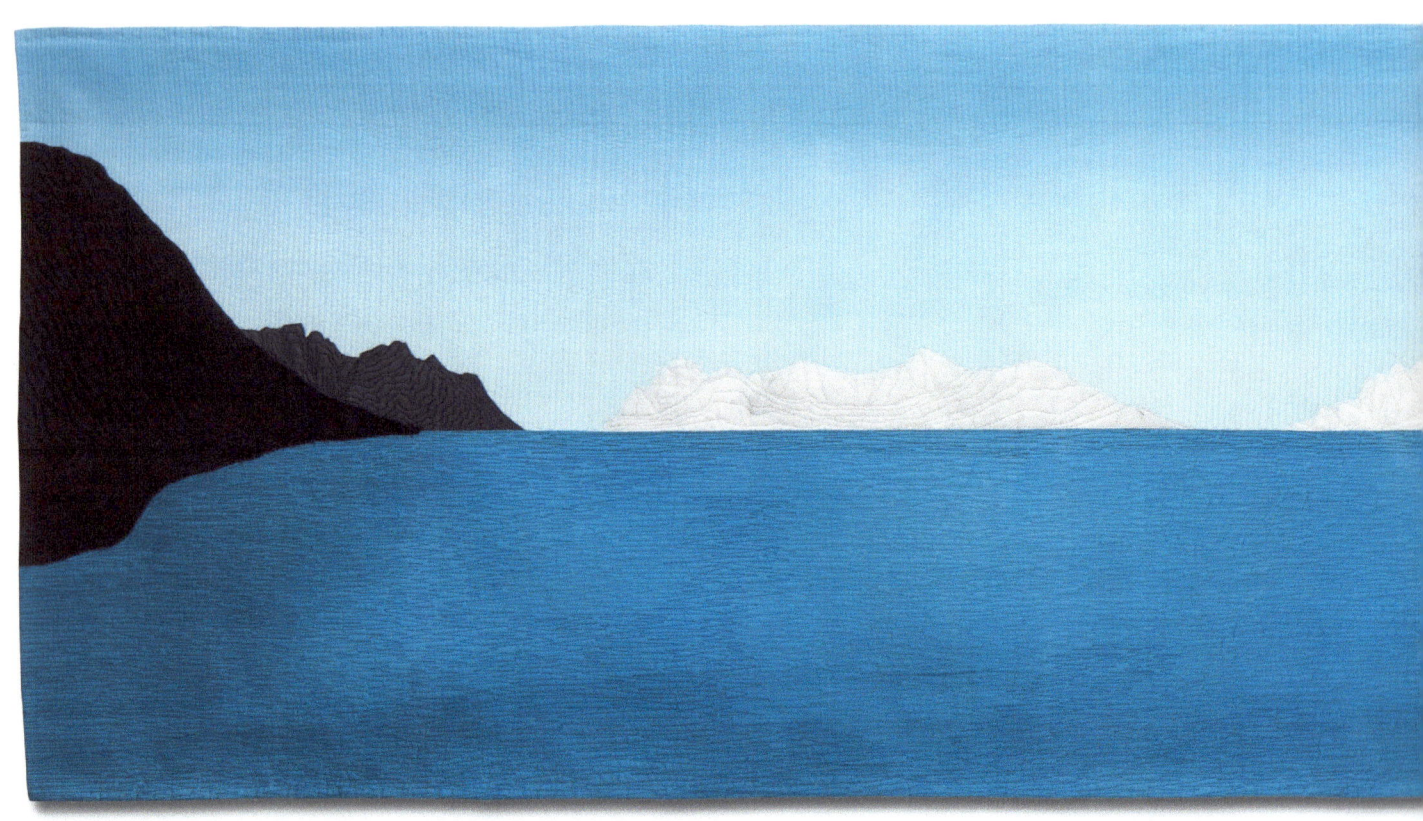

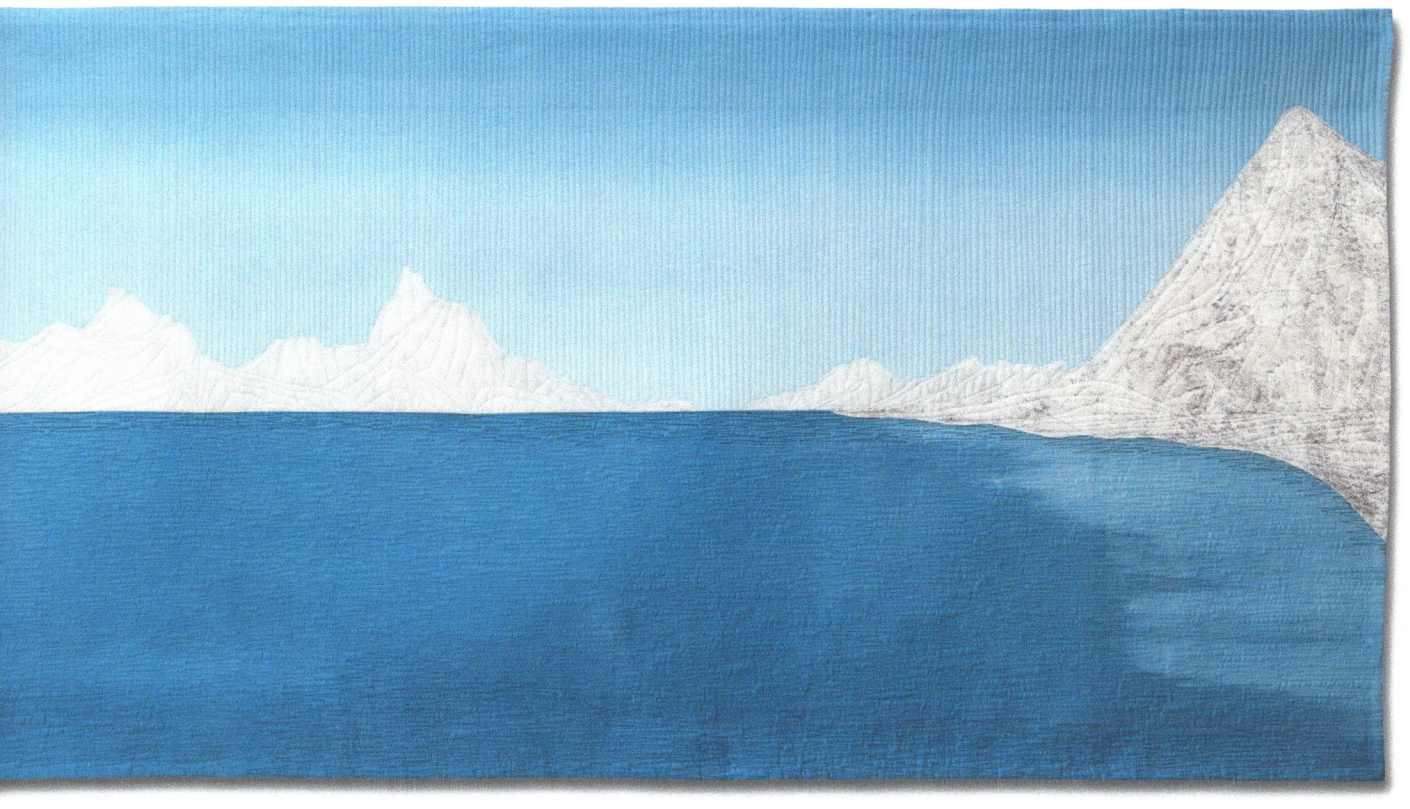

On the walk from our mine back to the trailhead, we are standing eye level with the tops of the mountains. We have a broad view of many of the high peaks of Yosemite, from the dark scree of the Dana Plateau on the east to the light spires of the Cathedral Range farther west. Many peaks are identifiable from a distance by their unique shapes.

32" x 124" • Cotton sateen, low-water immersion dyed, hand printed and painted with dye, machine stitched. 2016

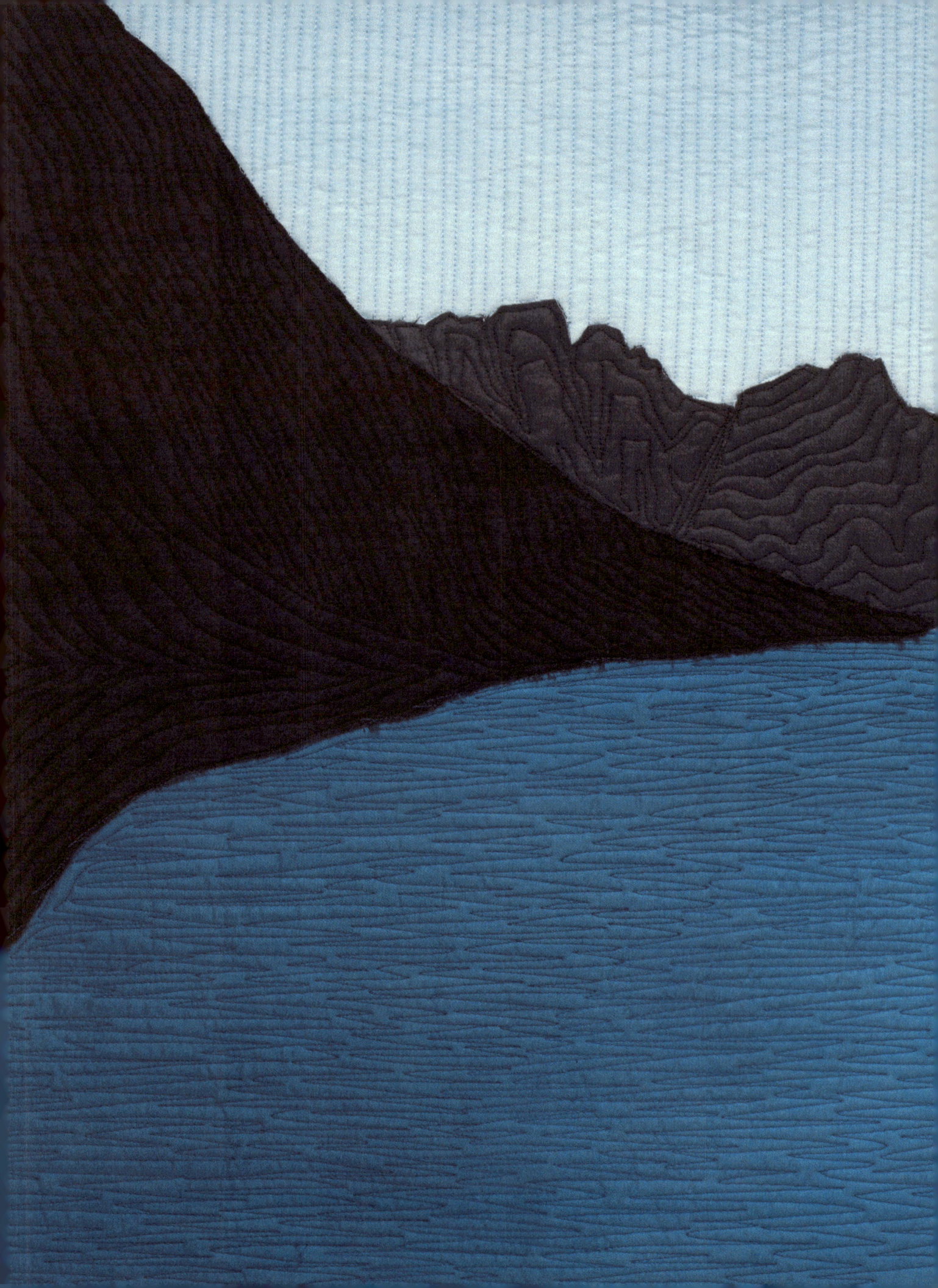

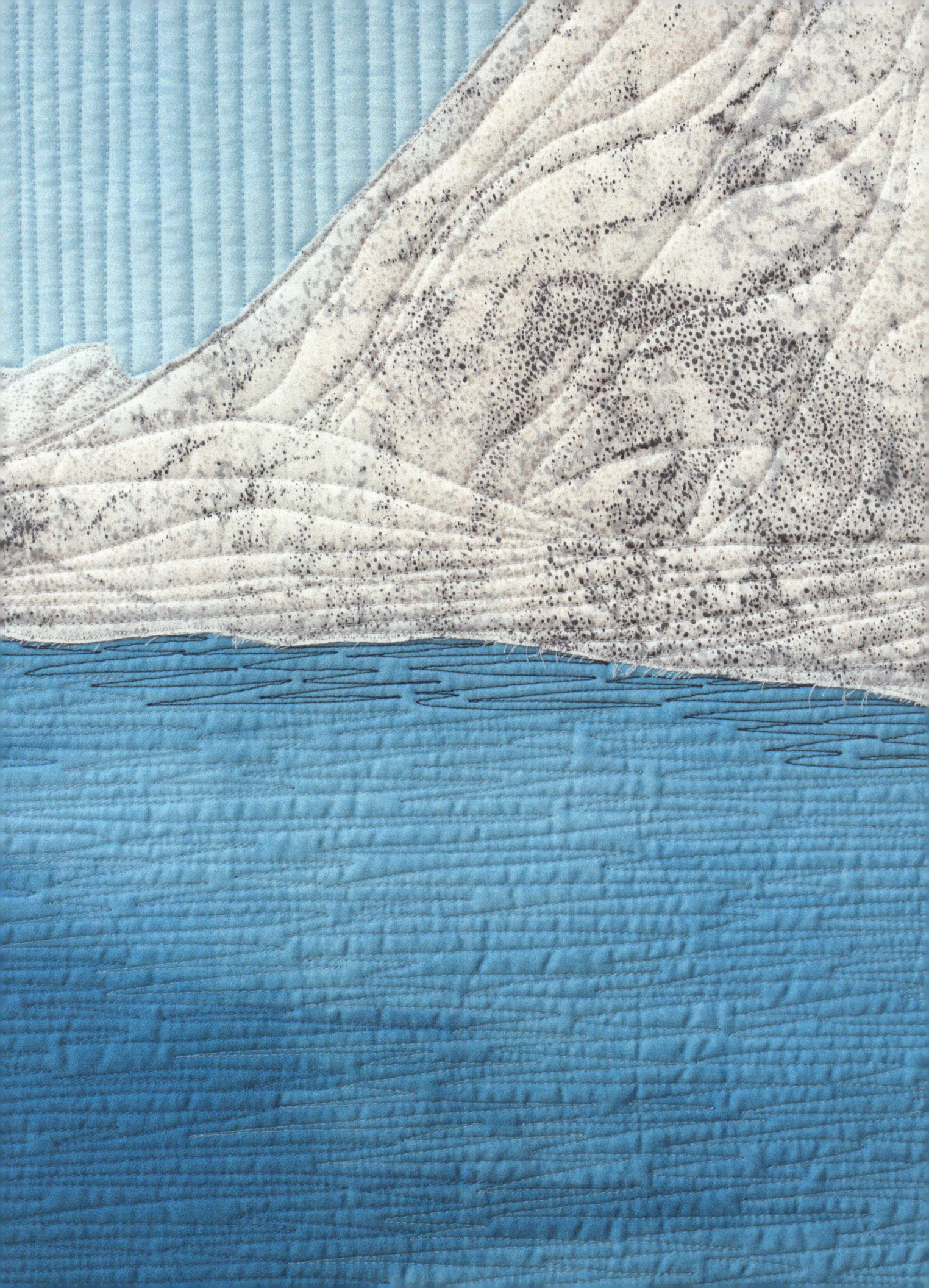

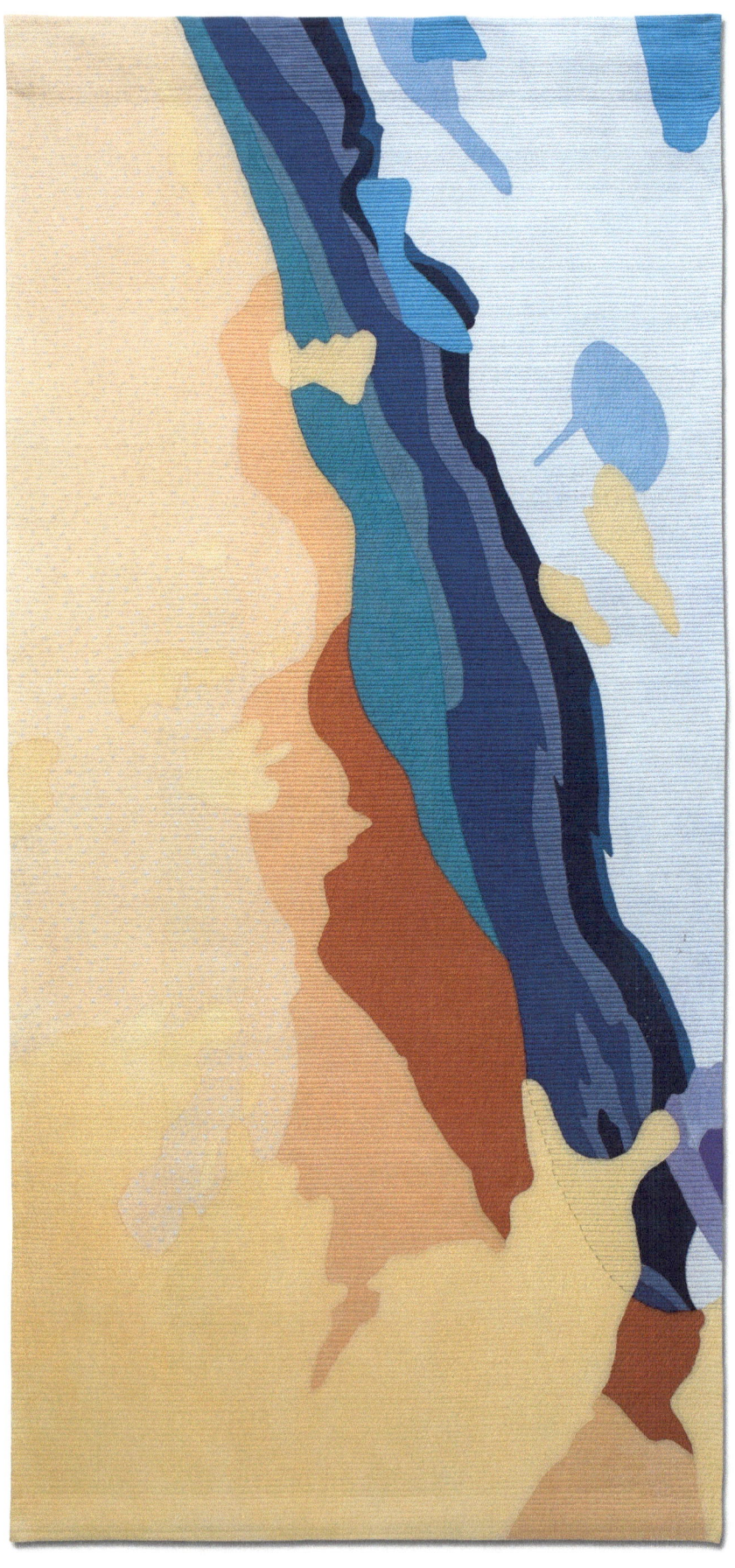

83" x 41" • Cotton sateen, low-water immersion dyed, machine assembled and quilted,
embellished with fabric paint and hand and machine embroidery. 2016

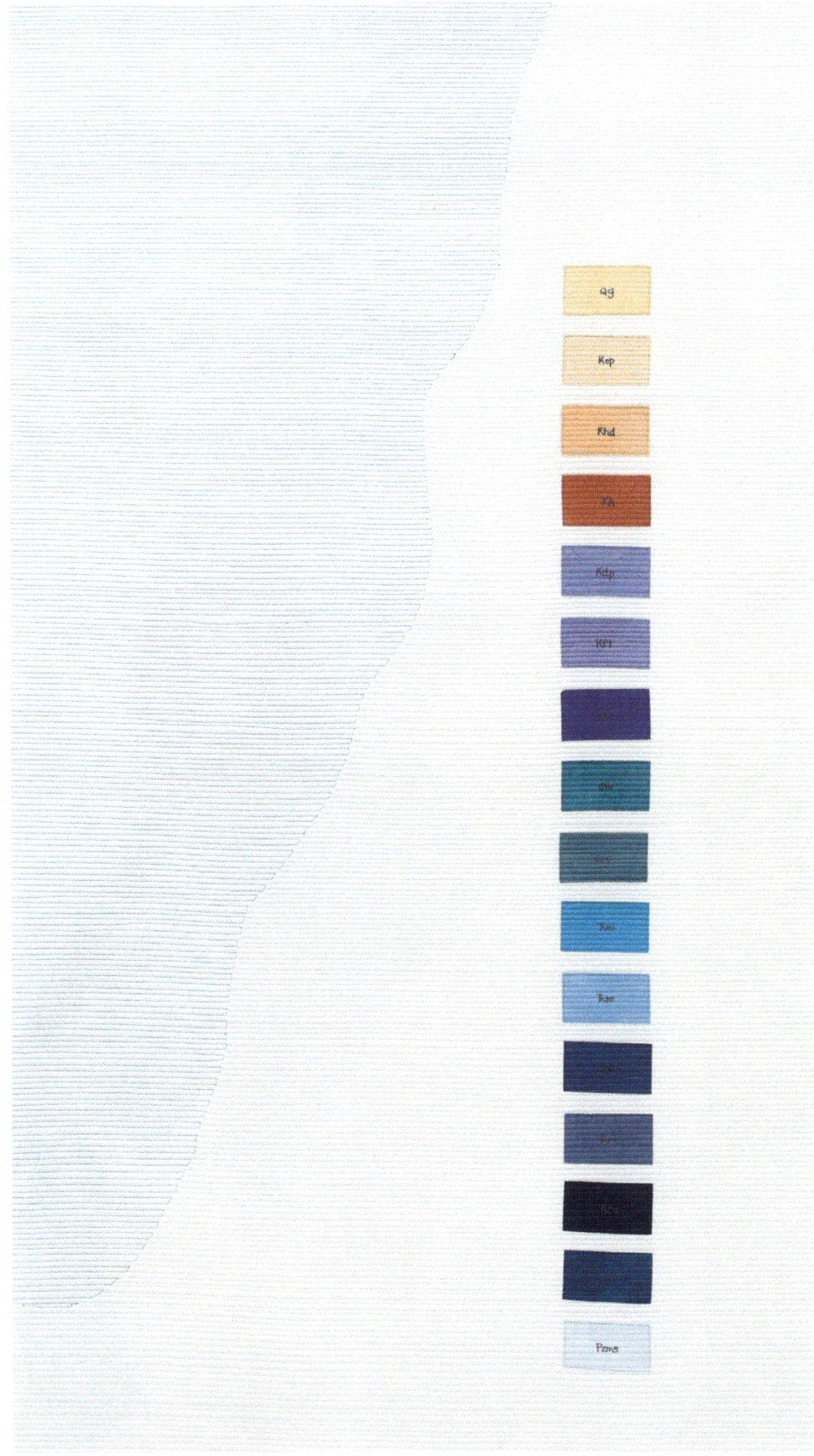

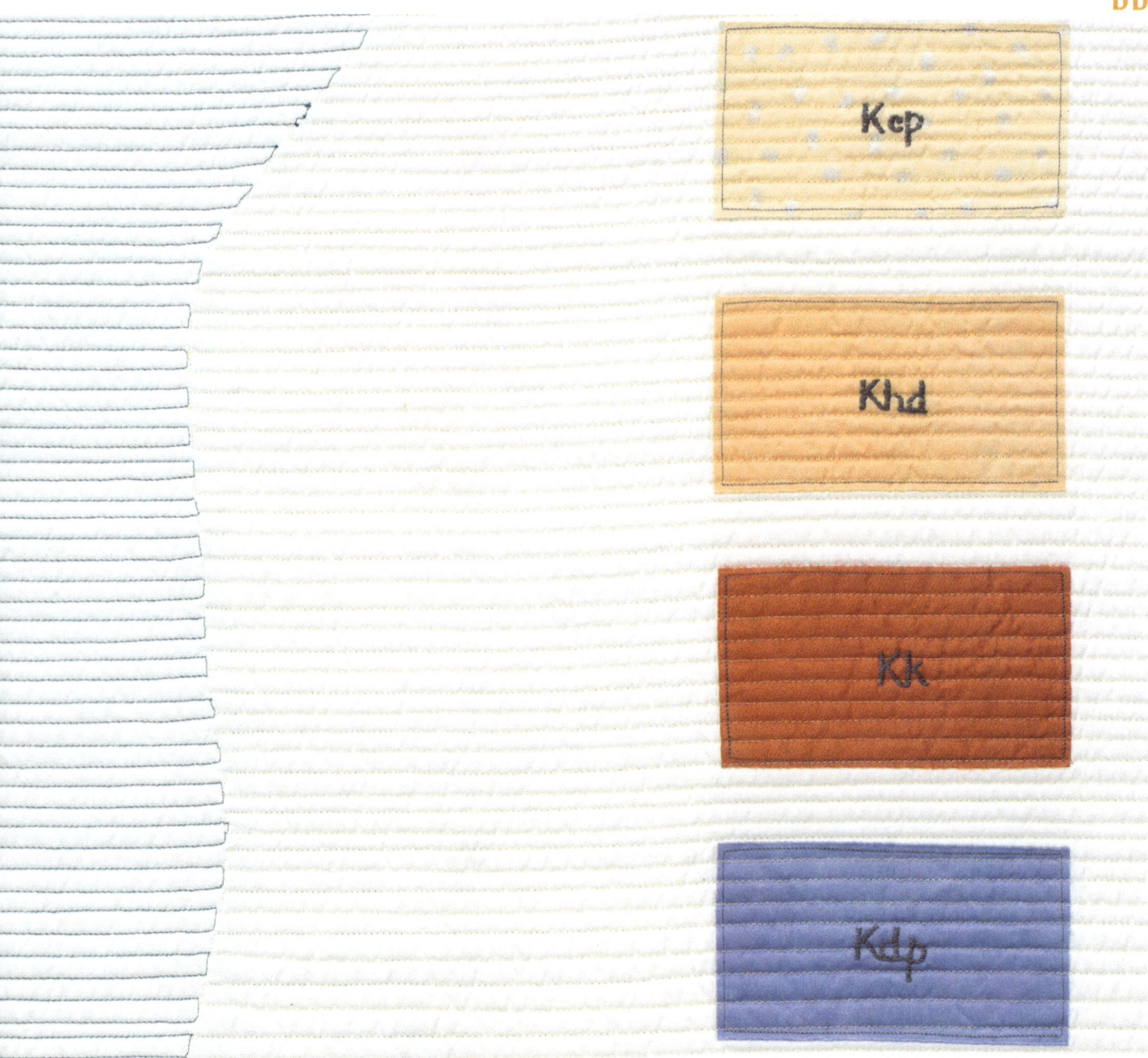

In 1860 a dentist named George Chase found a mineral lode on the east slope of the Sierra. He left a flattened tin can inscribed with his claim notice and broken shovel, keeping the knowledge to himself. A boy named William Brusky from Sonora found the claim in 1874 while tending his family's sheep. After a sample was found to be rich in silver he returned in 1878 to locate four claims along the lode for himself and his friends, with high hopes for another boomtown.

In May 1881 William and his brother James signed the deed selling one claim to my great grandfather, Daniel Doherty. According to a local newspaper, William "labored under an attack of insanity" when he committed suicide in August of the same year. Small thread marks indicate the prospects and cabin ruins of our claim on a map of the regional bedrock geology.

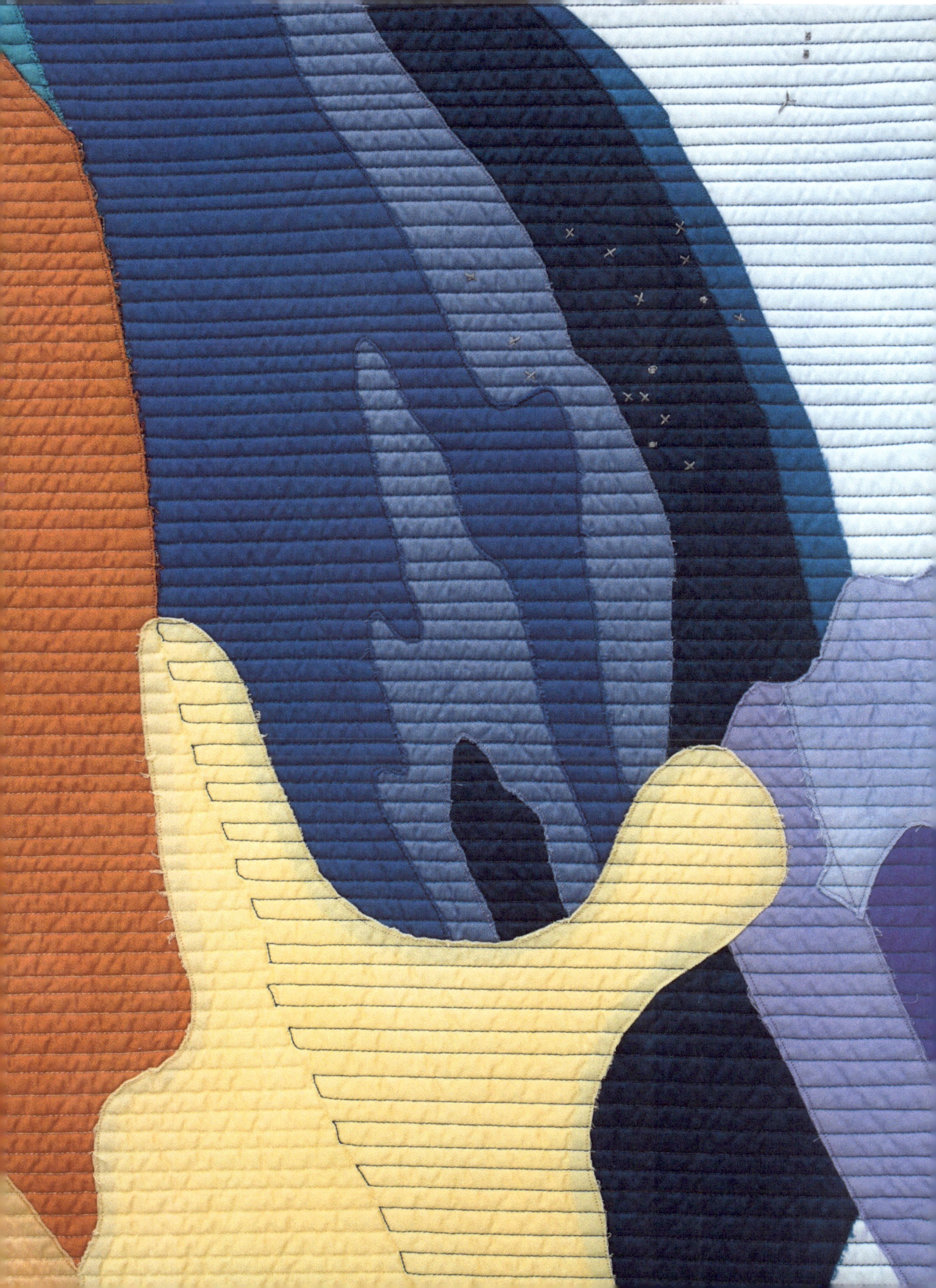

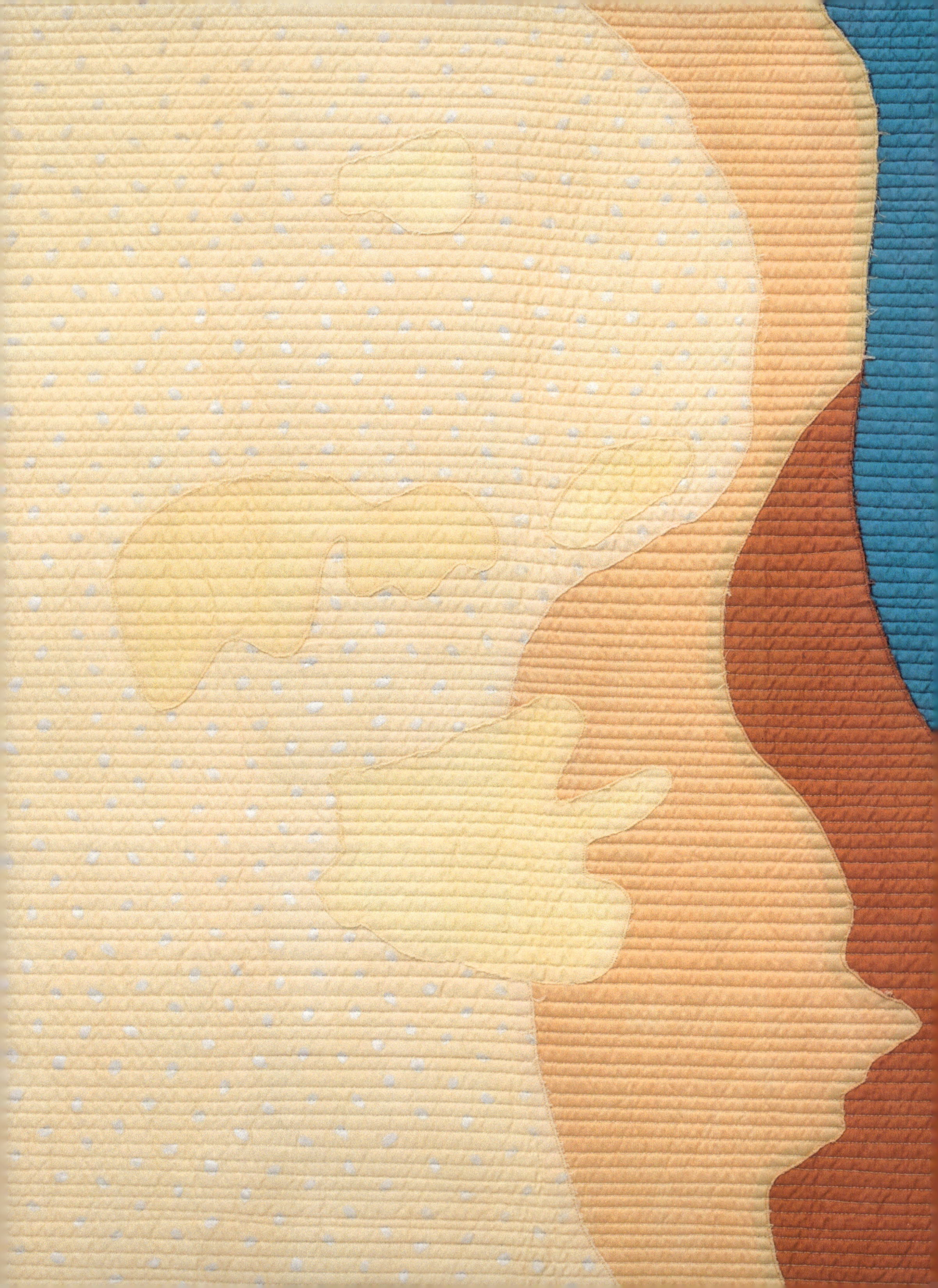

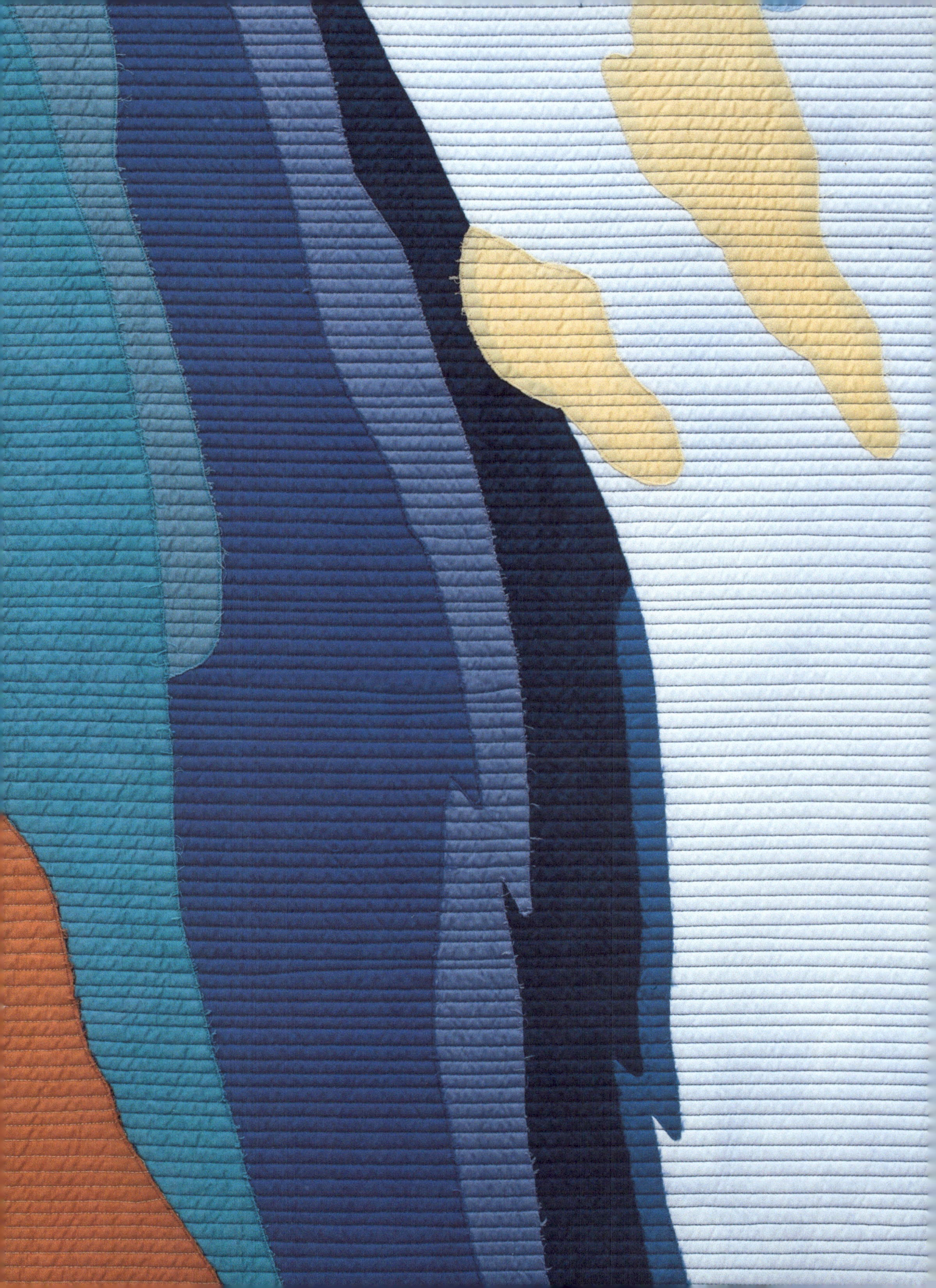

Above the tree line and across an expanse of meadow and scattered granite blocks, we have a perfect view of the contact of the eastern edge of the white Sierra Batholith and the mineralized Saddlebag Lake pendant where people labored fruitlessly for gold and silver 140 years ago. In the early summer this contact is covered with greenery, fed by tiny streams, headwaters of the Tuolumne River not too many miles away.

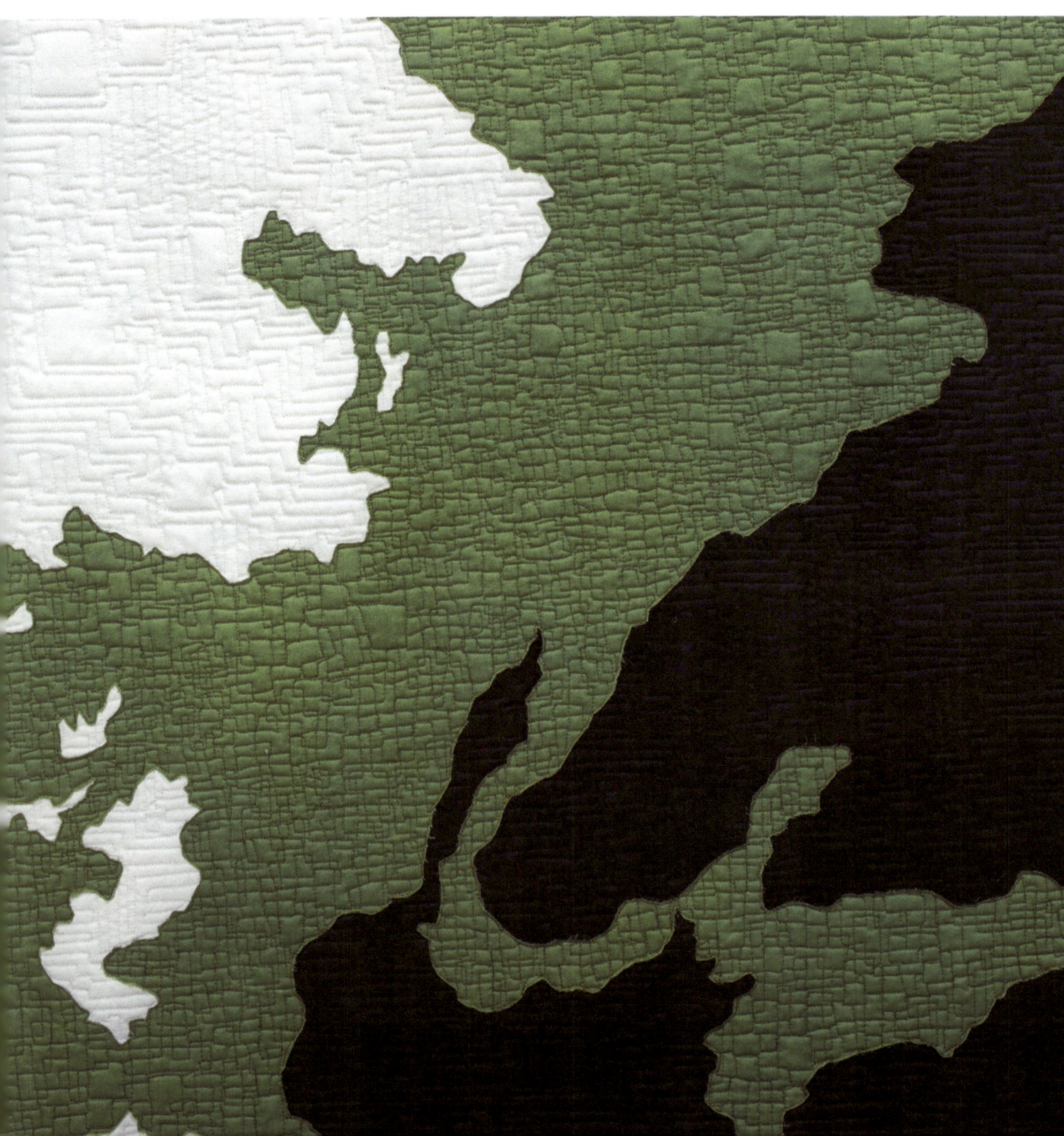

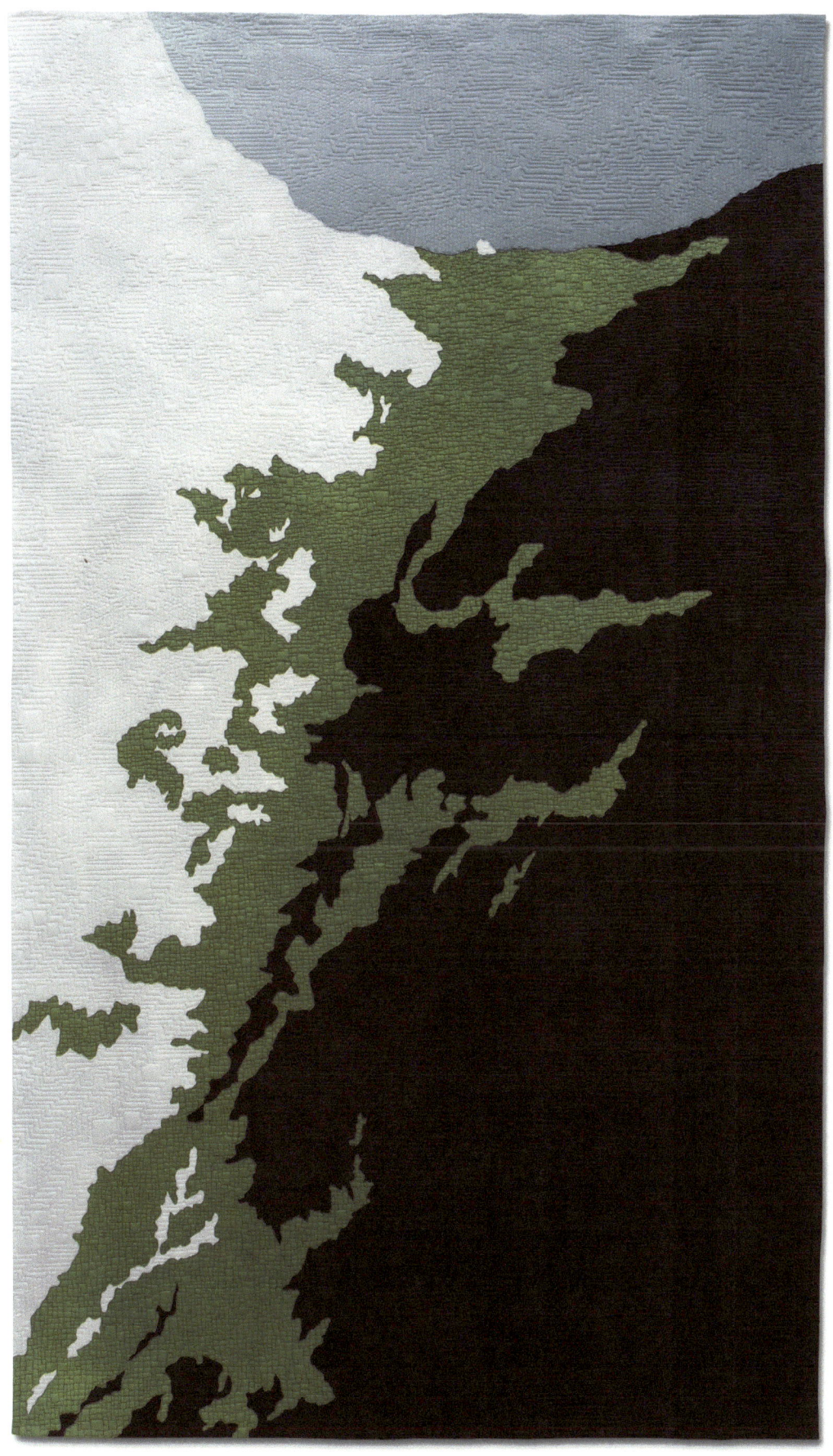

84" x 50" • Cotton sateen, low-water immersion dyed, machine stitched. 2016

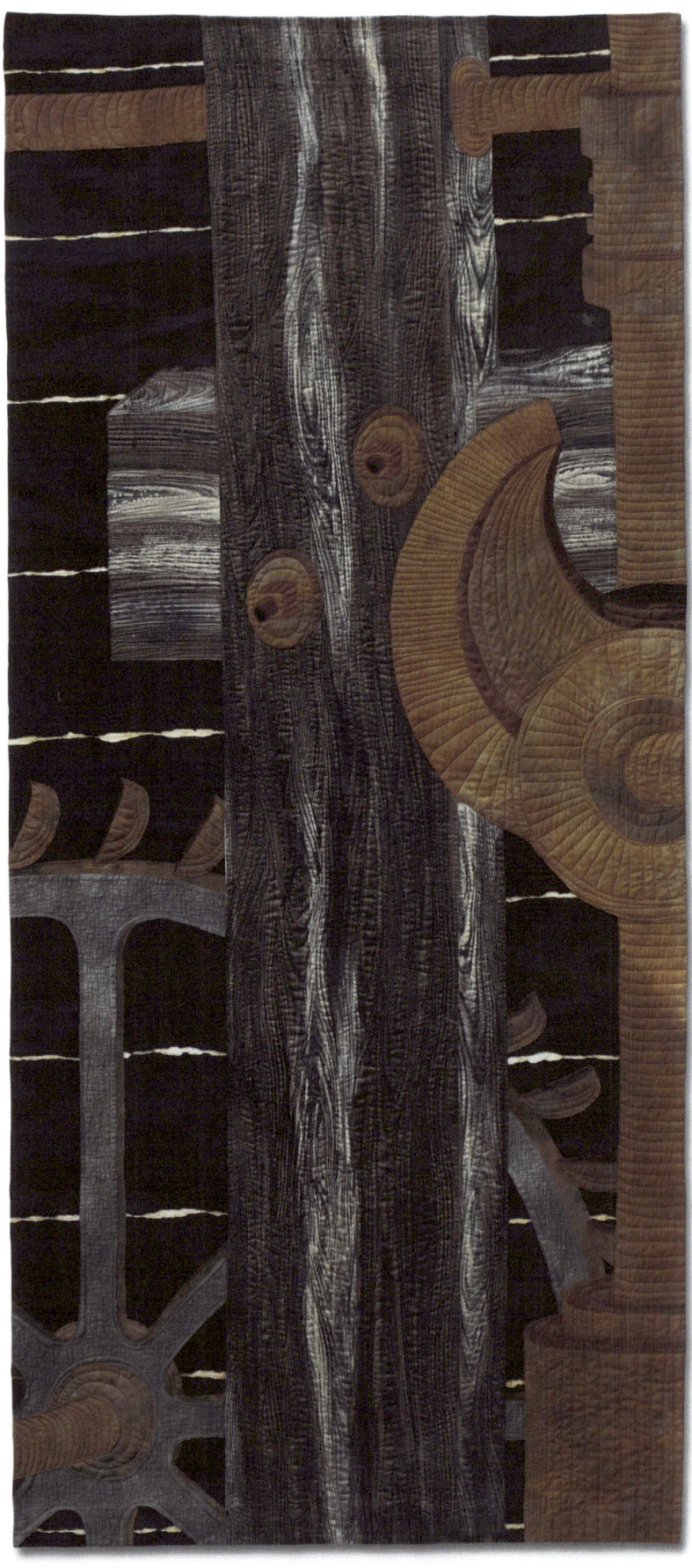

*84" x 39" • Cotton broadcloth and silk organza, low-water immersion dyed, hand printed
and painted with dye, machine stitched. 2013*

Walk in at the top level on the hillside, pass the ore cart hoppers and go down the steps, pass the grizzly and then the jaw crushers. Below, a Pelton water wheel teamed with wide leather belts lifts and drops iron stamps weighing 850 pounds each. In a day, a 60-stamp mill could pulverize 150 tons of rock to ready it for the mercury-coated plates and the concentrator tables—a green haze of arsenic dust floating over all. High grade ore returned about two to four ounces of gold per ton.

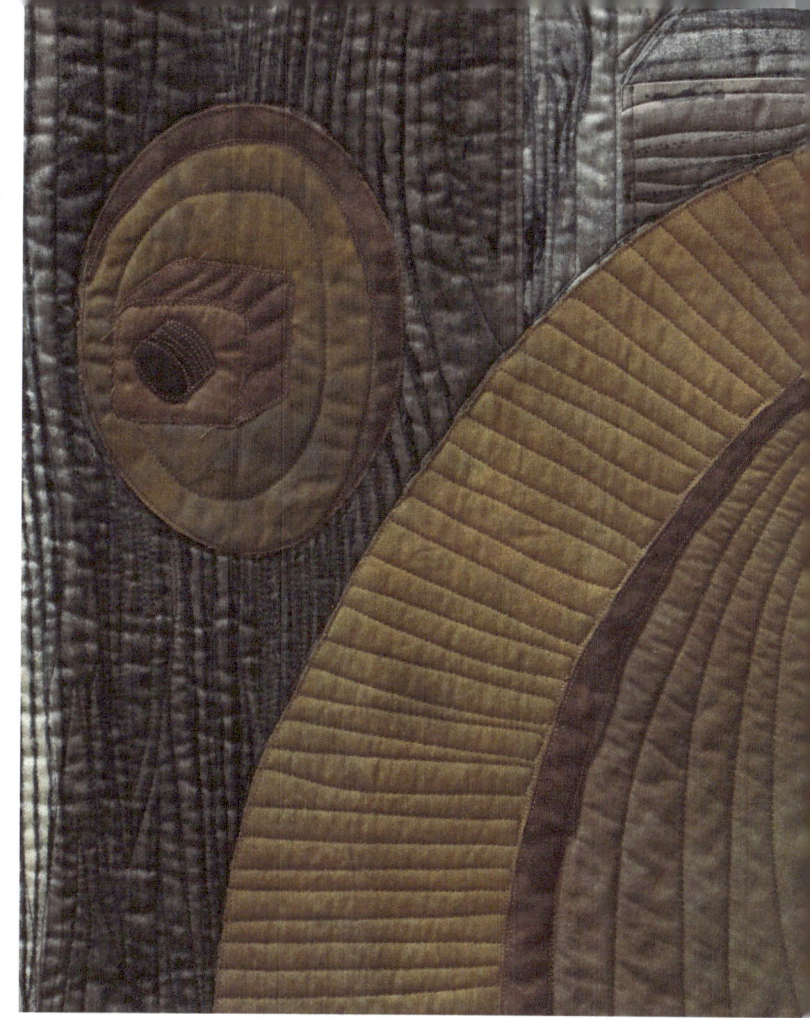

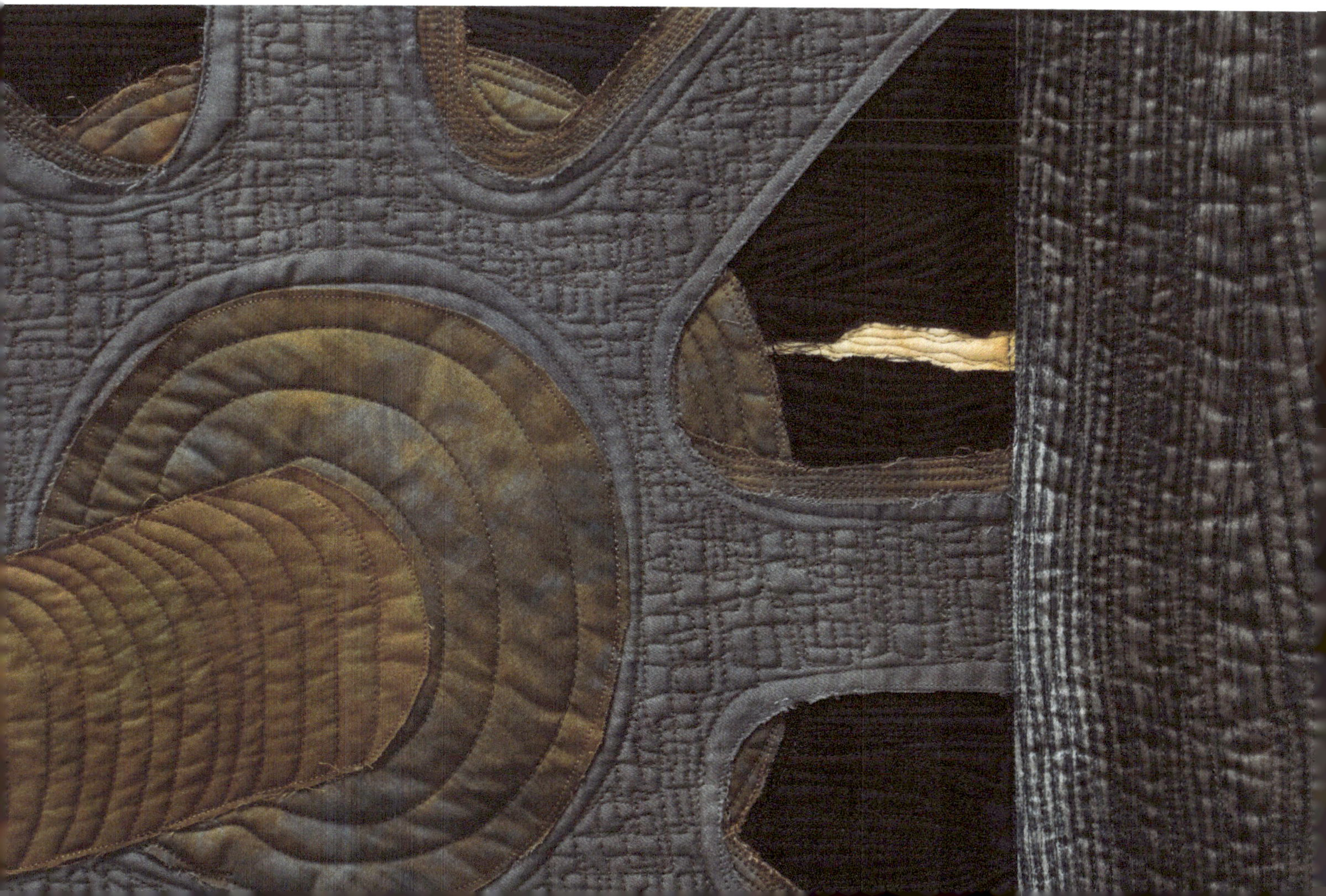

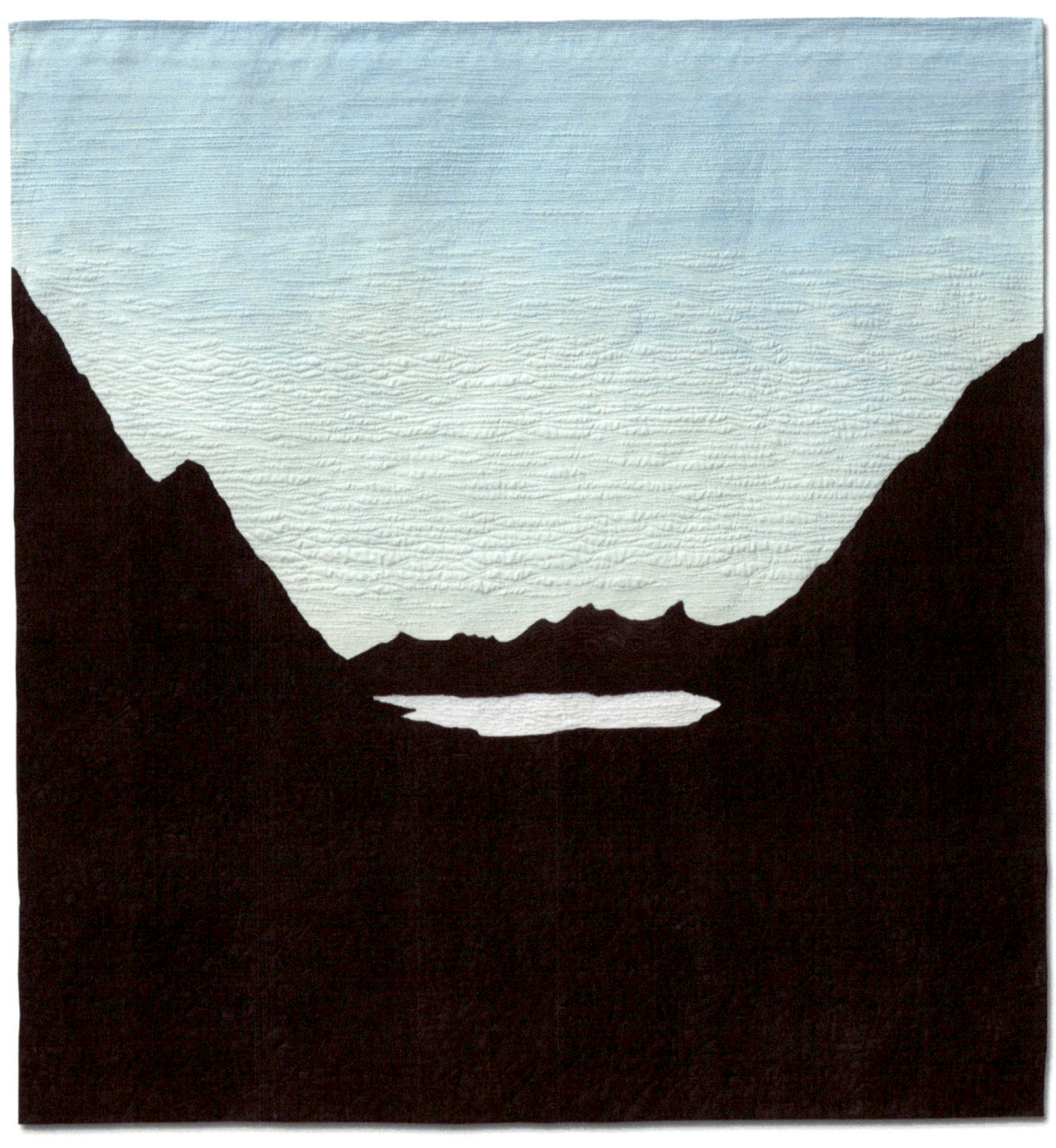

Sky and clouds appear and disappear quickly
in the evening at Golden Bear Lake, Center
Basin, CA, July 2012.

59" x 57" • Cotton sateen and organza, low-water immersion dyed, hand printed with dye, machine stitched. 2015

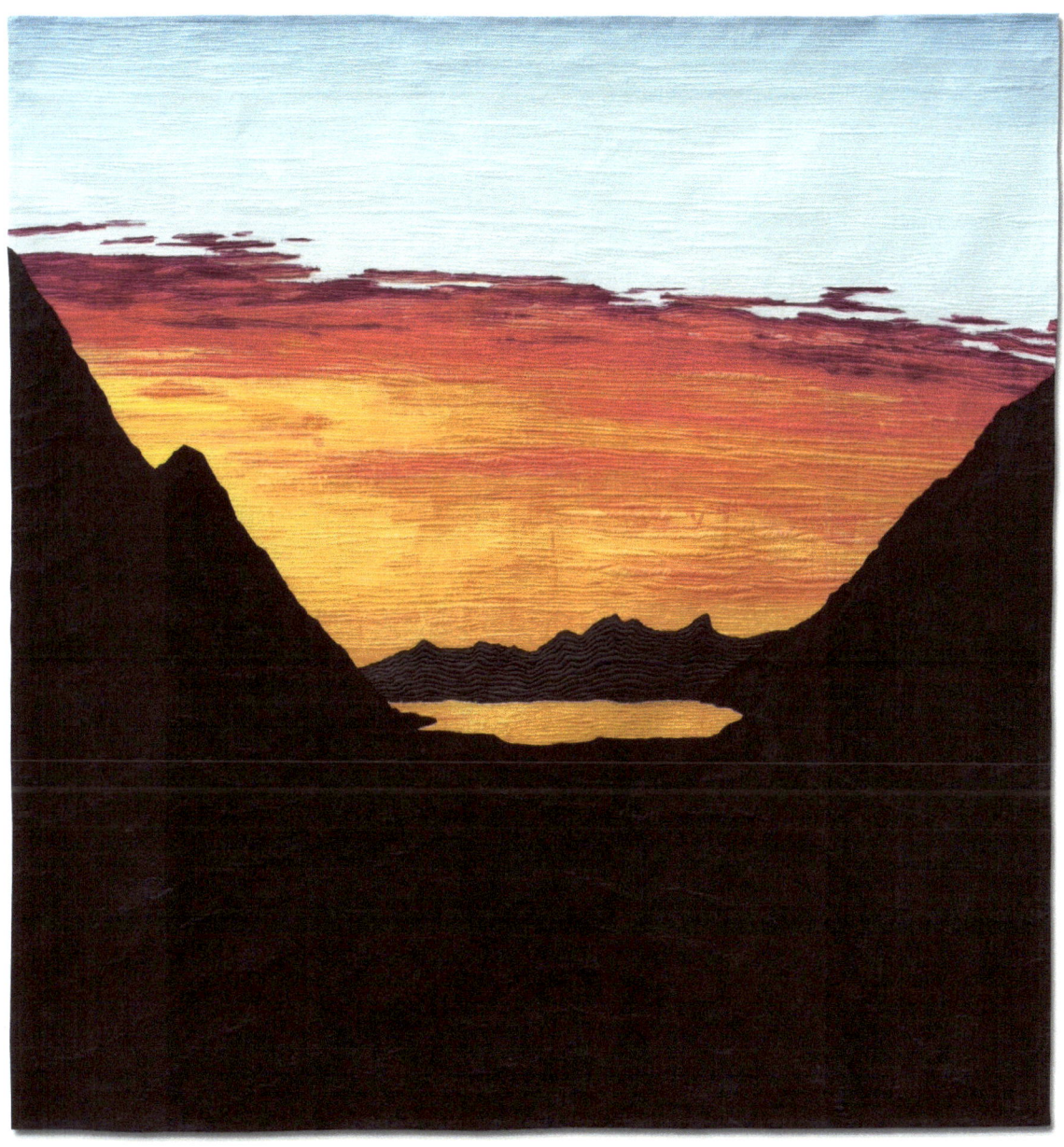

A deep, bowl-shaped landscape frames
eighteen different sunset-cloud formations in
eighteen minutes. These quilts show minute
one and minute eighteen.

59" x 57" • Cotton sateen, low-water immersion dyed, hand painted with dye, machine stitched. 2015

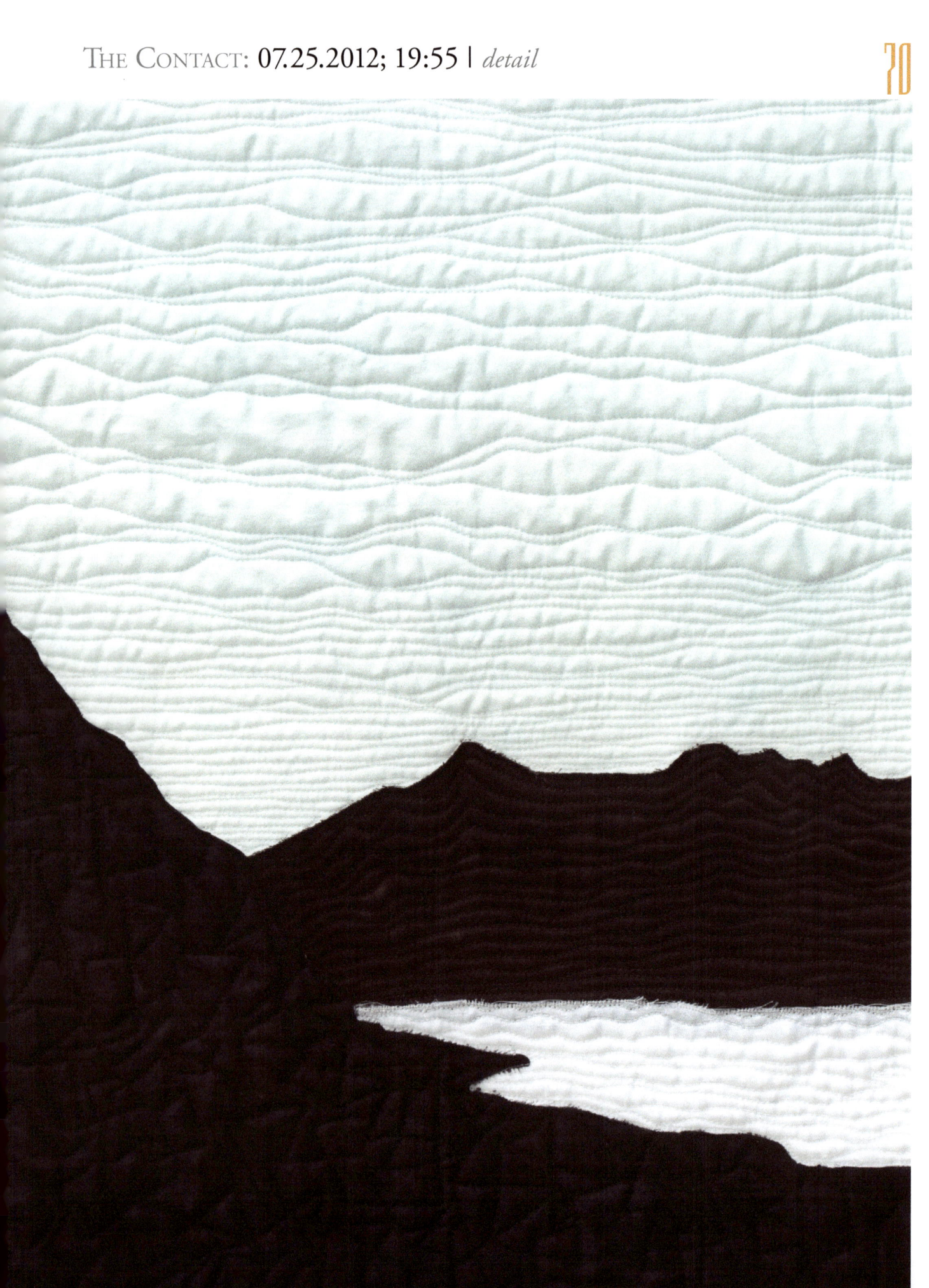

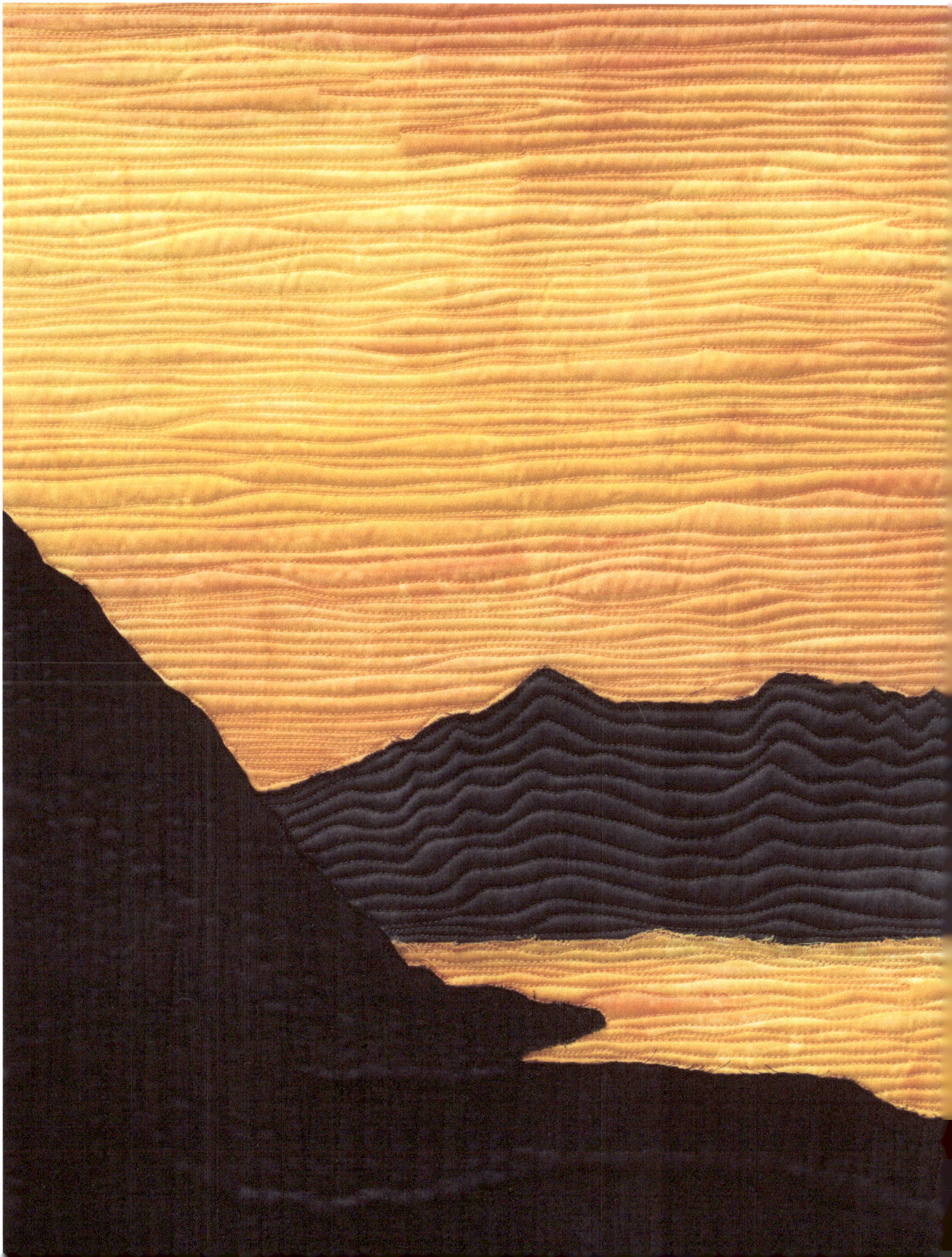

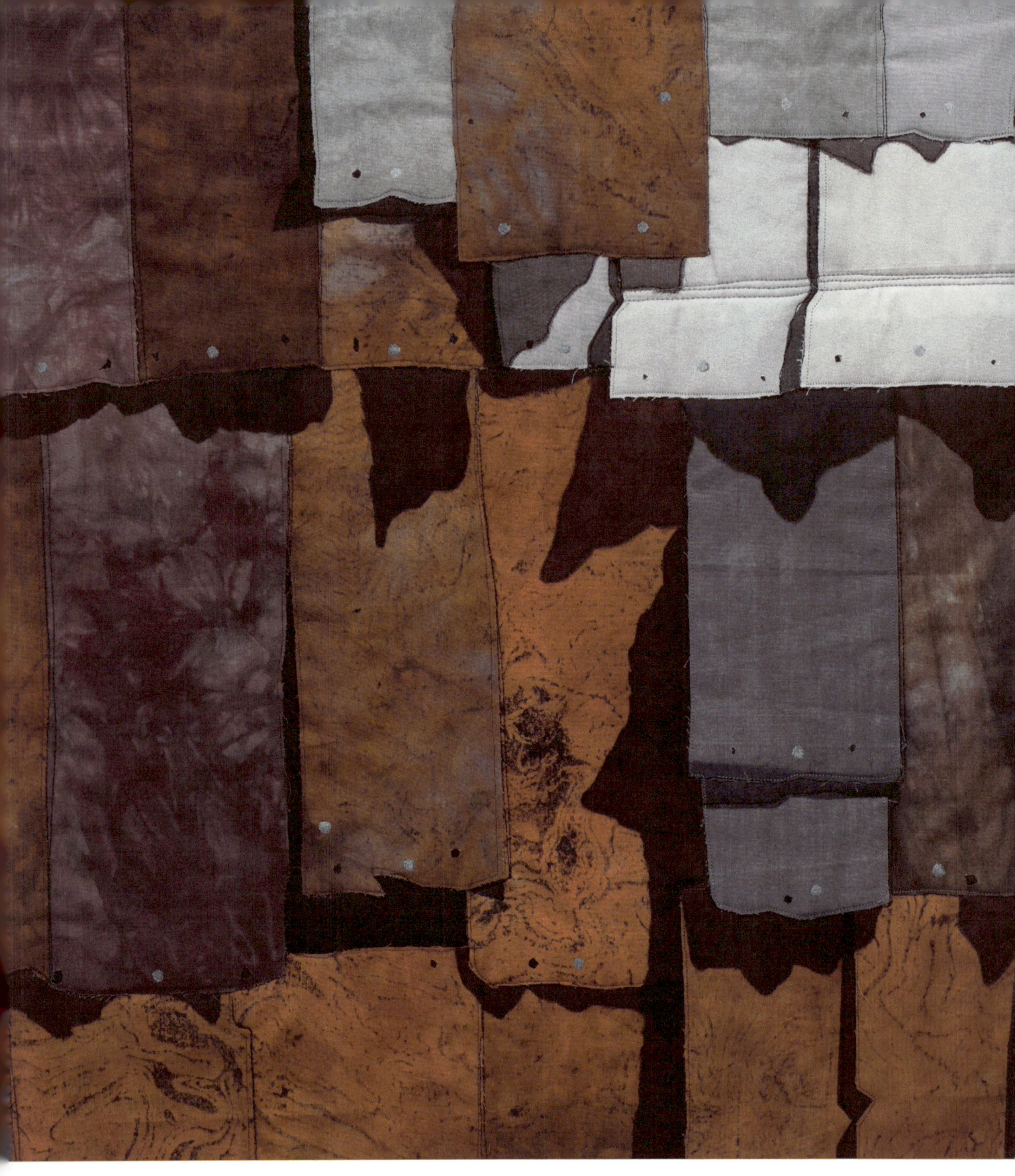

Restoration of a tin building gives us a feeling that it is the real thing from the old days. The original materials are there, though a bit rearranged. The giveaway, if you look closely, is the empty nail holes—dark dots—contrasting with the shiny new nail heads holding it all together now. The galvanized nails will hold up but never match.

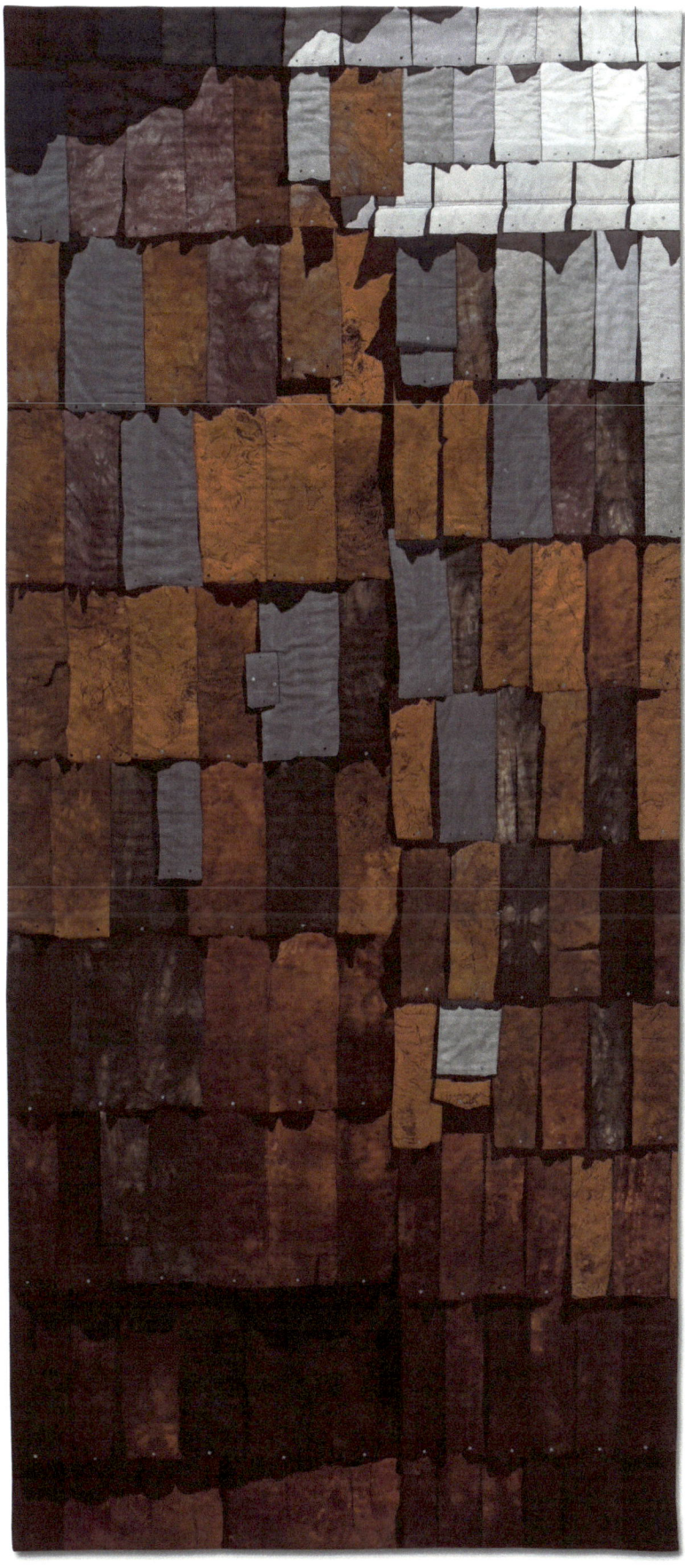

*84" x 38" • Cotton broadcloth and silk organza, low-water immersion dyed,
hand printed with dye, machine stitched. 2015*

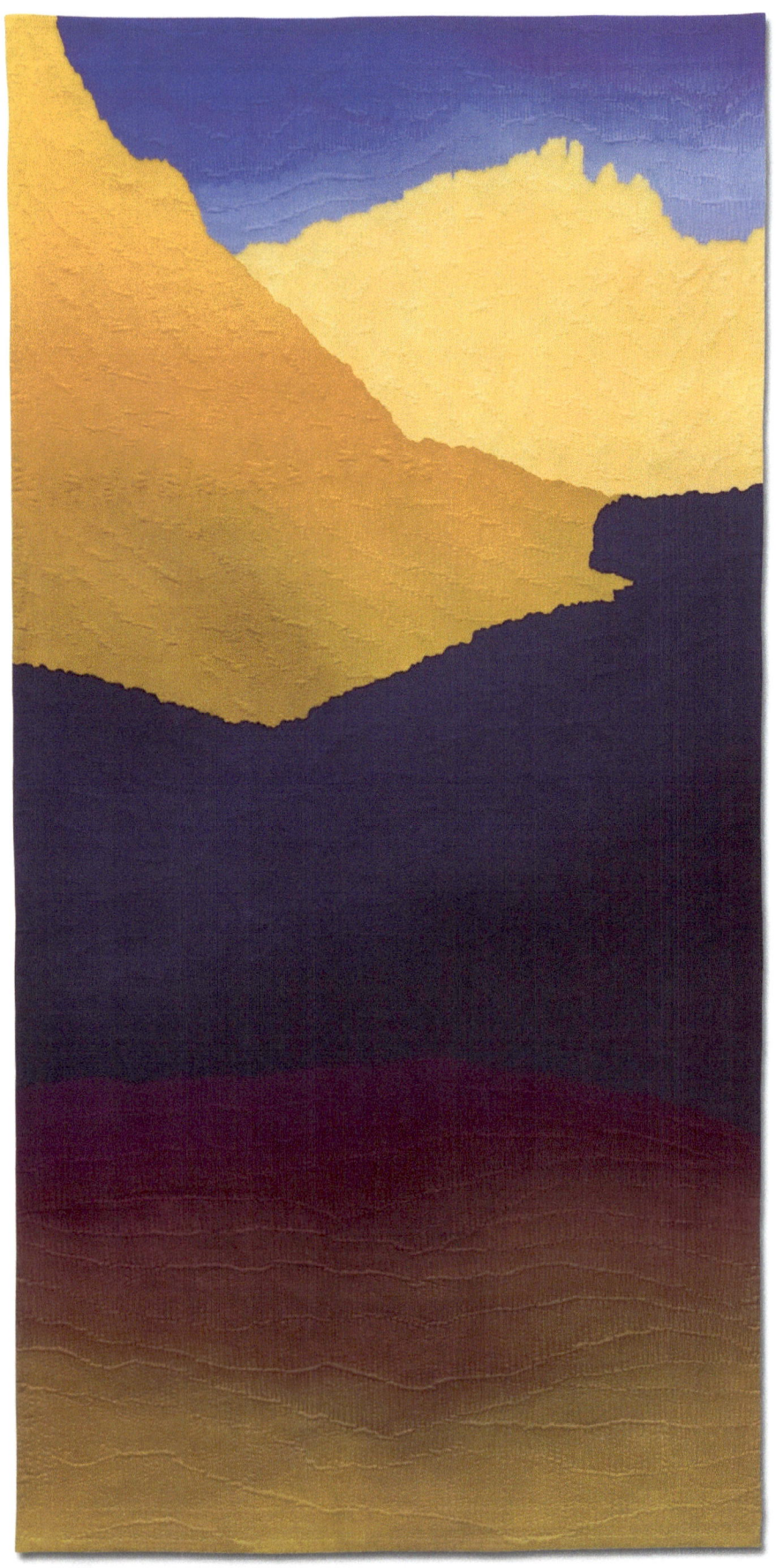

83" x 42" • Cotton sateen, low-water immersion dyed, machine stitched. 2014

Above the tree line, hungry and awestruck, we drink our rehydrated corn chowder by the light of the alpenglow on the peaks.

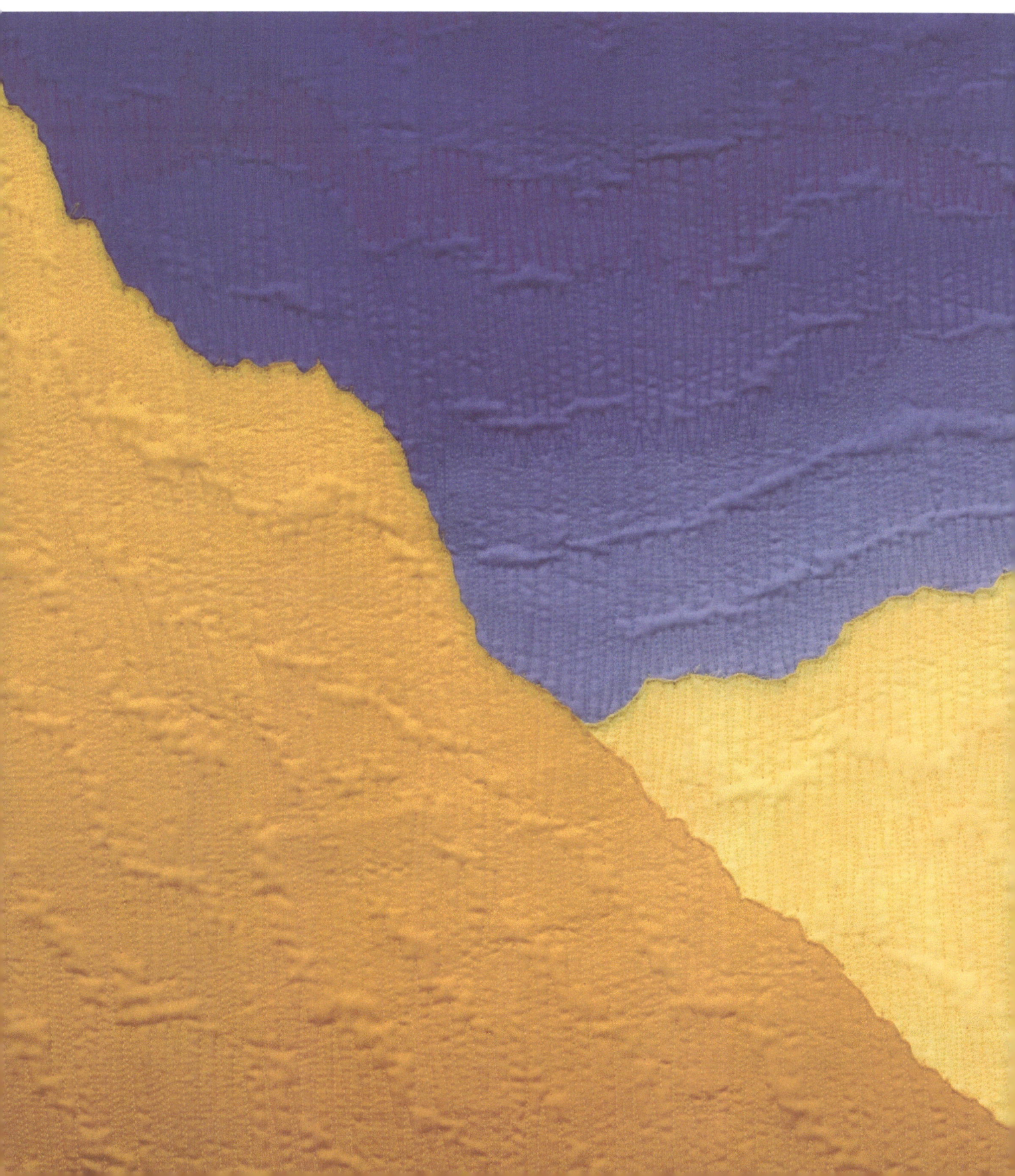

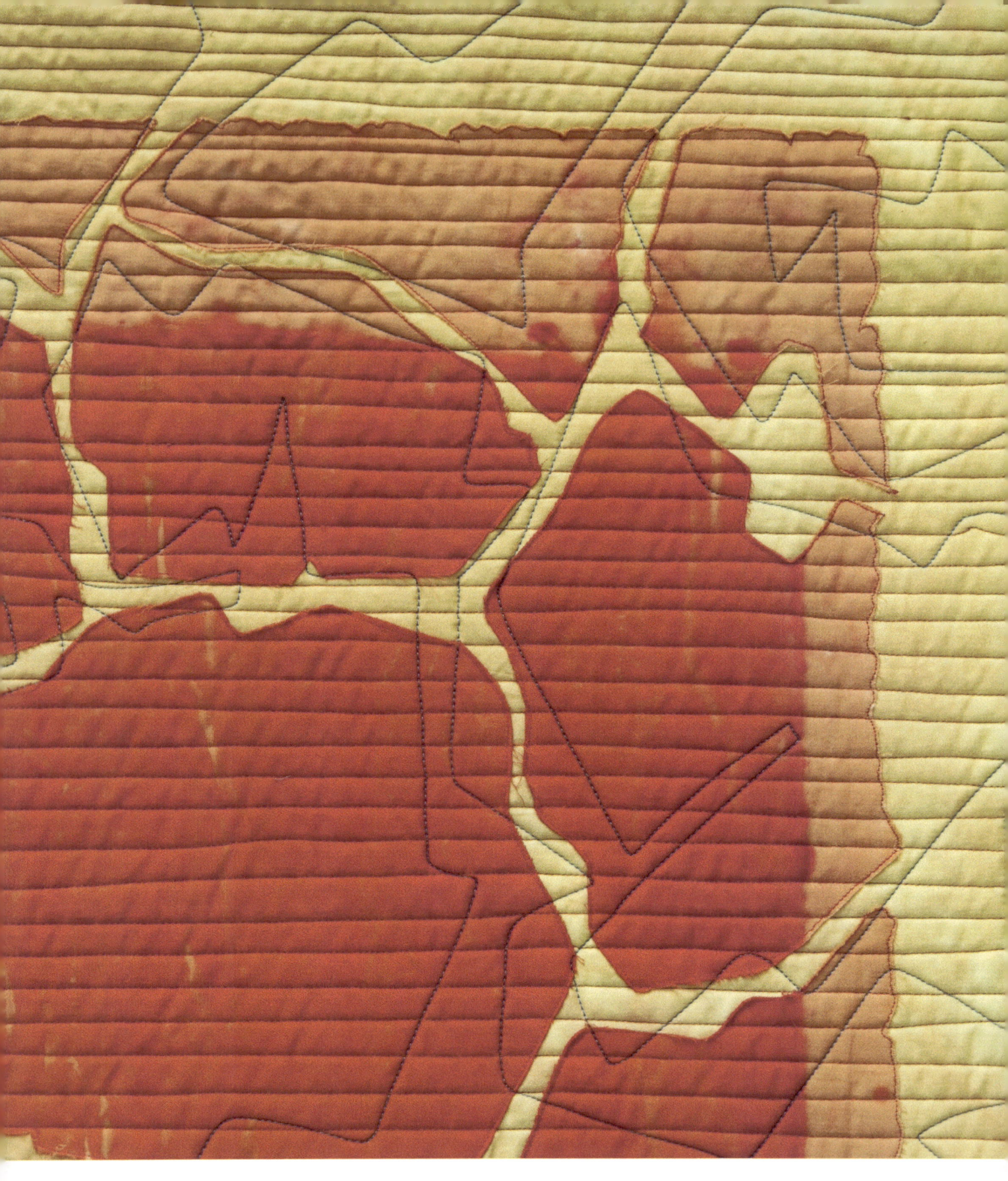

Drying mud and many other materials—from minerals to continents—break up according to the rules of chemistry and physics. They often have a characteristic look best described as tri-corner, that is, the angles around the breaking point are approximately 120° and create hexagon-like shapes that seem to repeat. My focus here is the emotion of seeing no water in the lake.

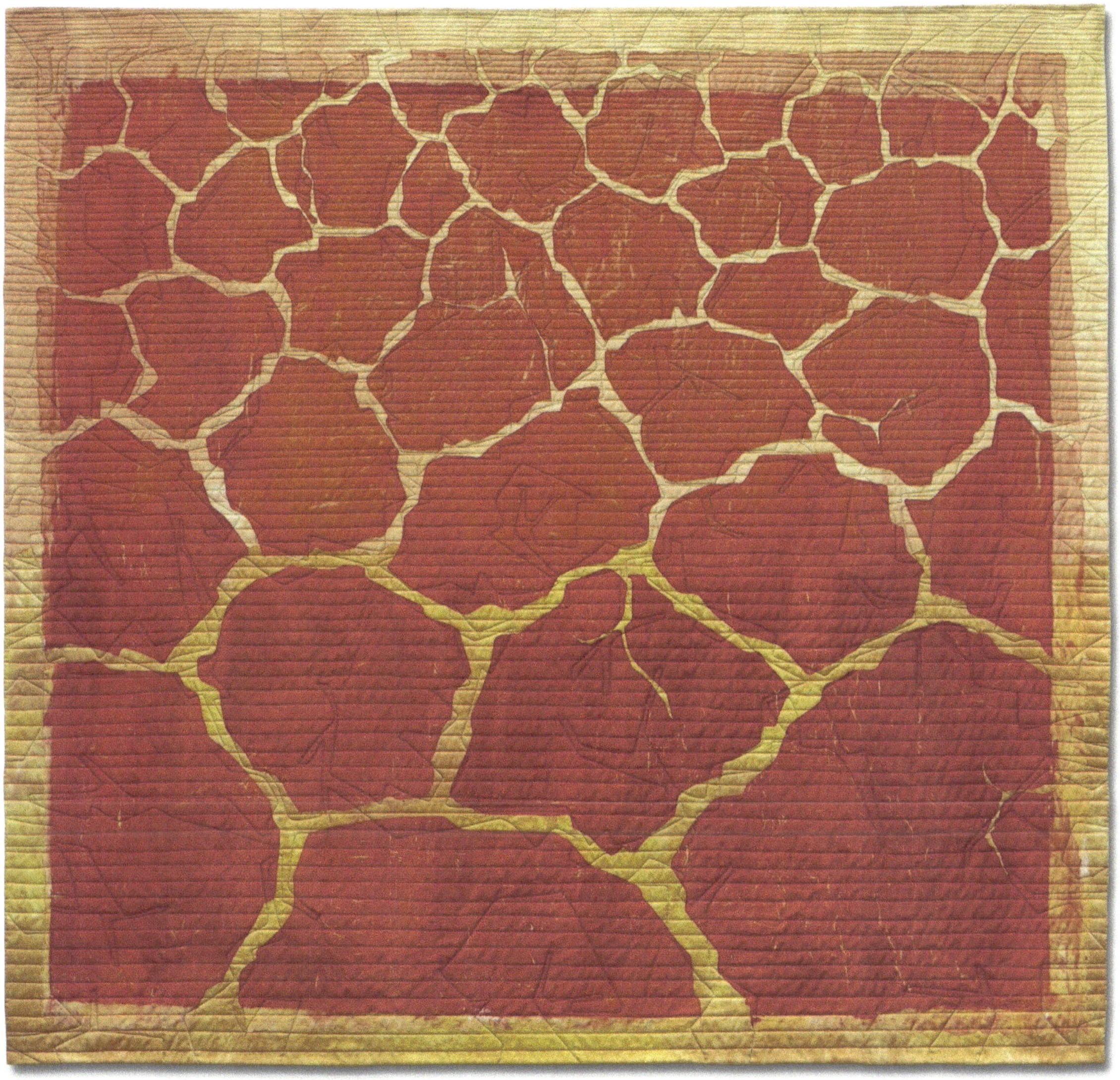

55" x 60" • Cotton sateen, hand painted and printed with dye, machine stitched. 2014

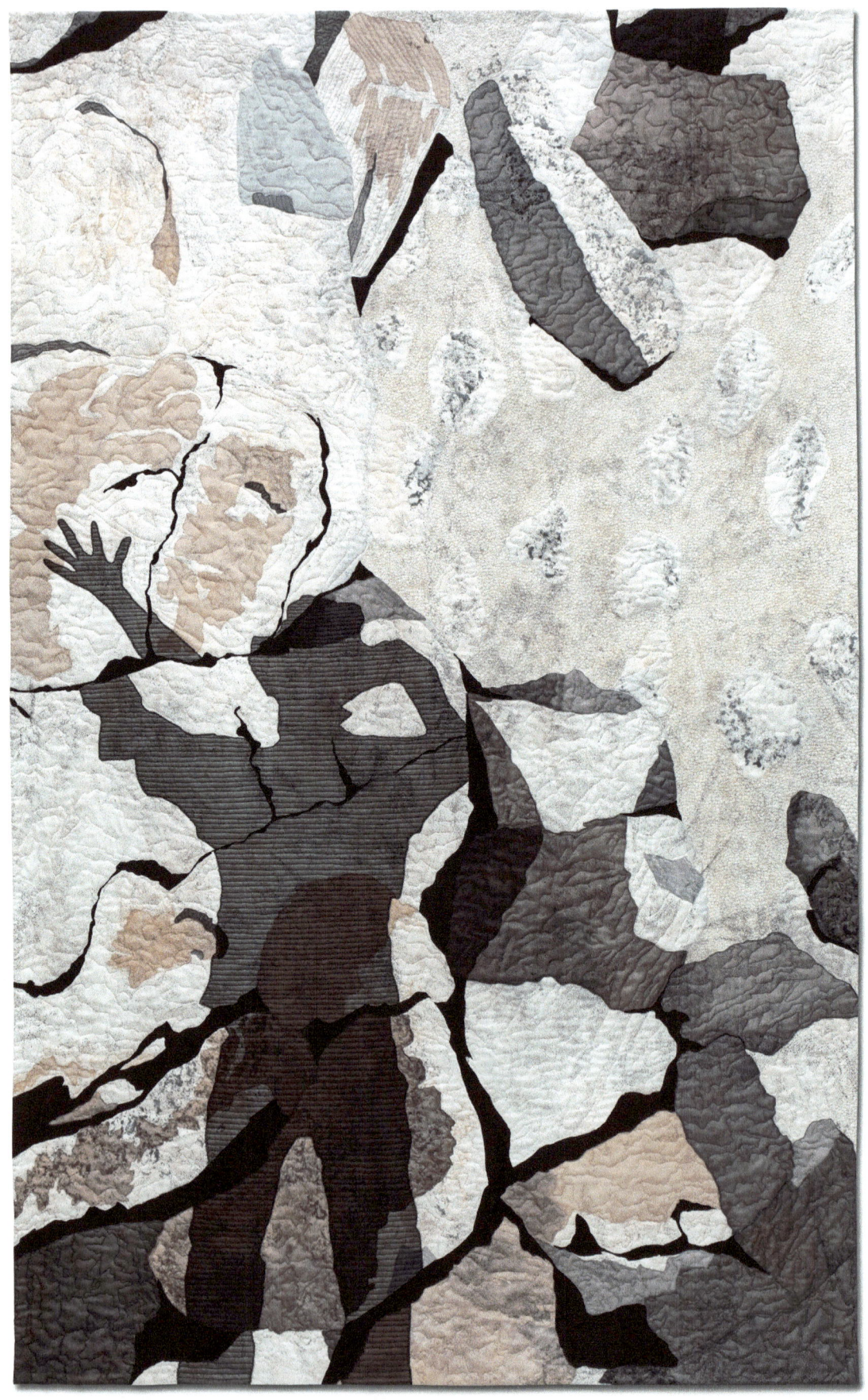

87" x 56" • Cotton sateen and silk organza, hand painted and printed with dye, machine stitched. 2016

Midday sun casts small, sharp shadows on granite fallen from cliffs above. Some pieces are fresh and look like they broke off yesterday; others are overgrown by lichen or weathered to sand. We arrive to cast shadows and squint in the brightness, diminished by the grandeur.

Back detail.

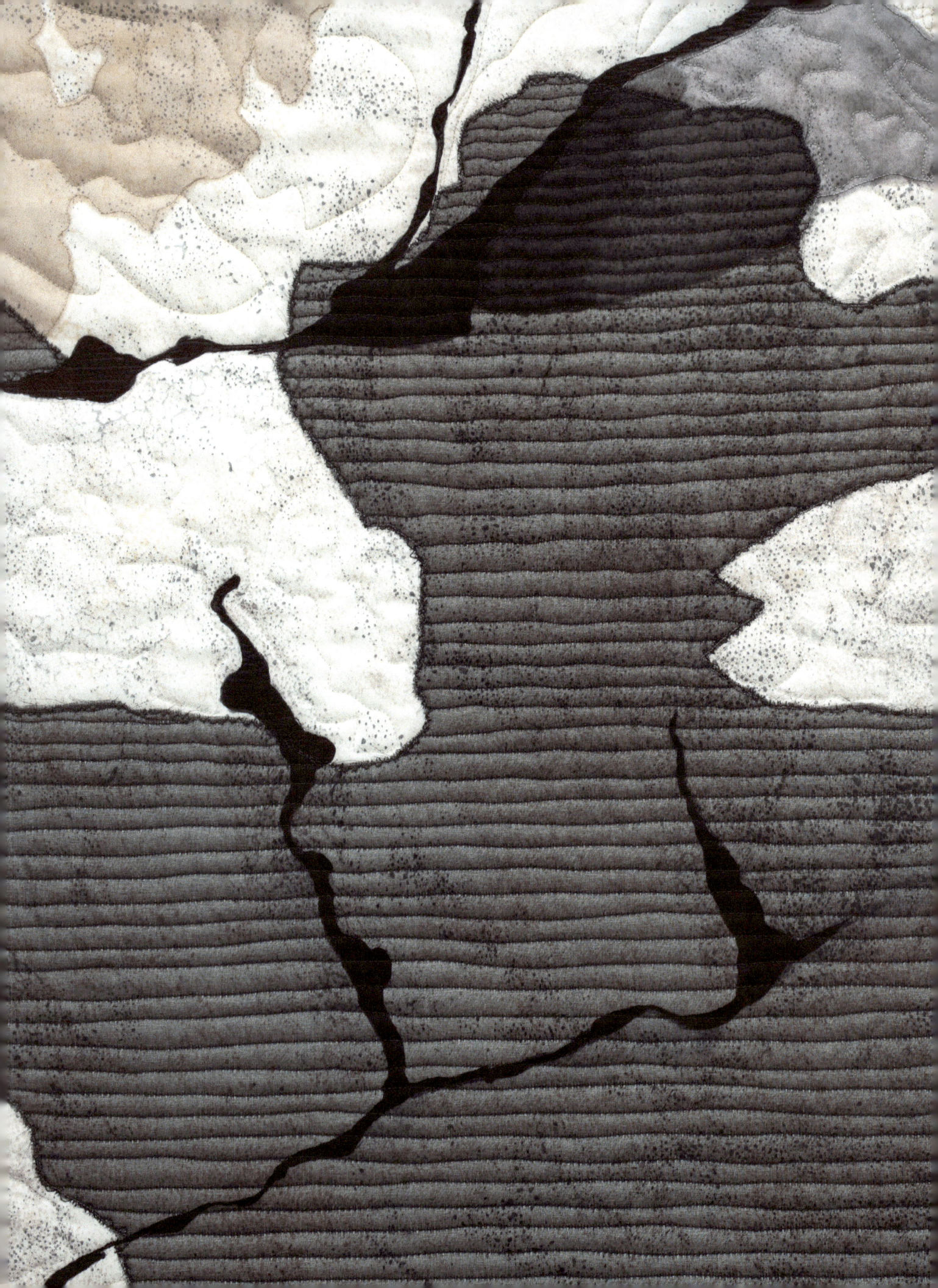

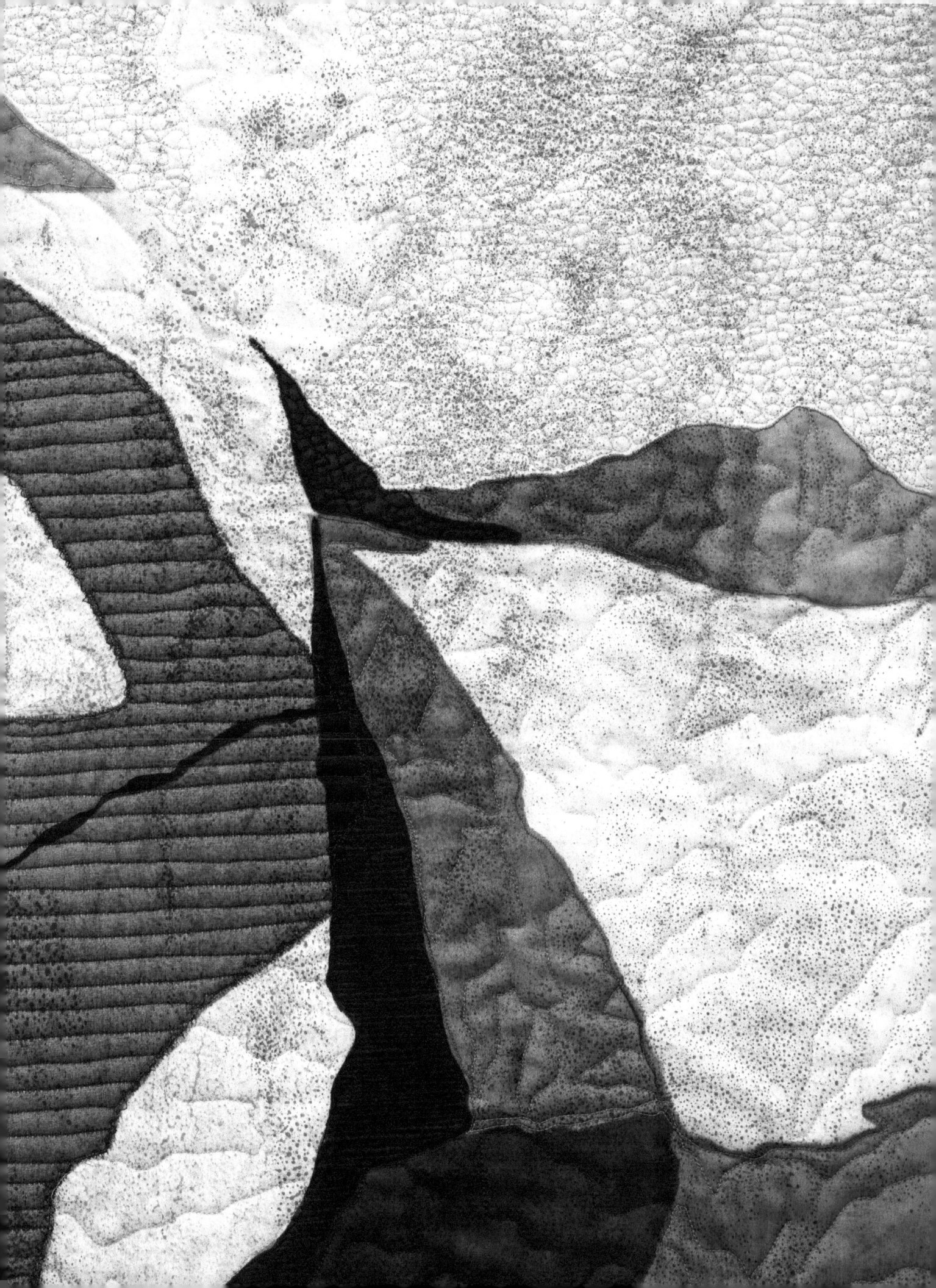

As we cooked dinner at sunset in a hemlock grove near Peeler Lake on the crest of the Sierra, white flakes of ash drifted down on us from a forest fire more than 50 miles to the west. The full moon was red all night long.

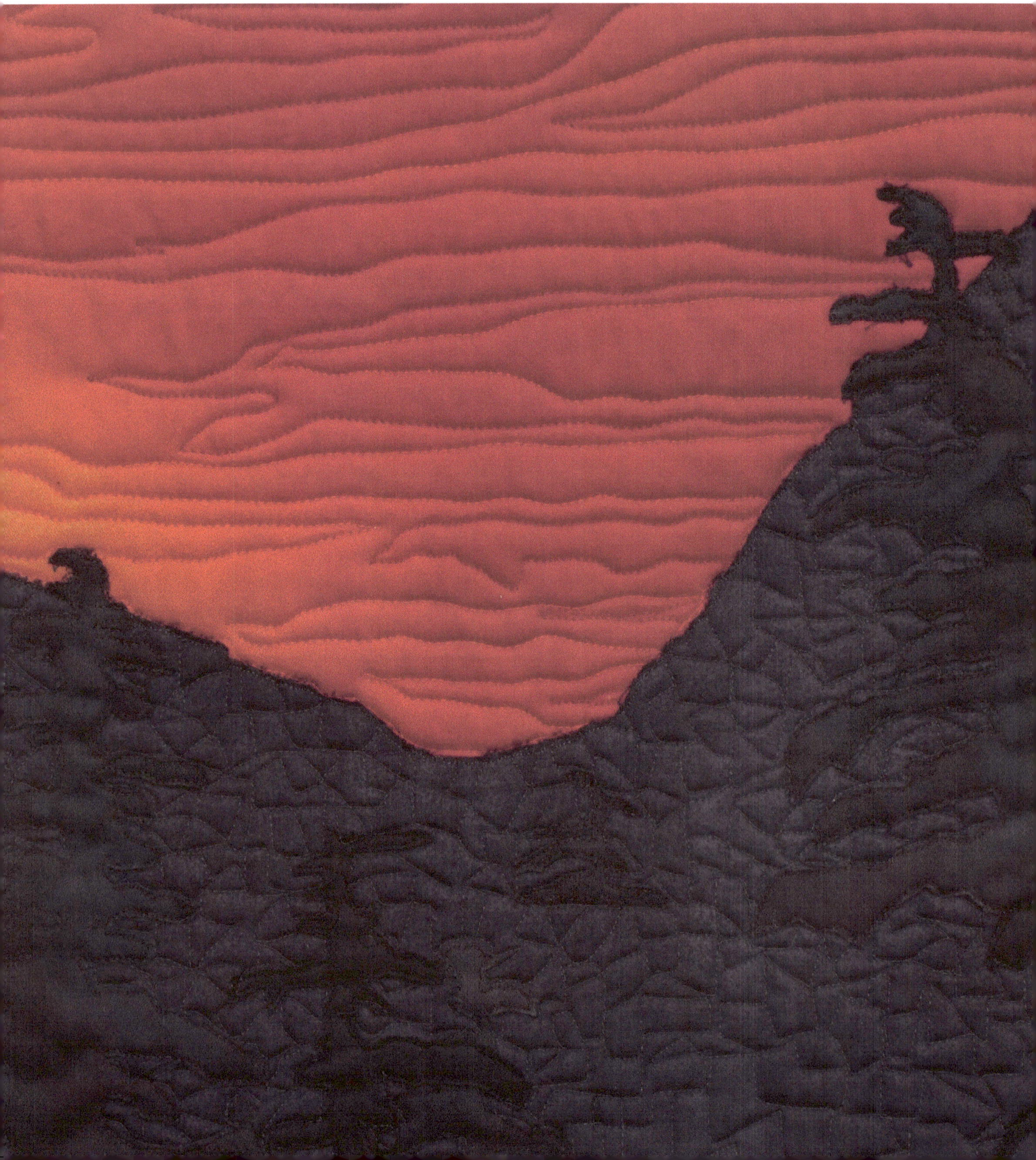

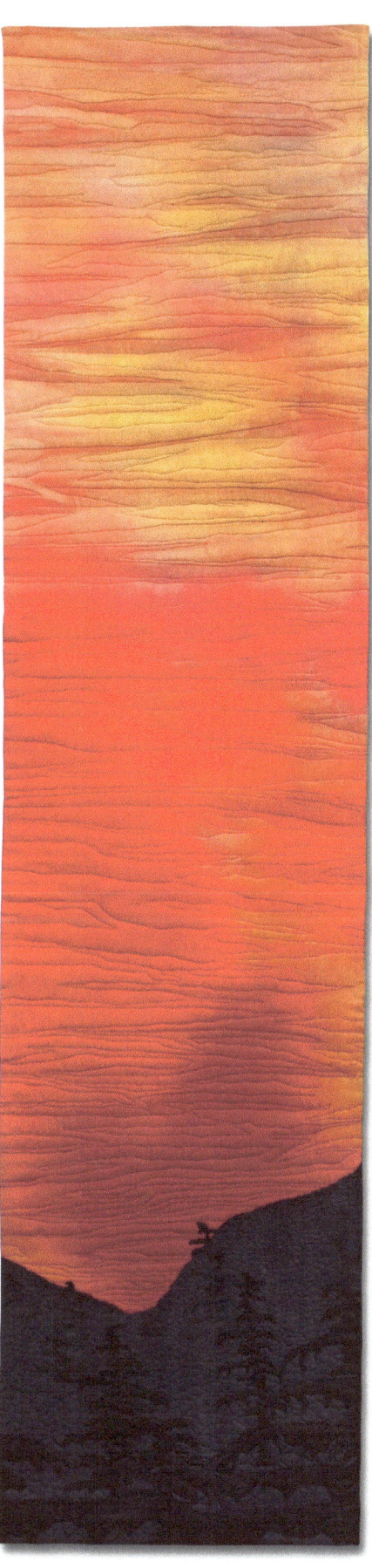

84″ x 21″ • Cotton sateen, low-water immersion dyed,
hand printed with dye, machine stitched. 2012

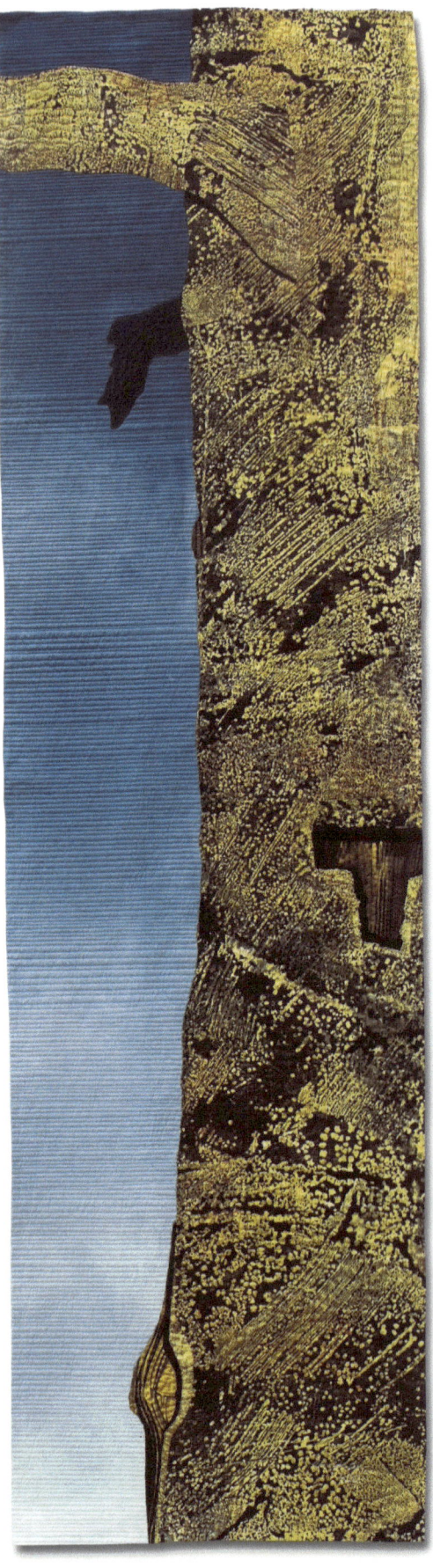

*84" x 24" • Cotton sateen, low-water immersion dyed, hand printed
and painted with dye, hand and machine stitched. 2011*

It is amazing to be in a mature forest where the dominant species of tree has been able to grow to its fullest. I have walked in the High Sierra, in protected places, where "T" shaped blazes cut into the trees in the mid-1800s by the park's early guardians, army soldiers, still mark the trails.

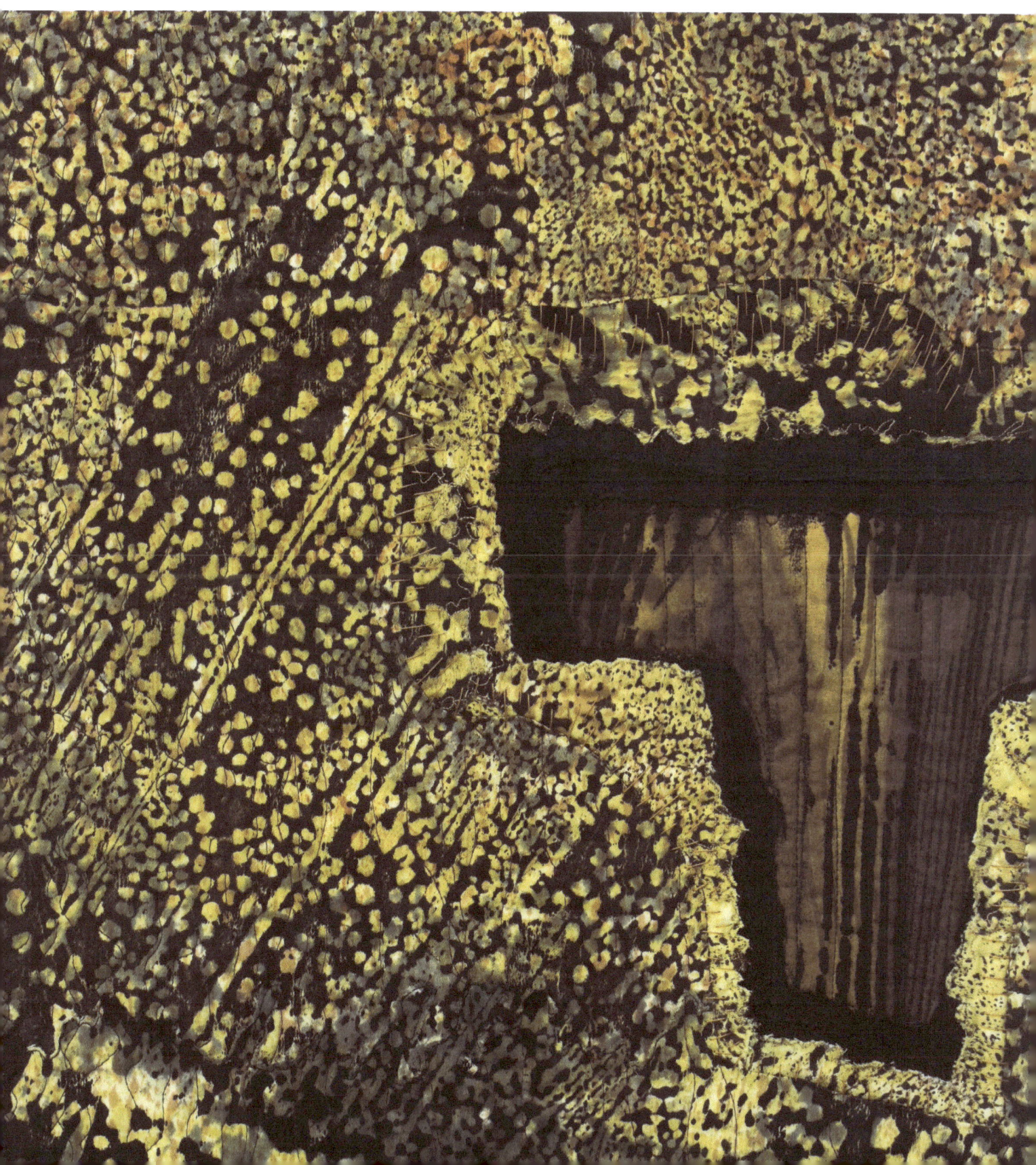

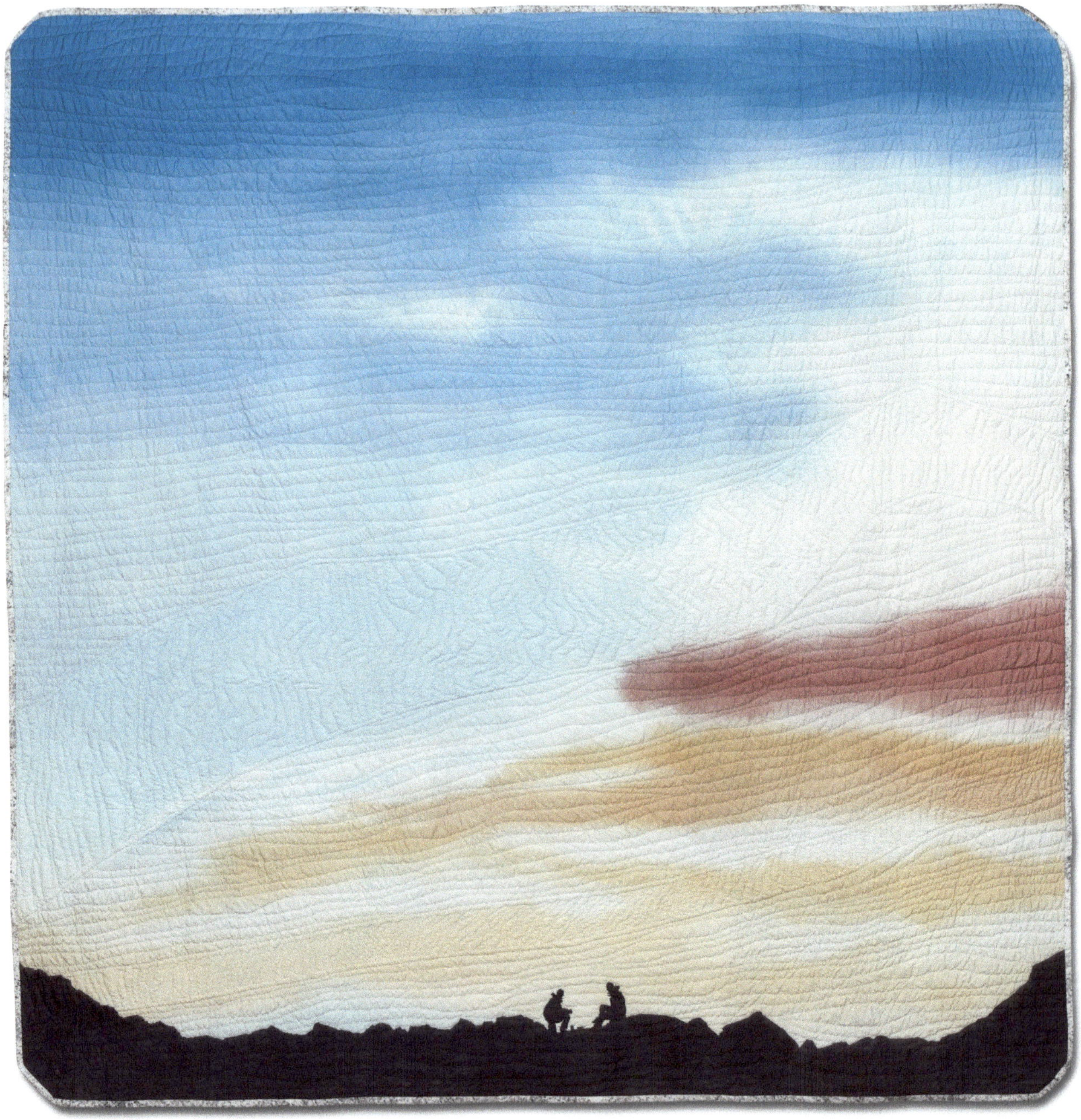

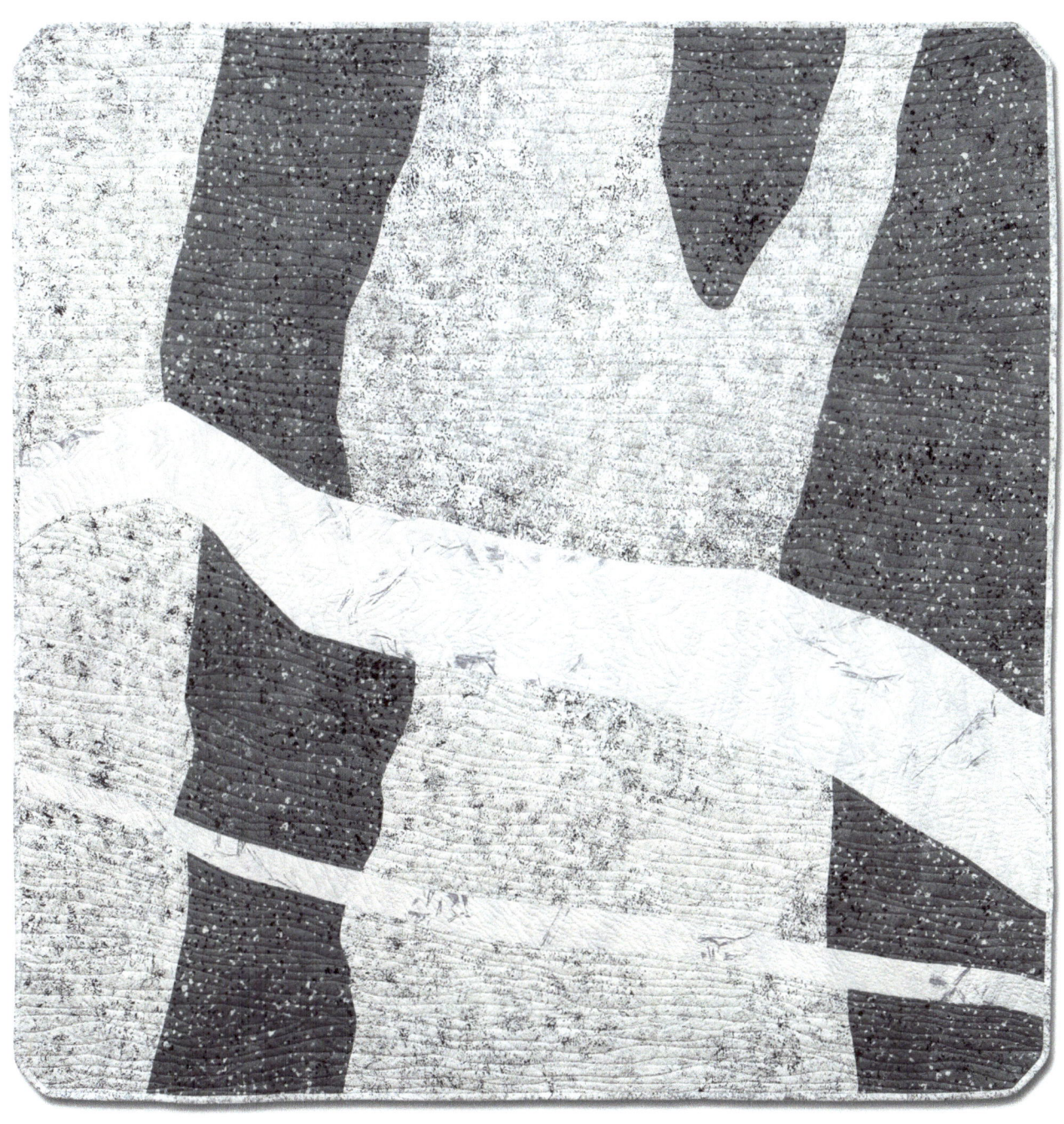

104" x 104" • Cotton sateen, hand painted and printed with dye. Back: low-water immersion dyed, hand painted with dye.
Pieced and marked by Ann. Hand quilted by the Oswego Quilters. 2015

Intruding magma seals two rocks. A sunset shared in the High Sierra binds two people in the space between sky and earth.

Back detail.

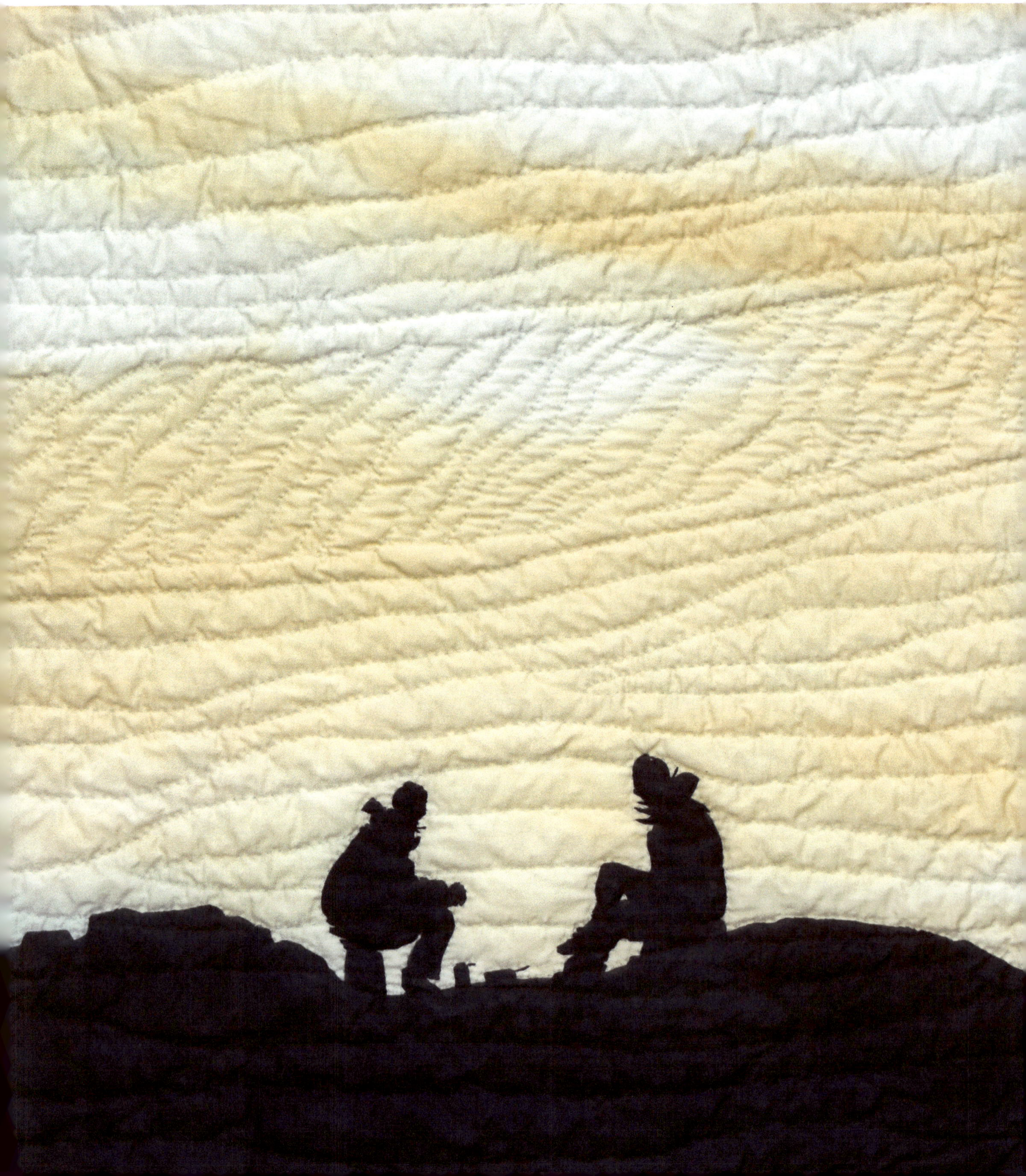

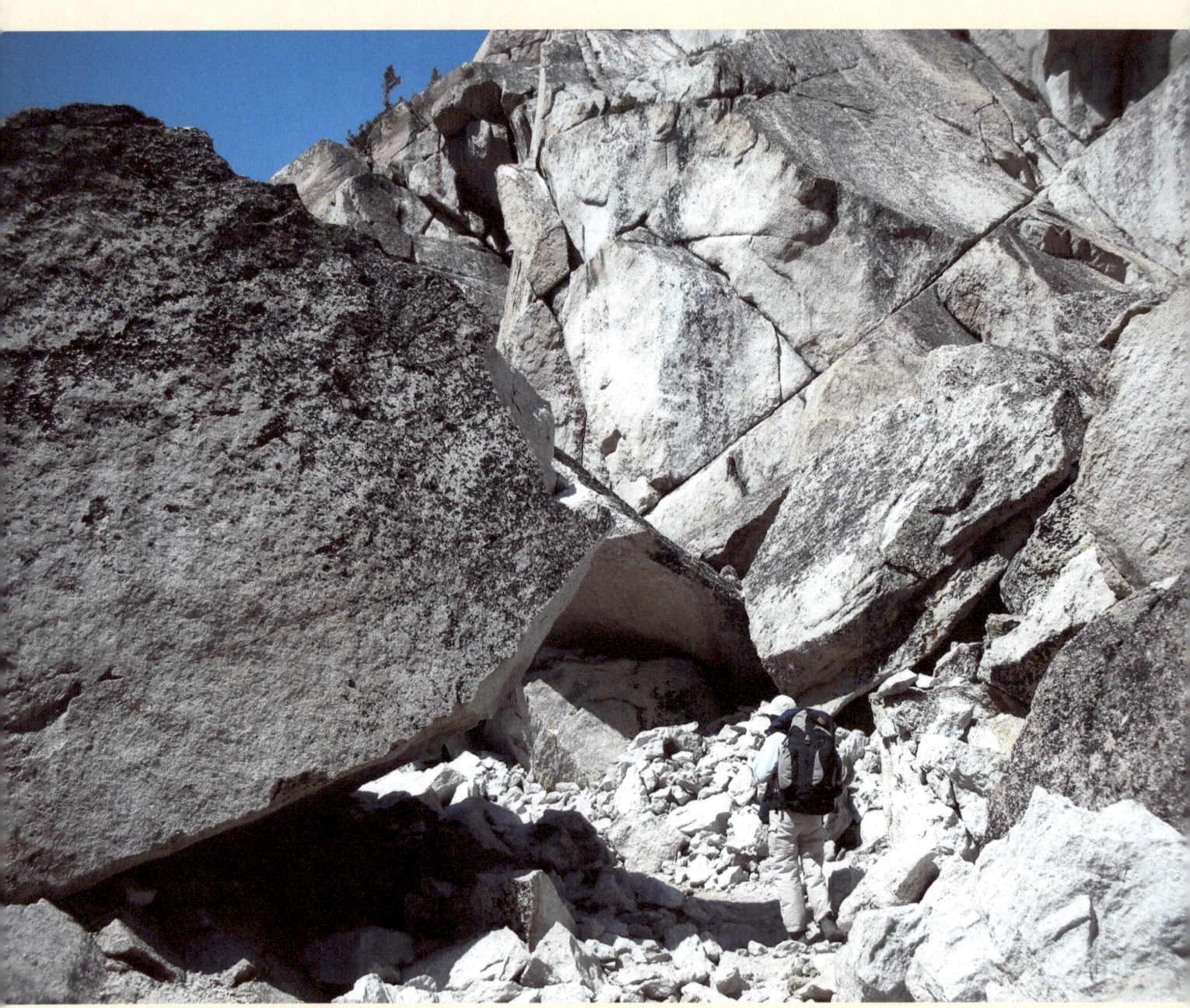

Inspiration

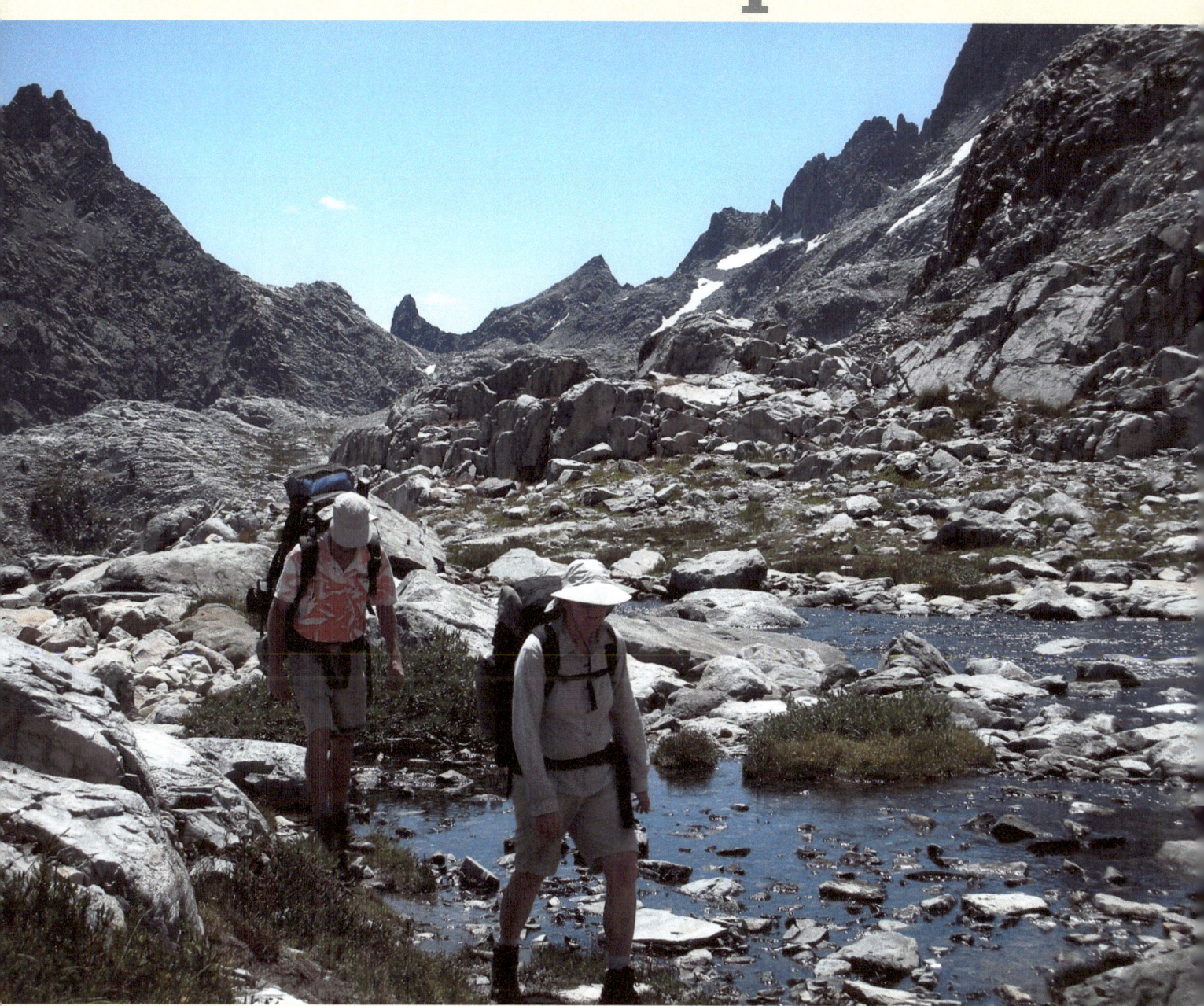

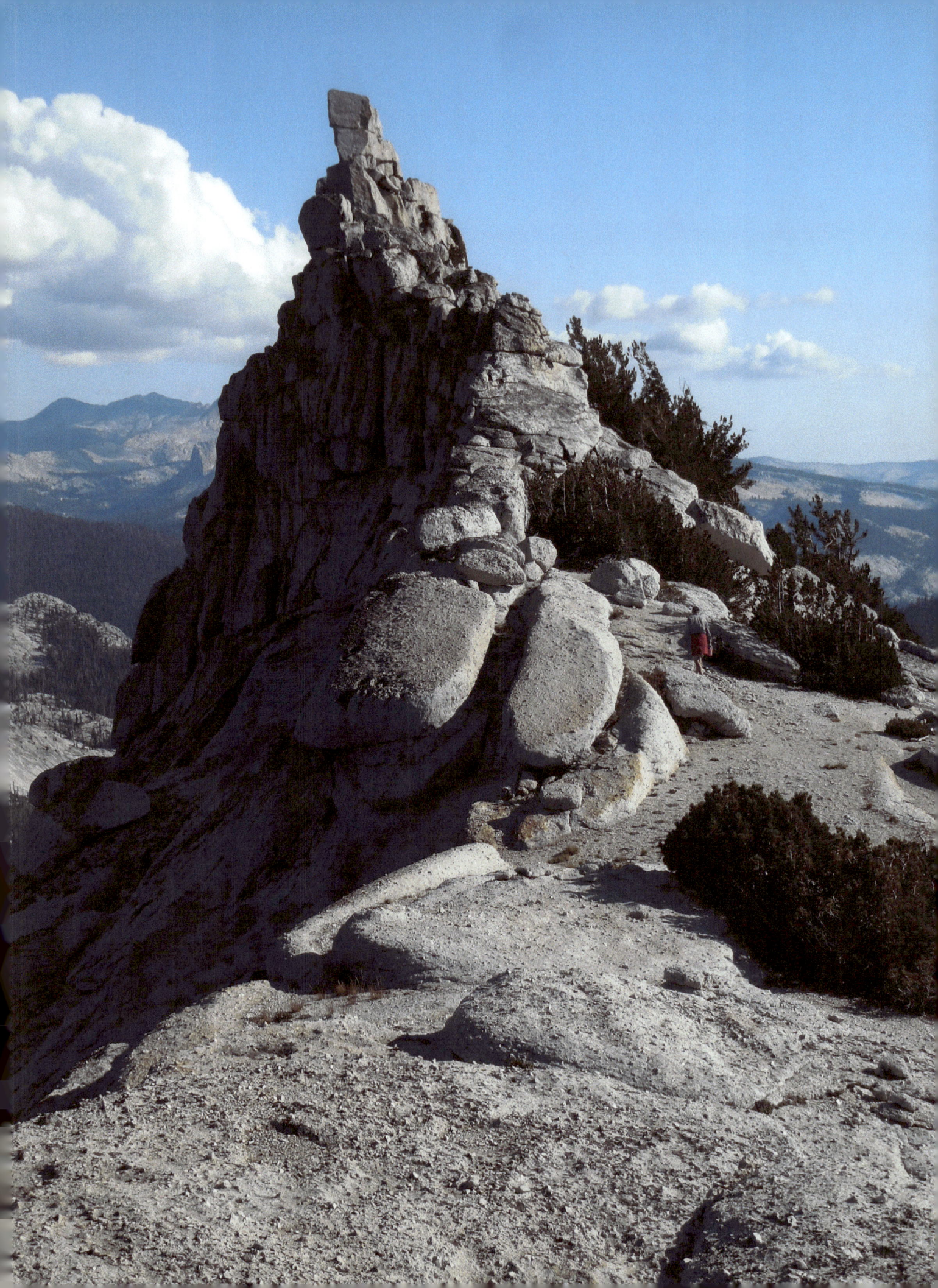

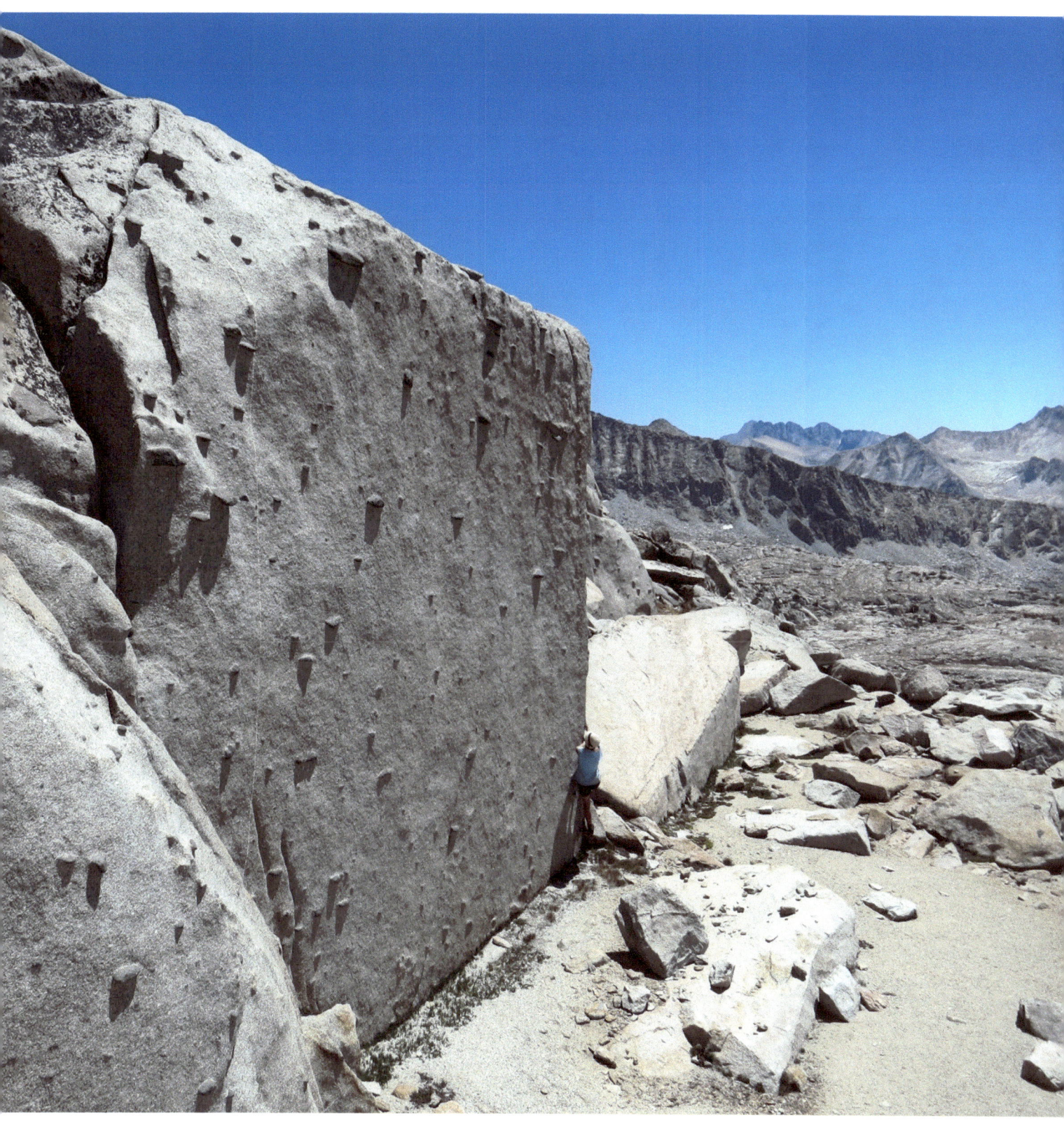

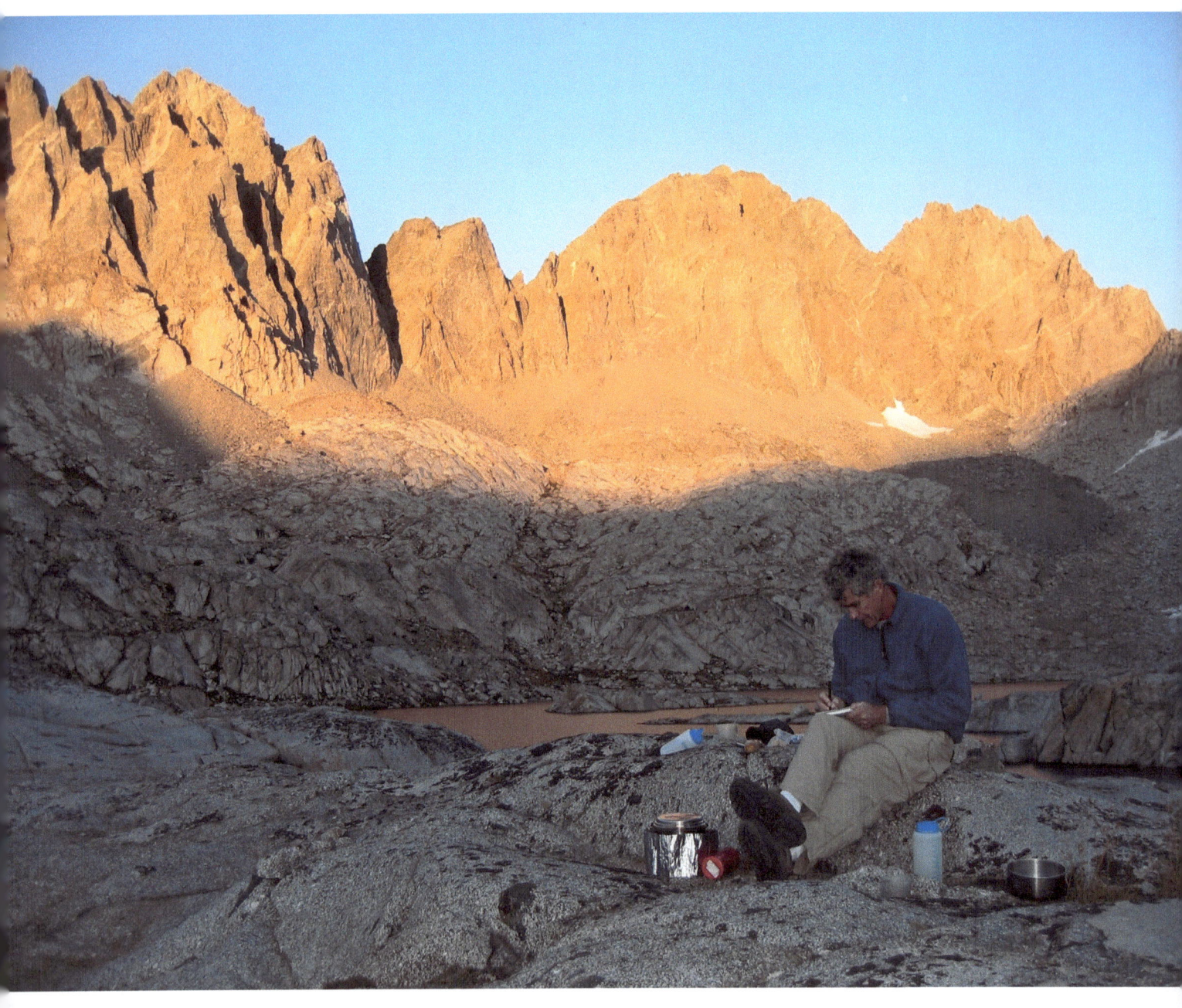

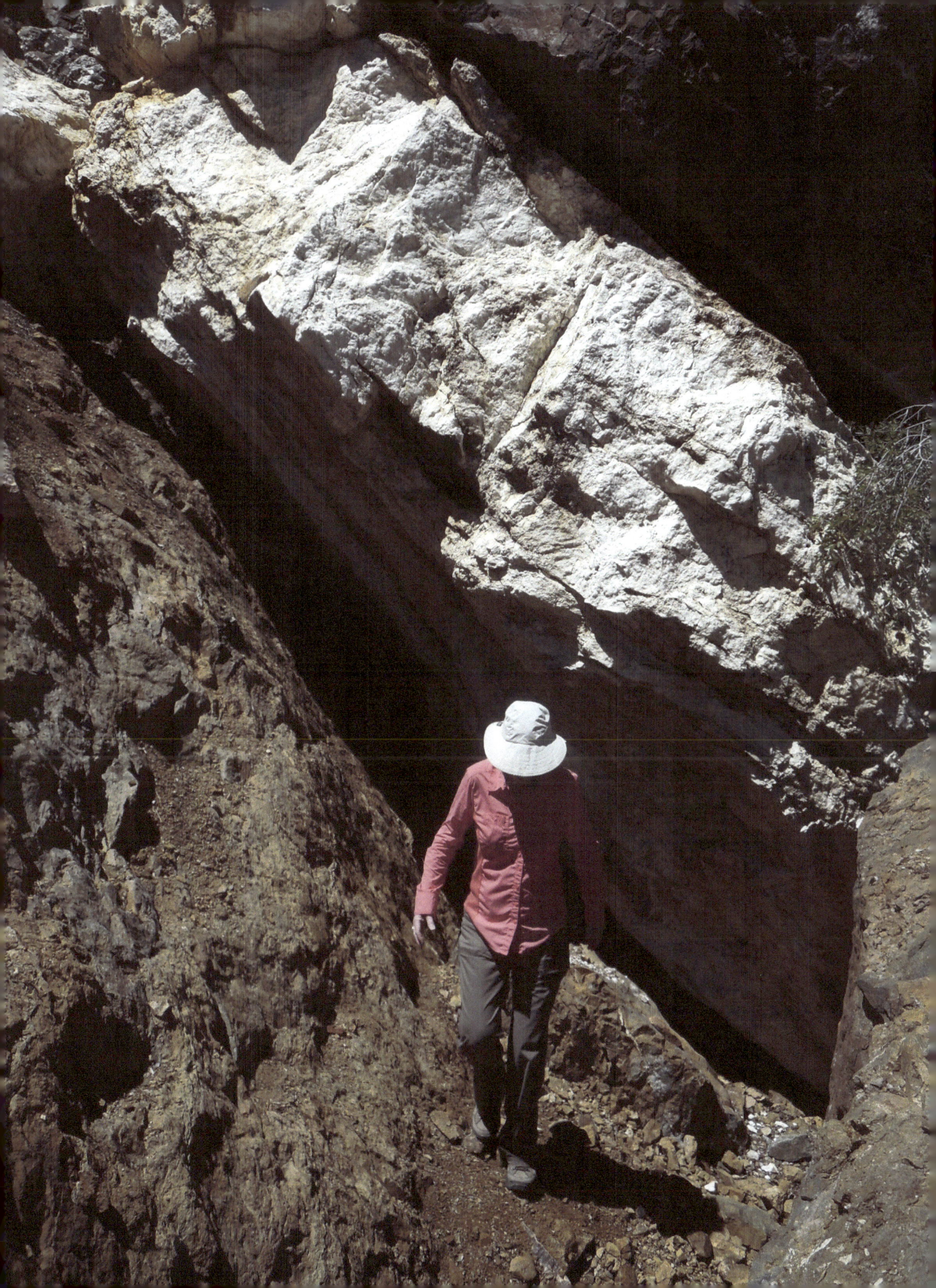

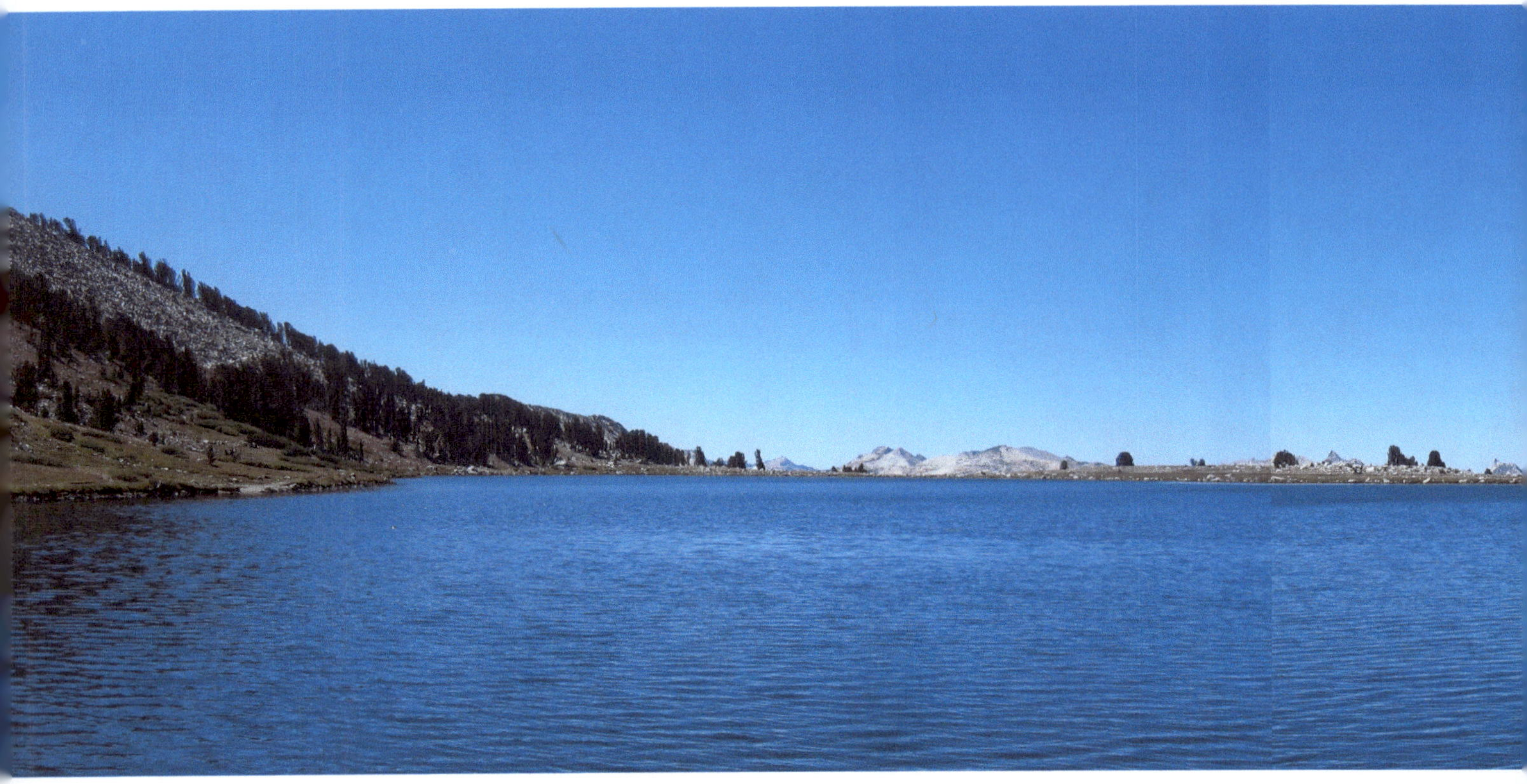

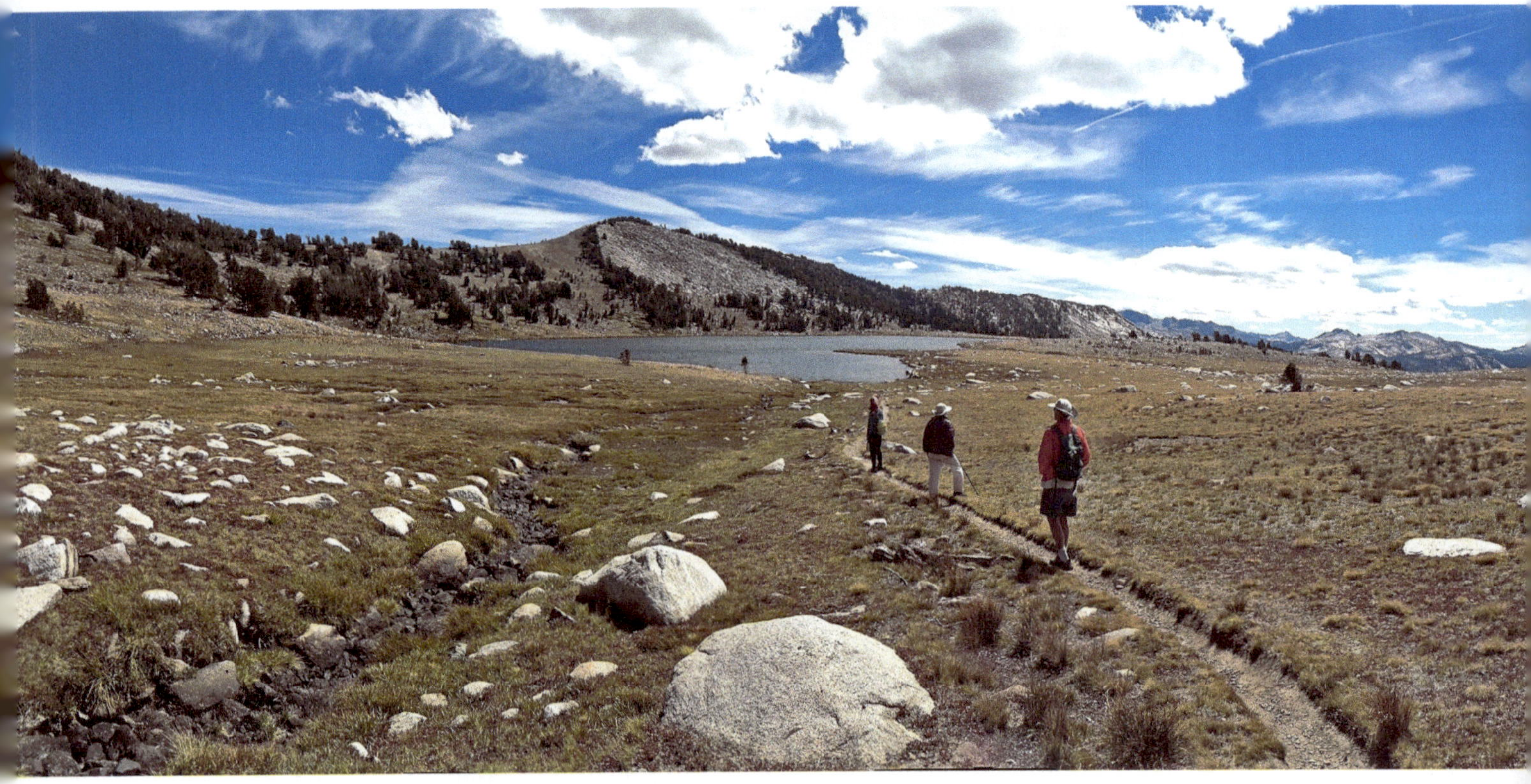

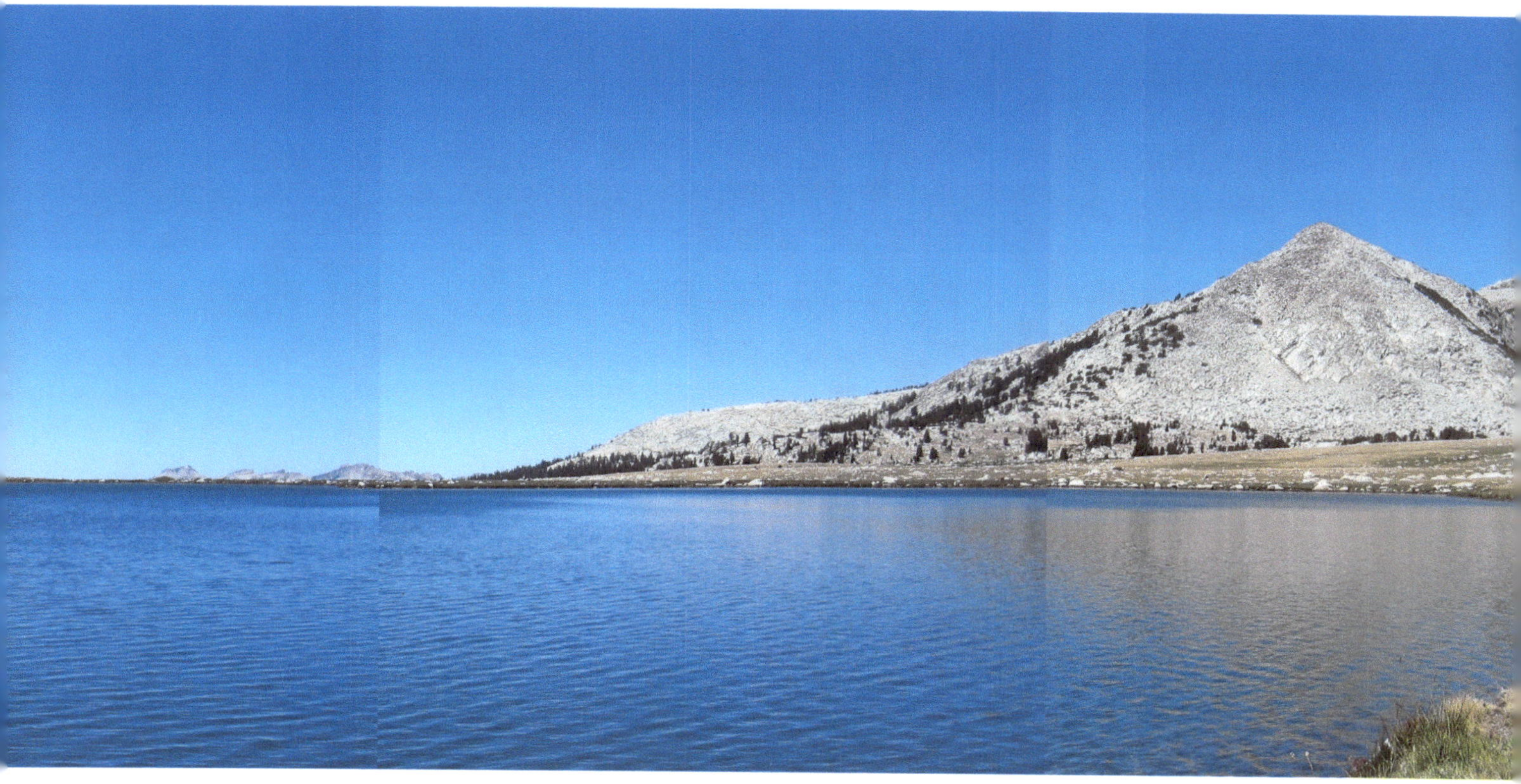

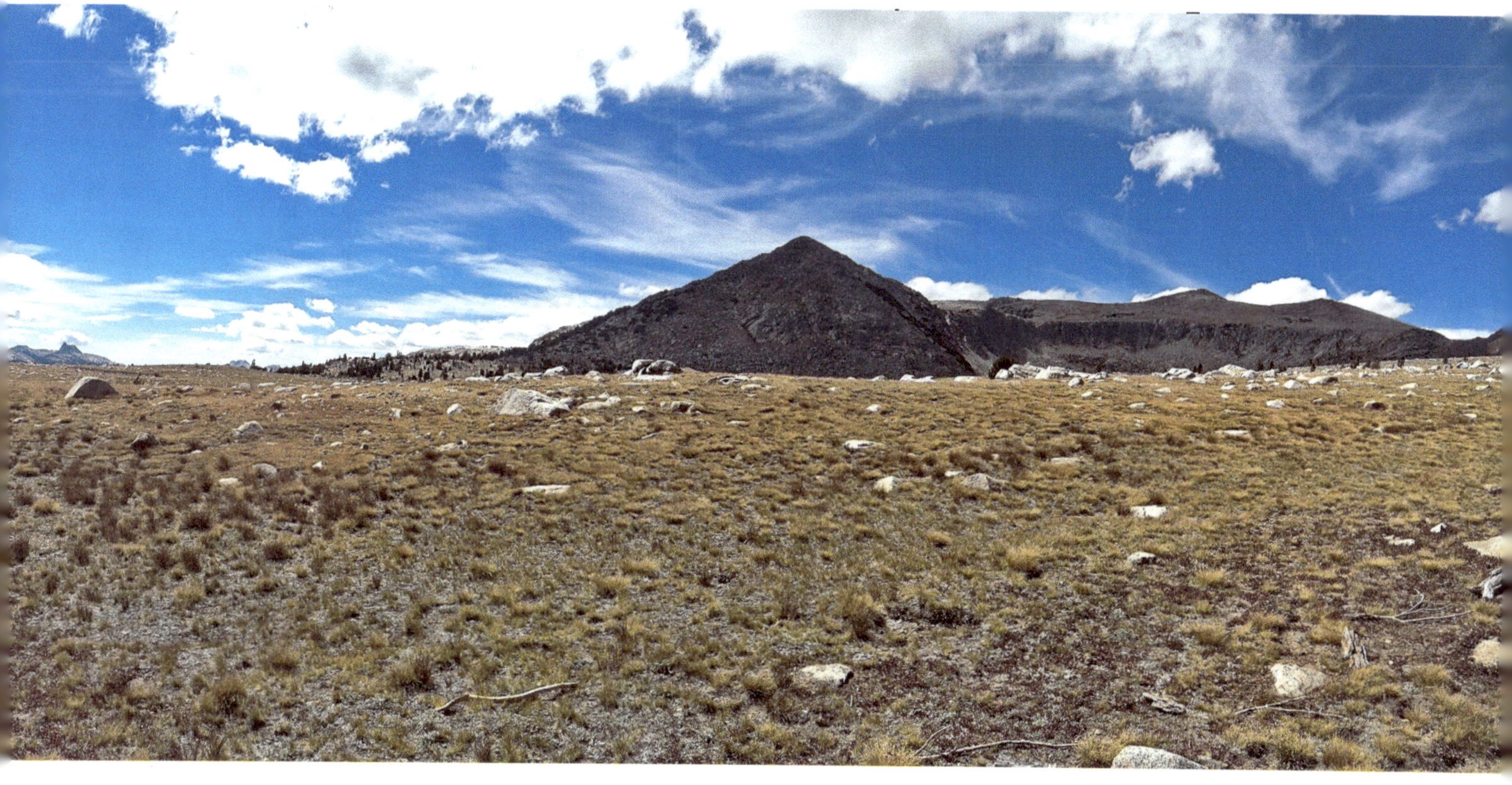

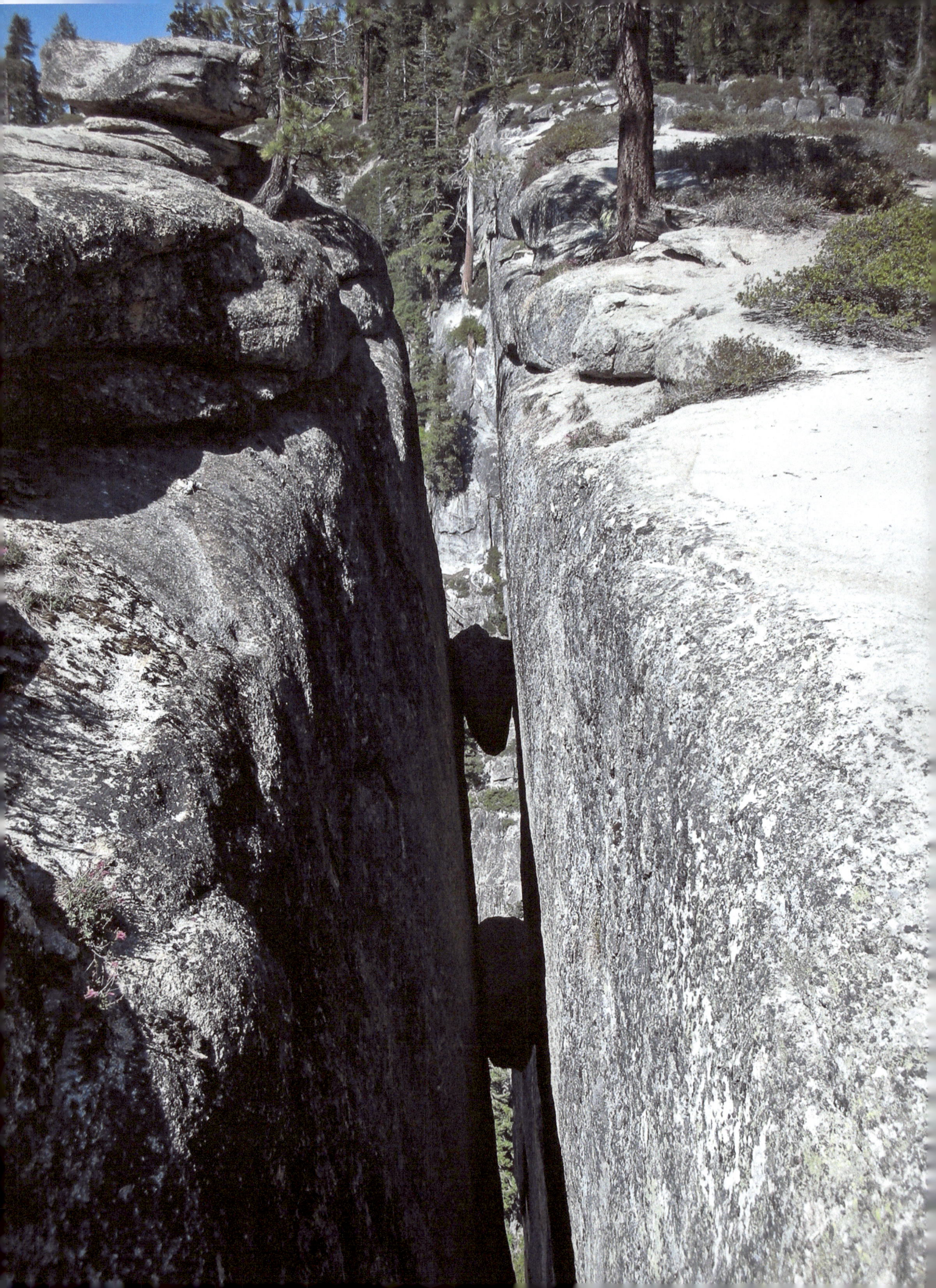

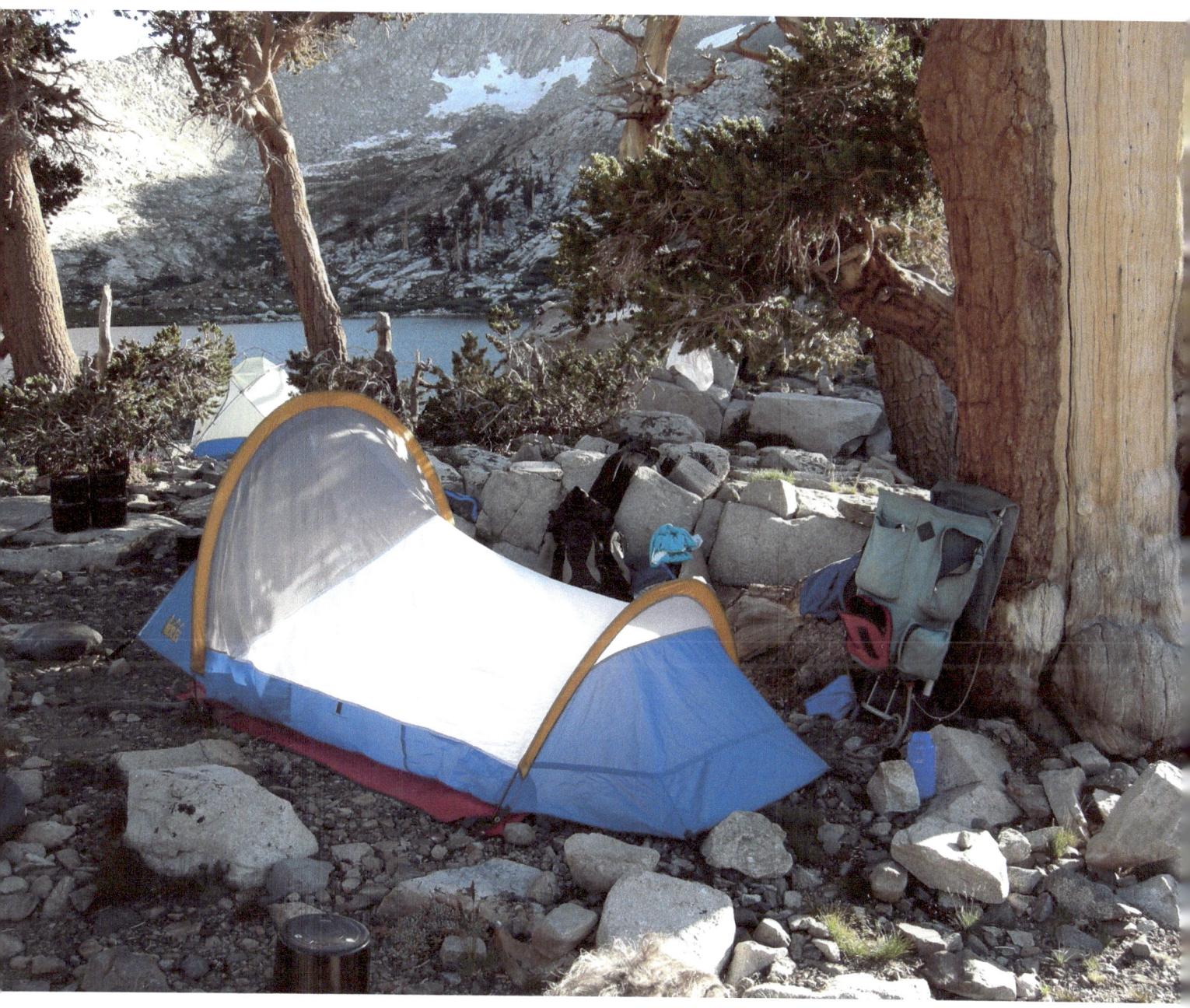

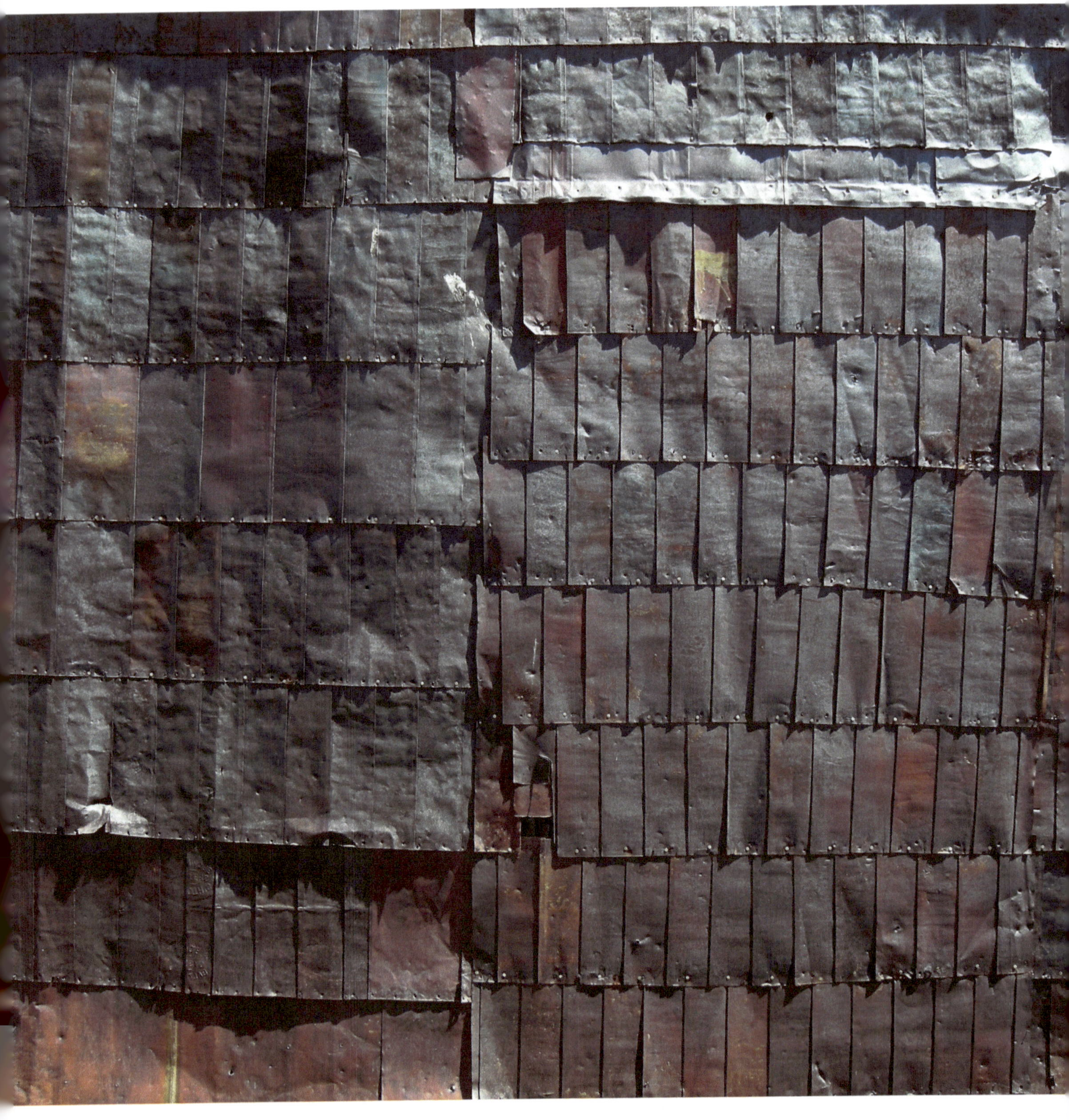

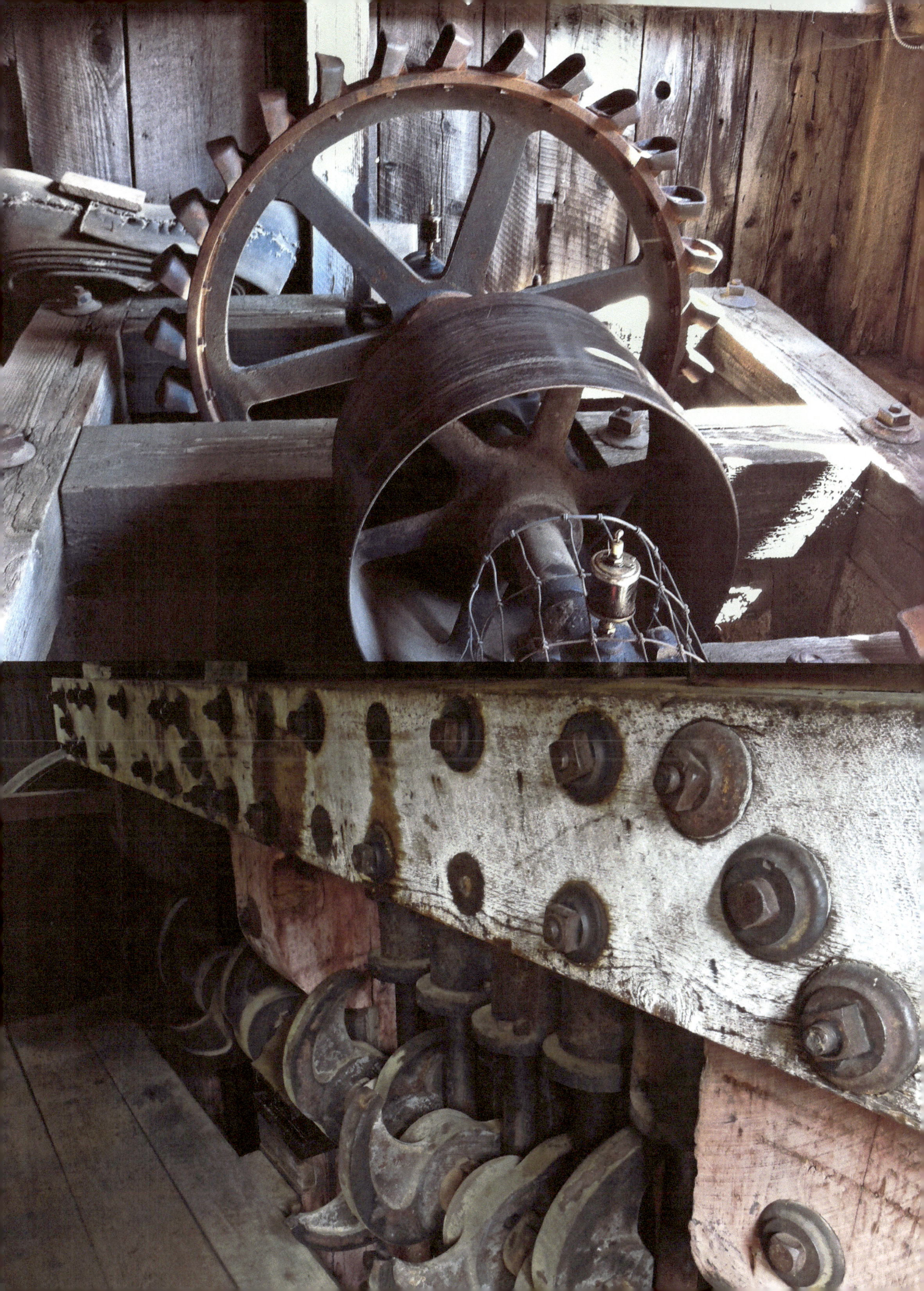

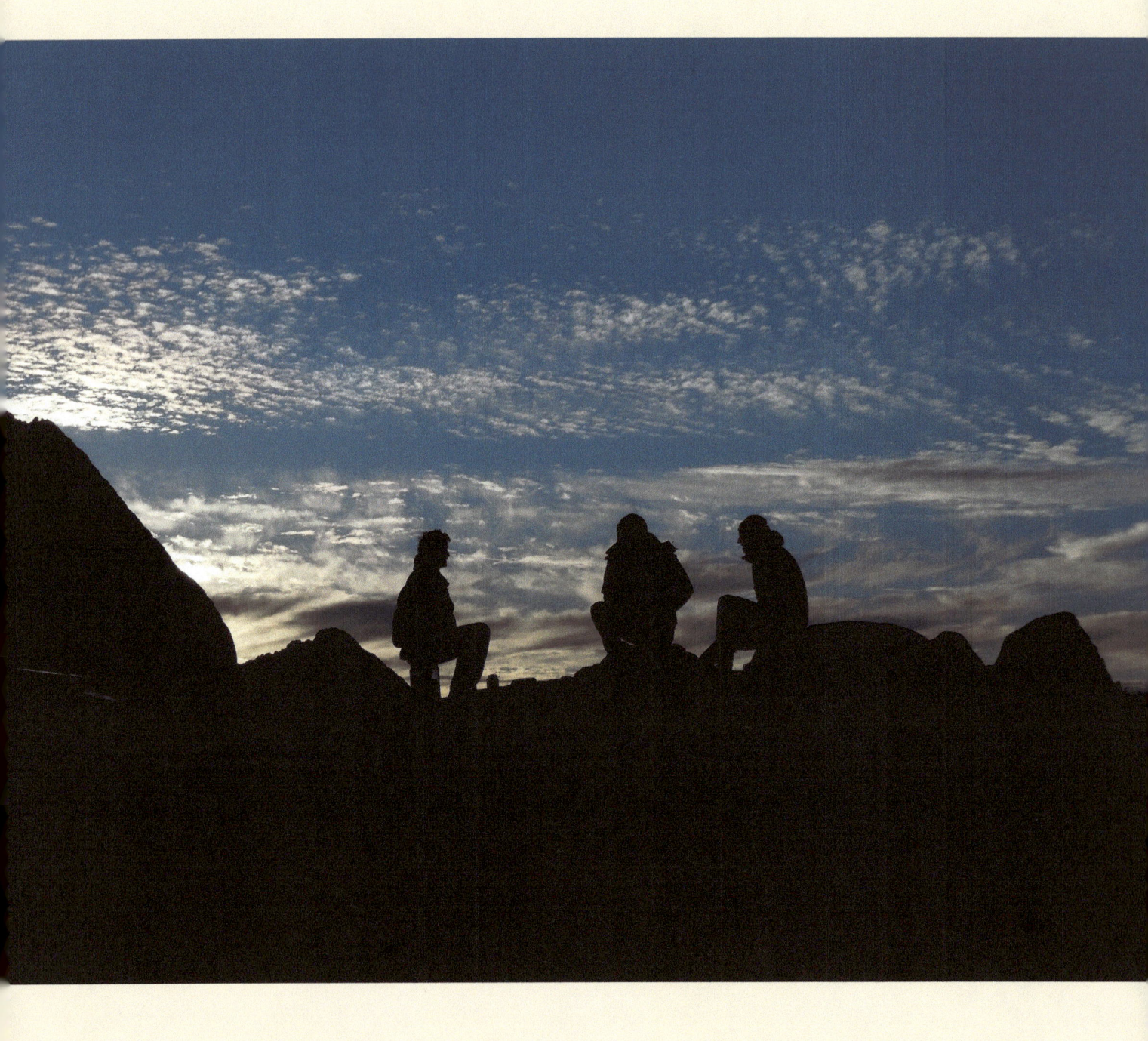

Process

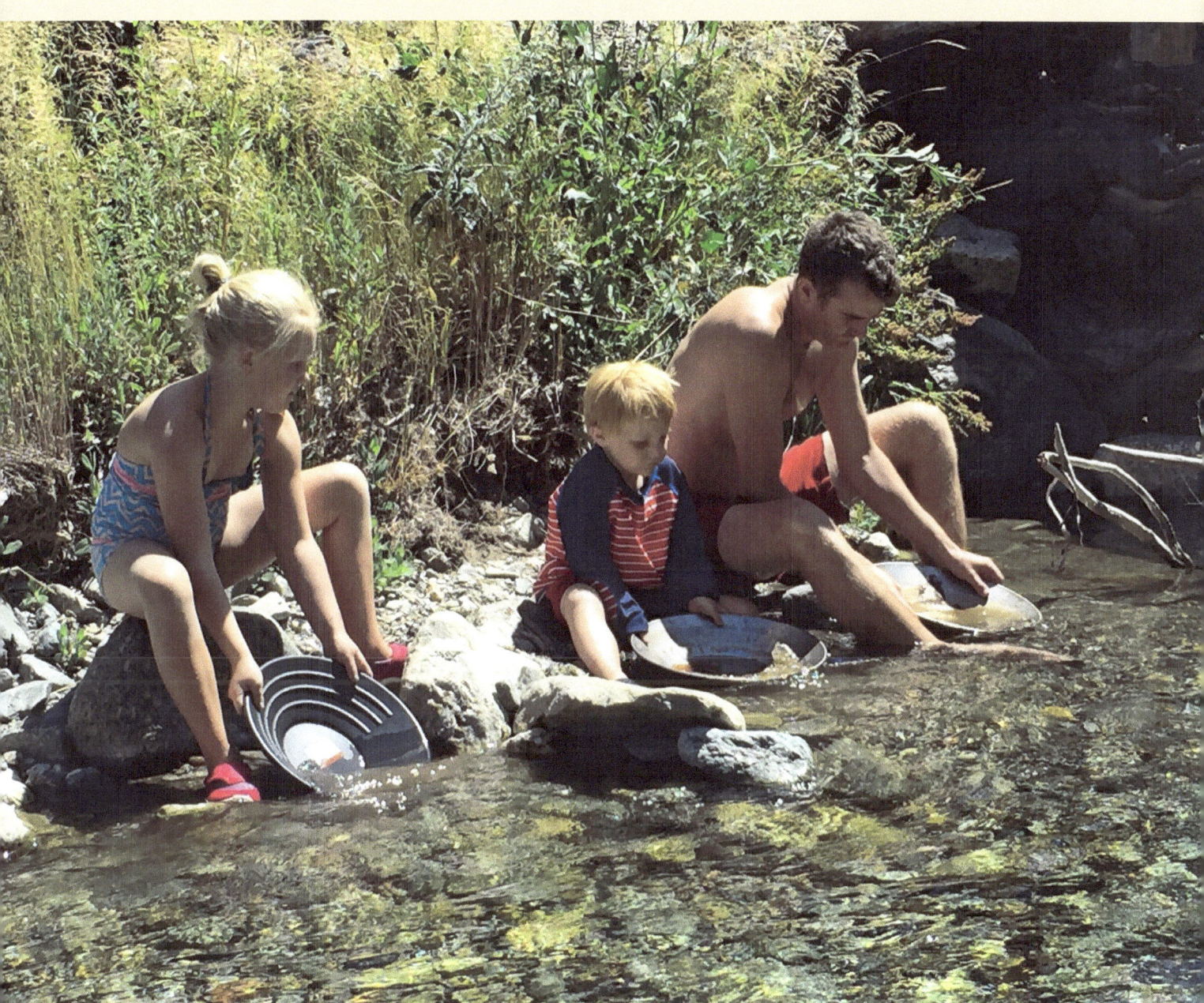

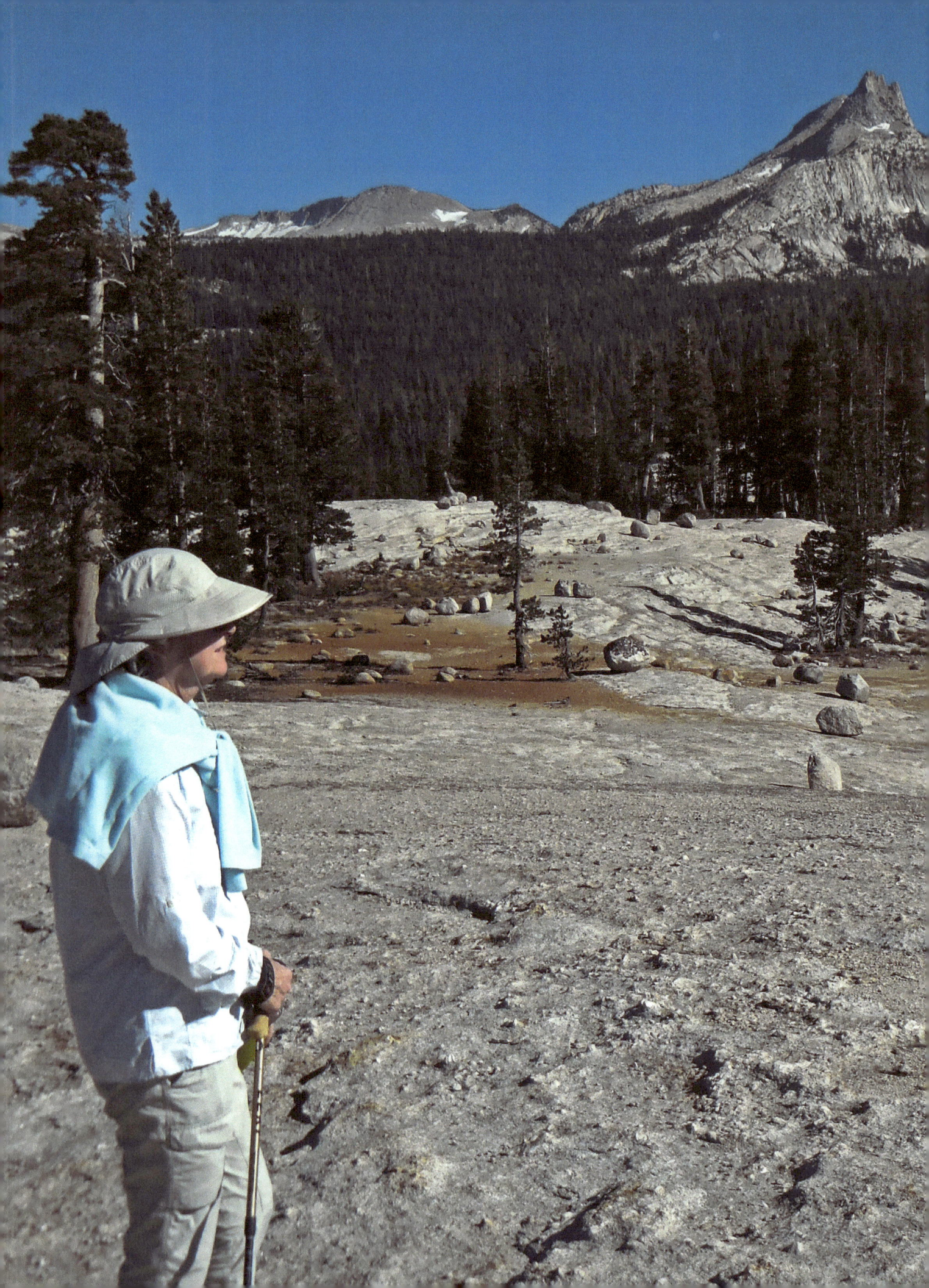

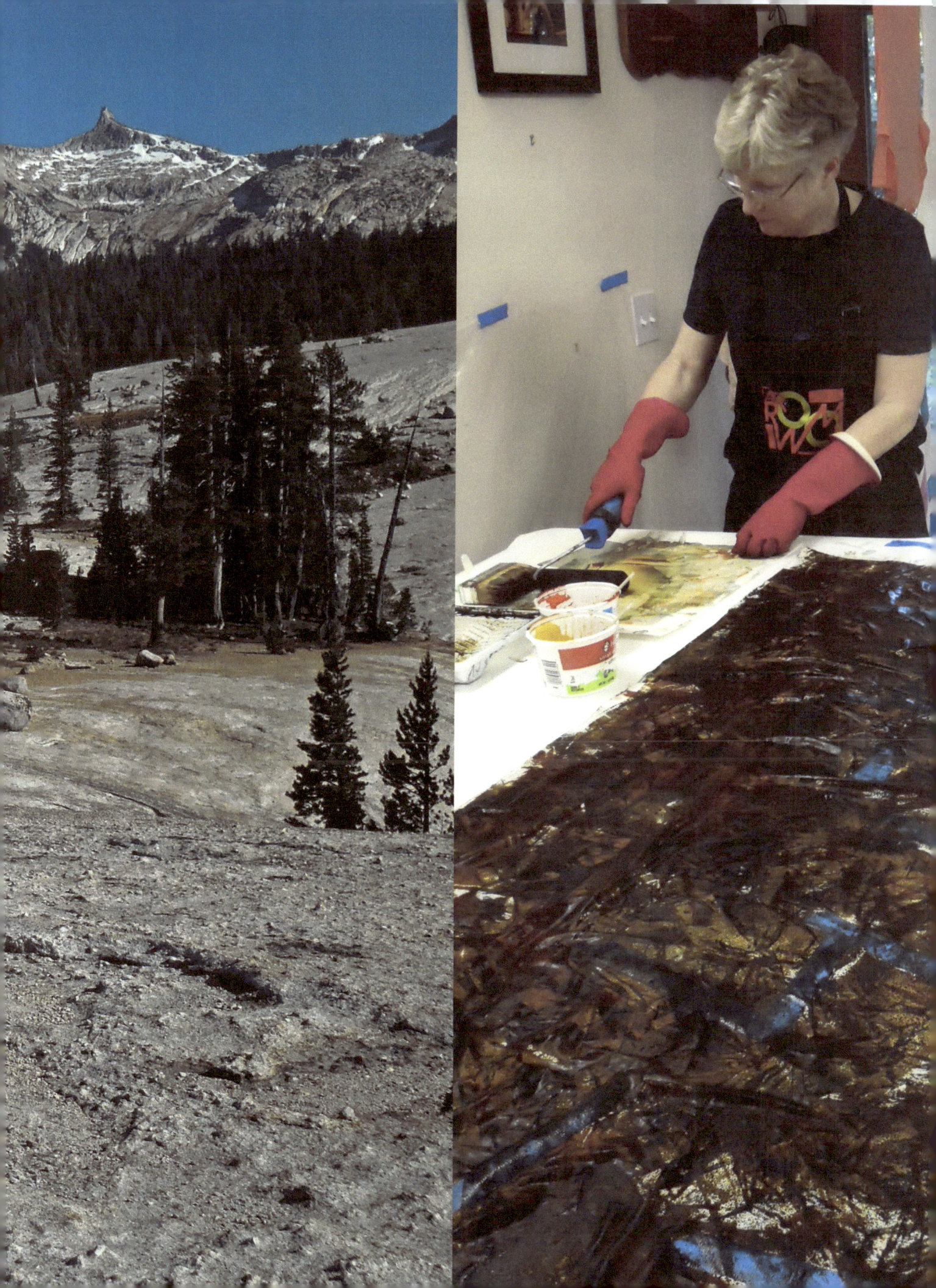

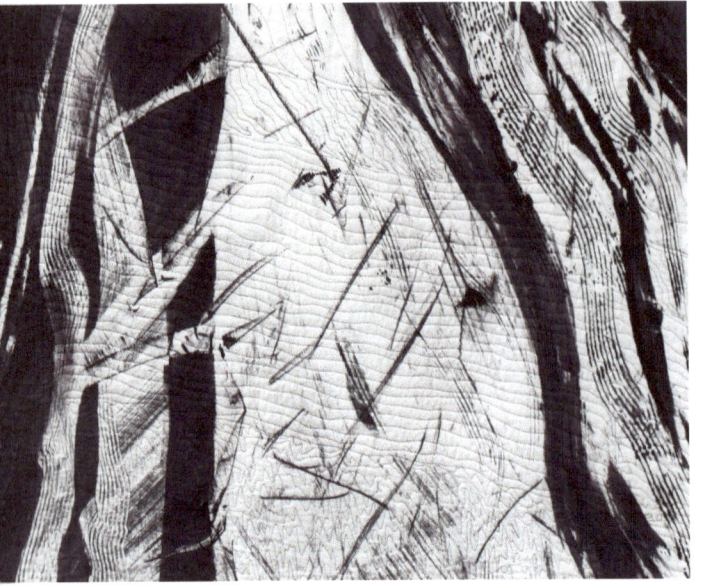

Monoprinting dye on fabric that is larger than my table requires printing it in sections. I apply the dye directly on the surface, and lay the fabric over it. Here, I have smooth vinyl on the back table and absorbent foam in the foreground where the fabric is still face down with only one half printed. After the dye fixed, I painted more dye over the front. I used potato dextrin resist for the gold texture.

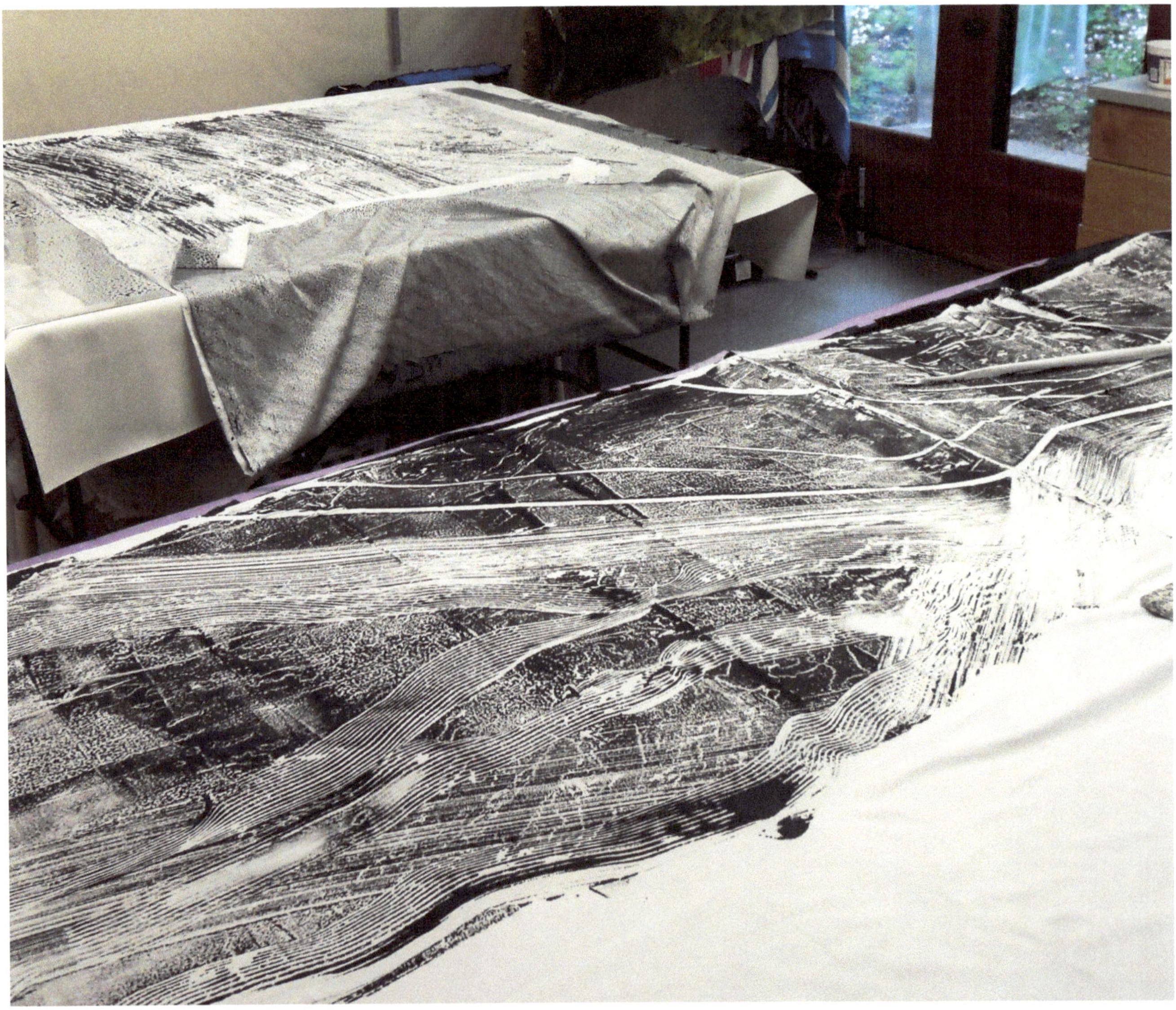

See quilt page 16.

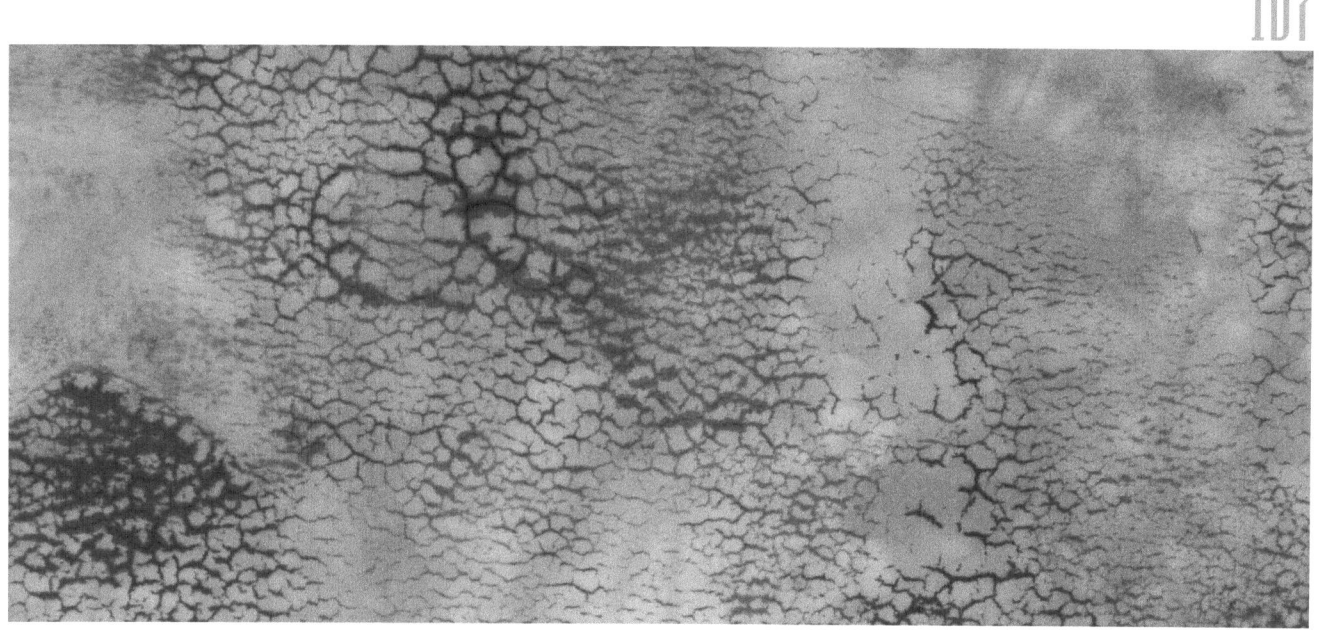

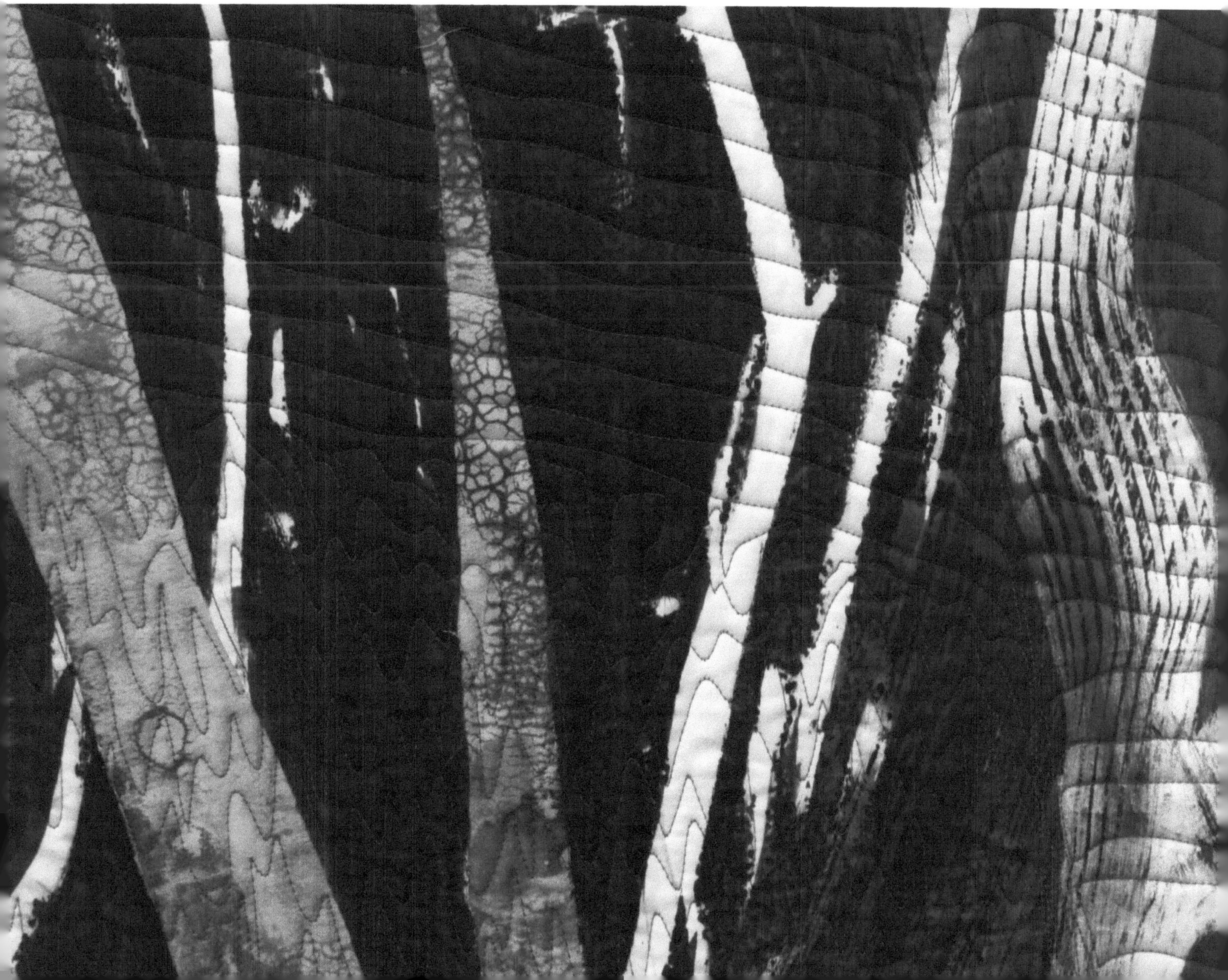

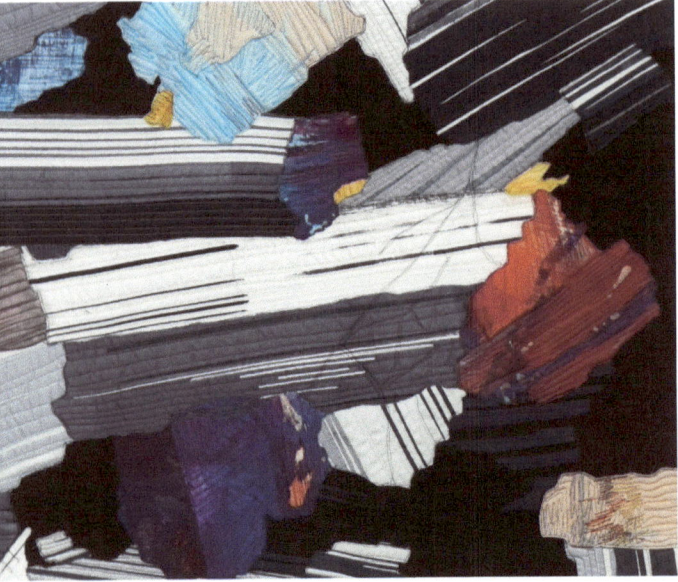

See quilt page 18.

A microscope with a camera that had two polarizing filters over very thin slices of rock provided references for me to dye fabric for these quilts. My goal was to make the crystal types recognizable to a geologist. I selected and enlarged and printed some of the crystals to help visualize. The most difficult was figuring out how I would dye the infinitely diverse linear markings and values of gray in the plagioclase feldspars. The brightly colored, less linear minerals would be another puzzle.

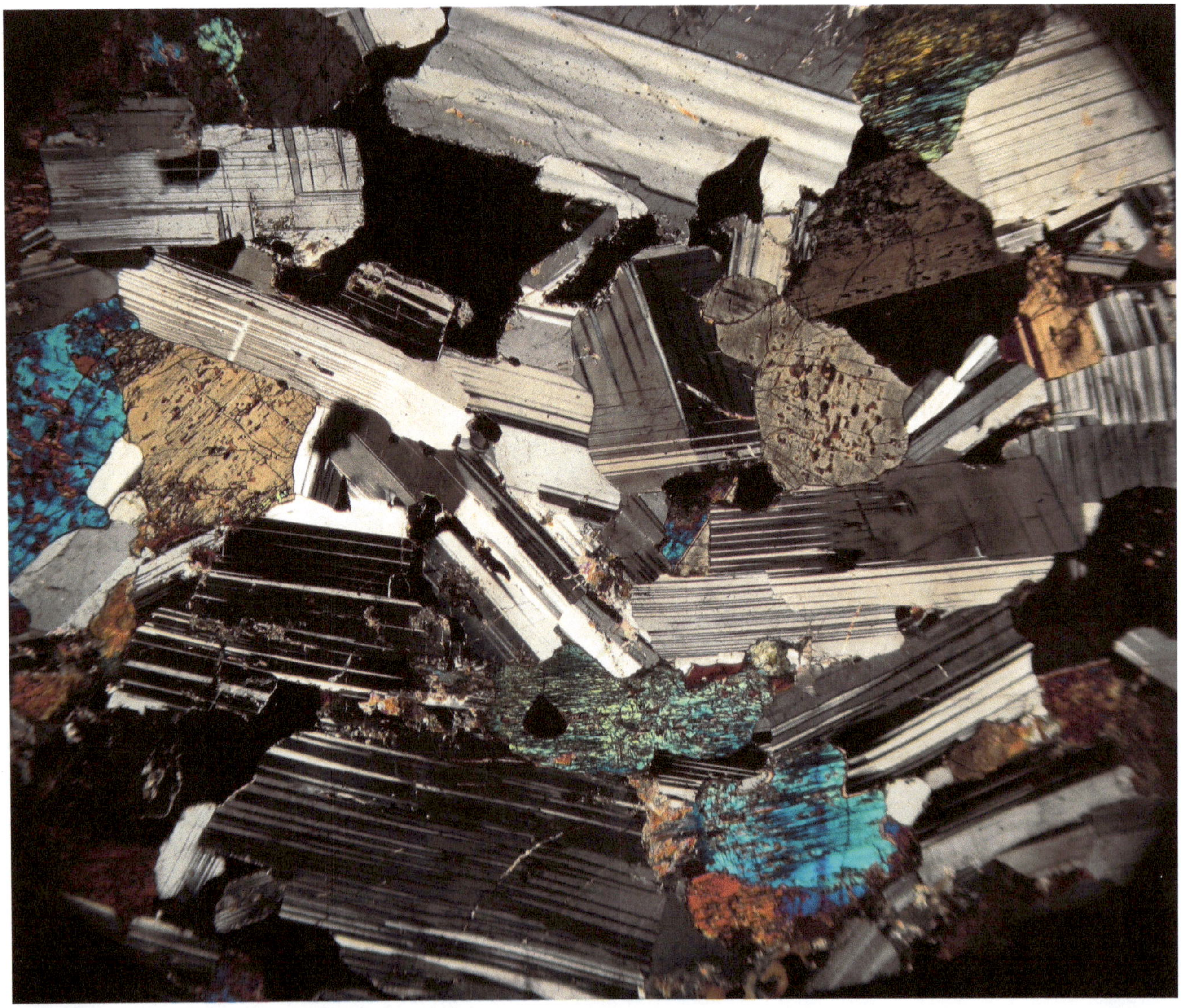

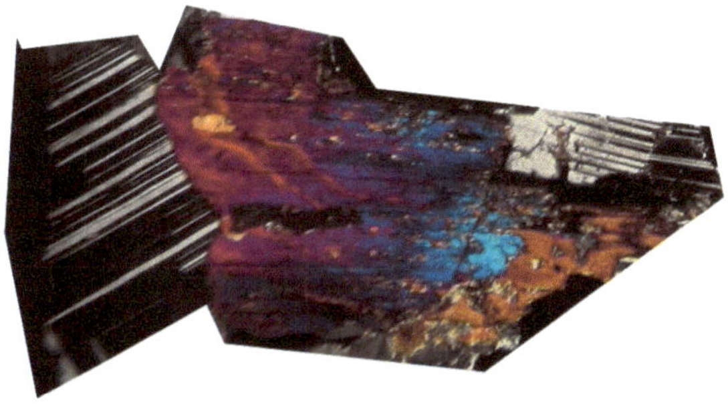

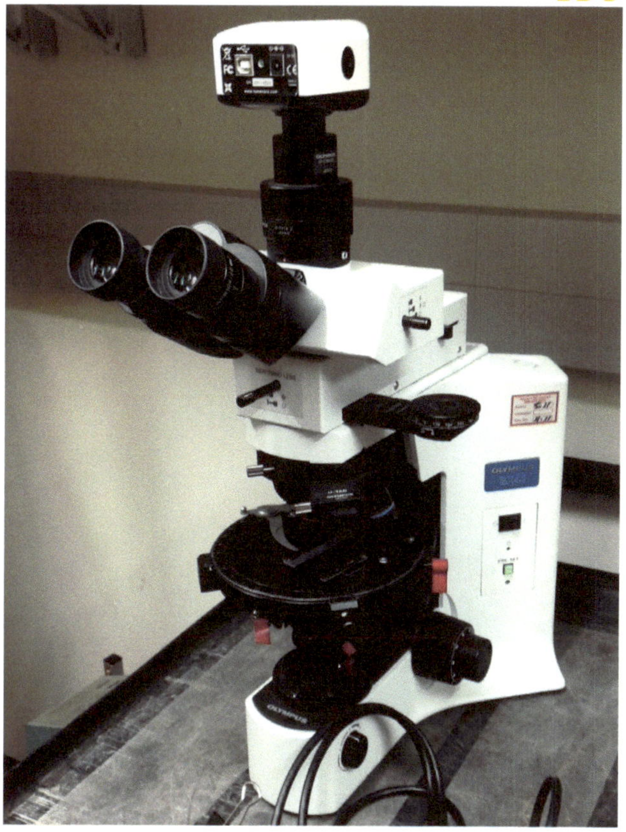

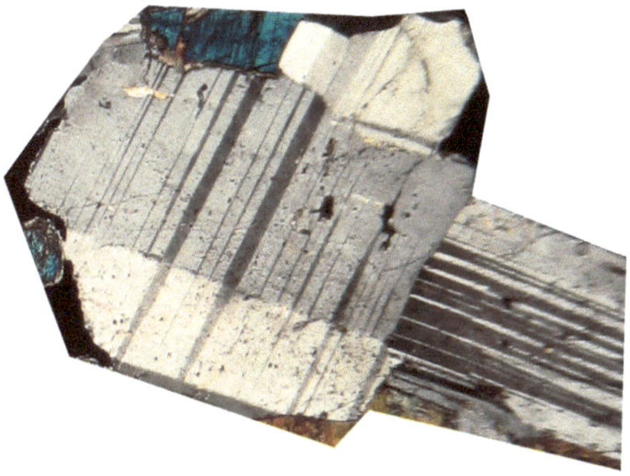

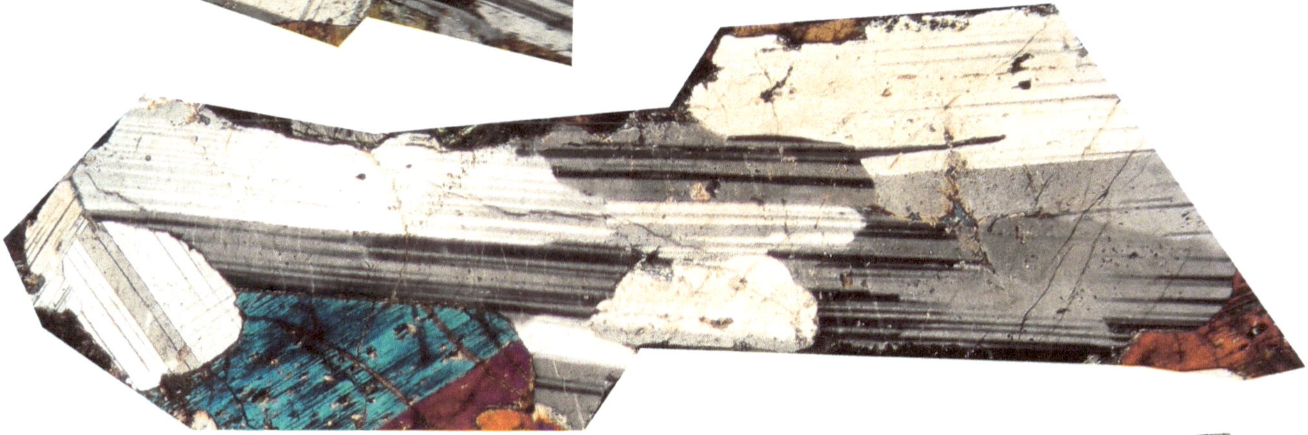

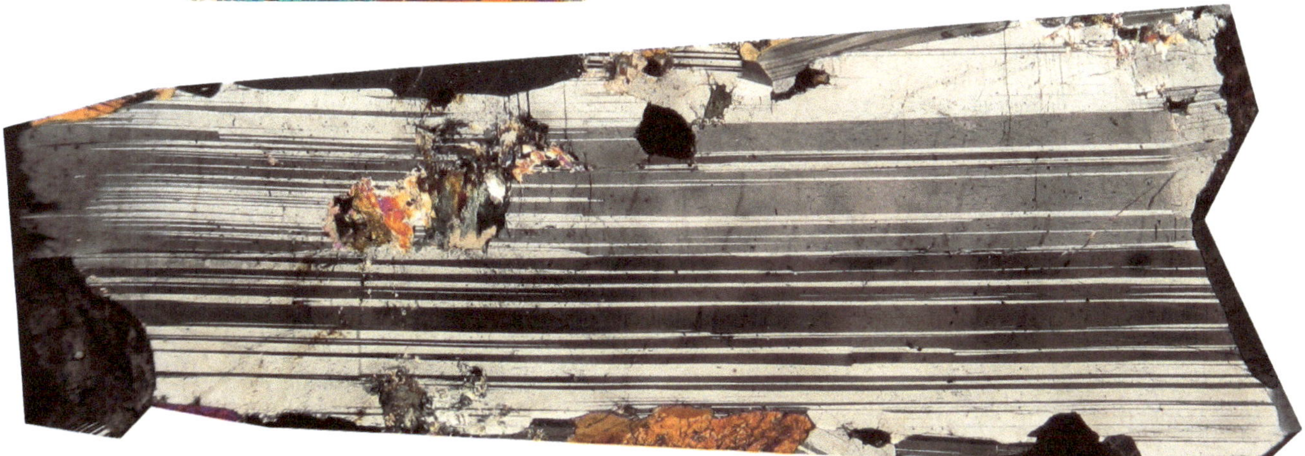

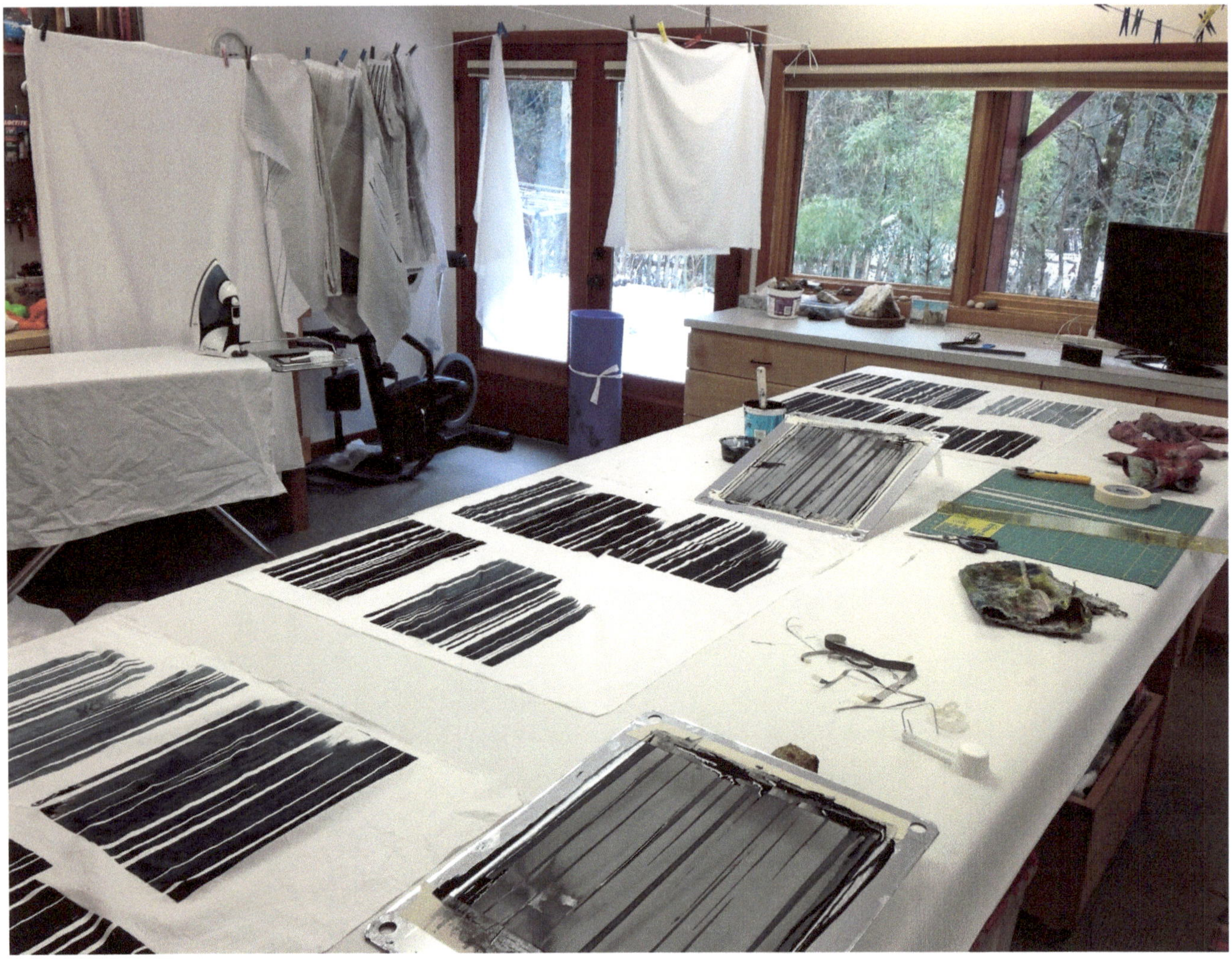

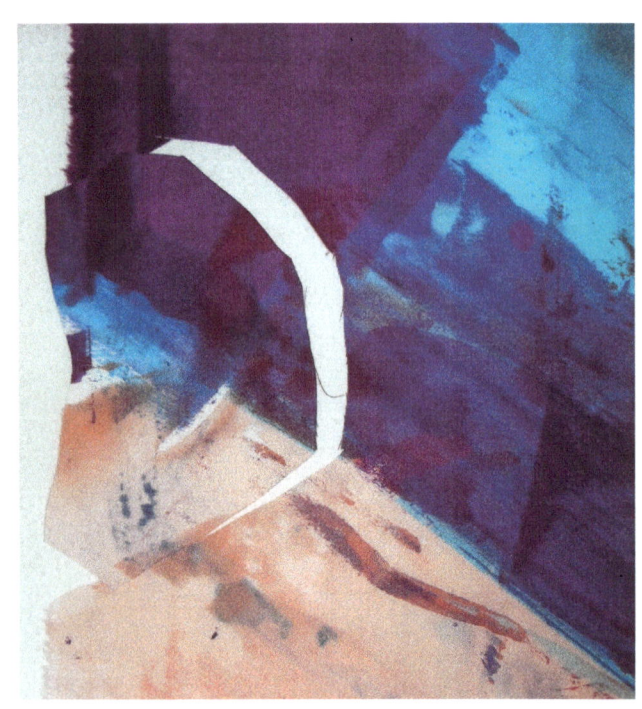

I settled on screen printing for the feldspars, moving or removing the masked lines on the screen each time I pulled the dye. For the colored minerals, I used immersion dyeing, breakdown printing, monoprinting, and brush-painted dyes.

Fabrics being auditioned on my wall have blue tape indicating the edges of the quilt. I took pieces down a few at a time, sewed edges together, right sides up, cut away the excess, repeated, and rearranged. Off to the side I had extra pieces and transparent silk organza ready to use.

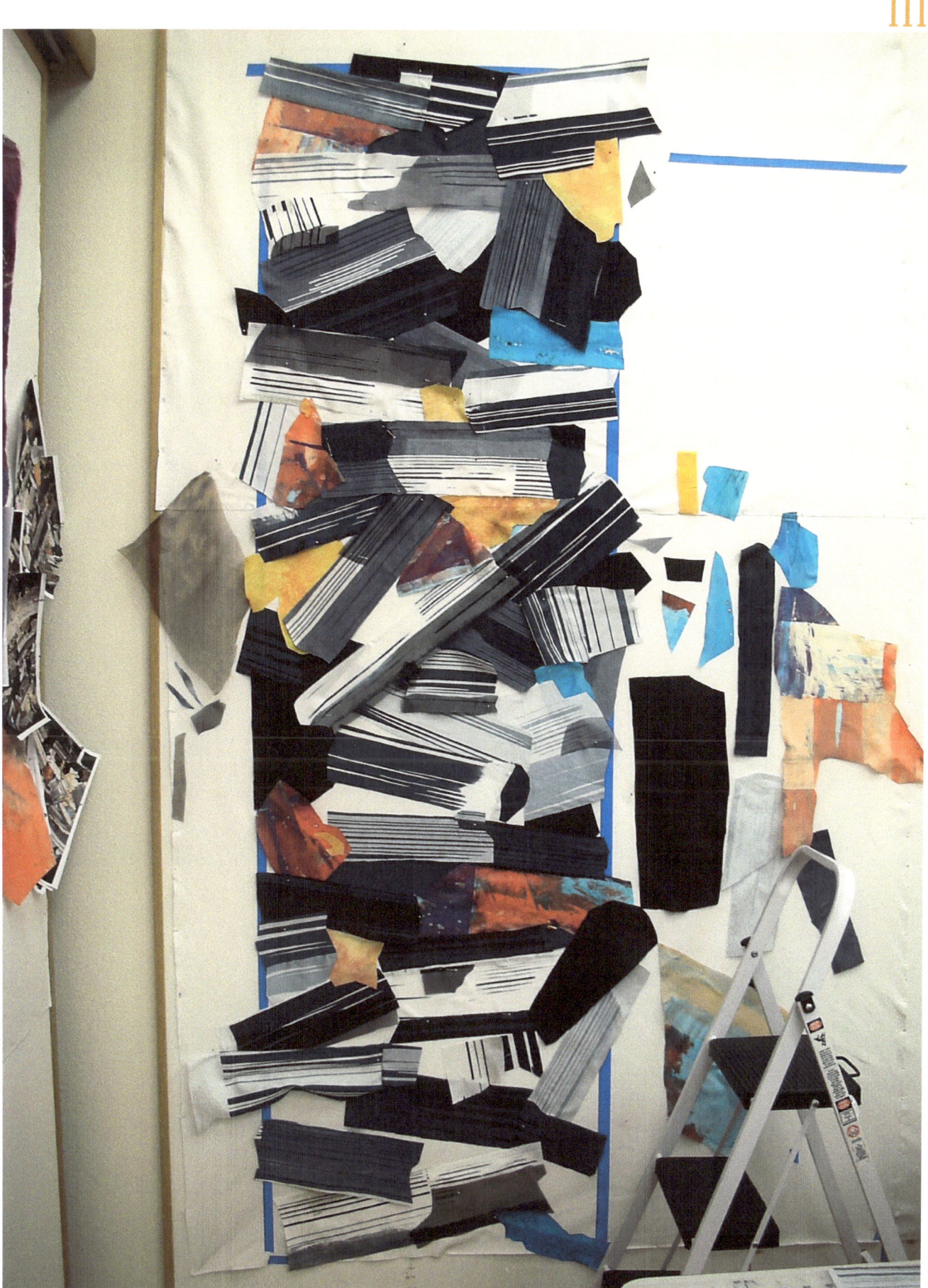

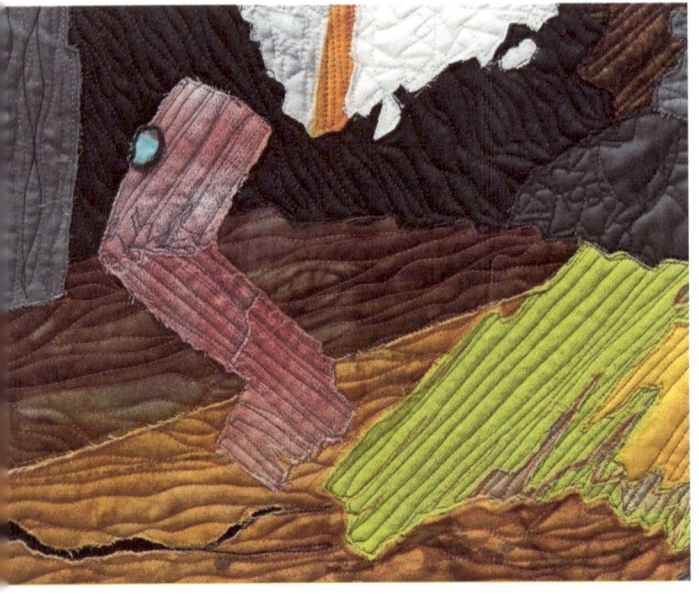

See quilt page 19.

The characteristic minerals in granite are not as distinct as gabbro. I dyed about 20 yards of textures and used any small pieces that seemed to fit the mineral. After the draft on the wall, I worked on the table to join the clusters of pieces together, pinning them exactly in place.

I first quilted with one color, stitching only where it blended visually. Then I went back with specific colors, using different patterns to work with specific minerals.

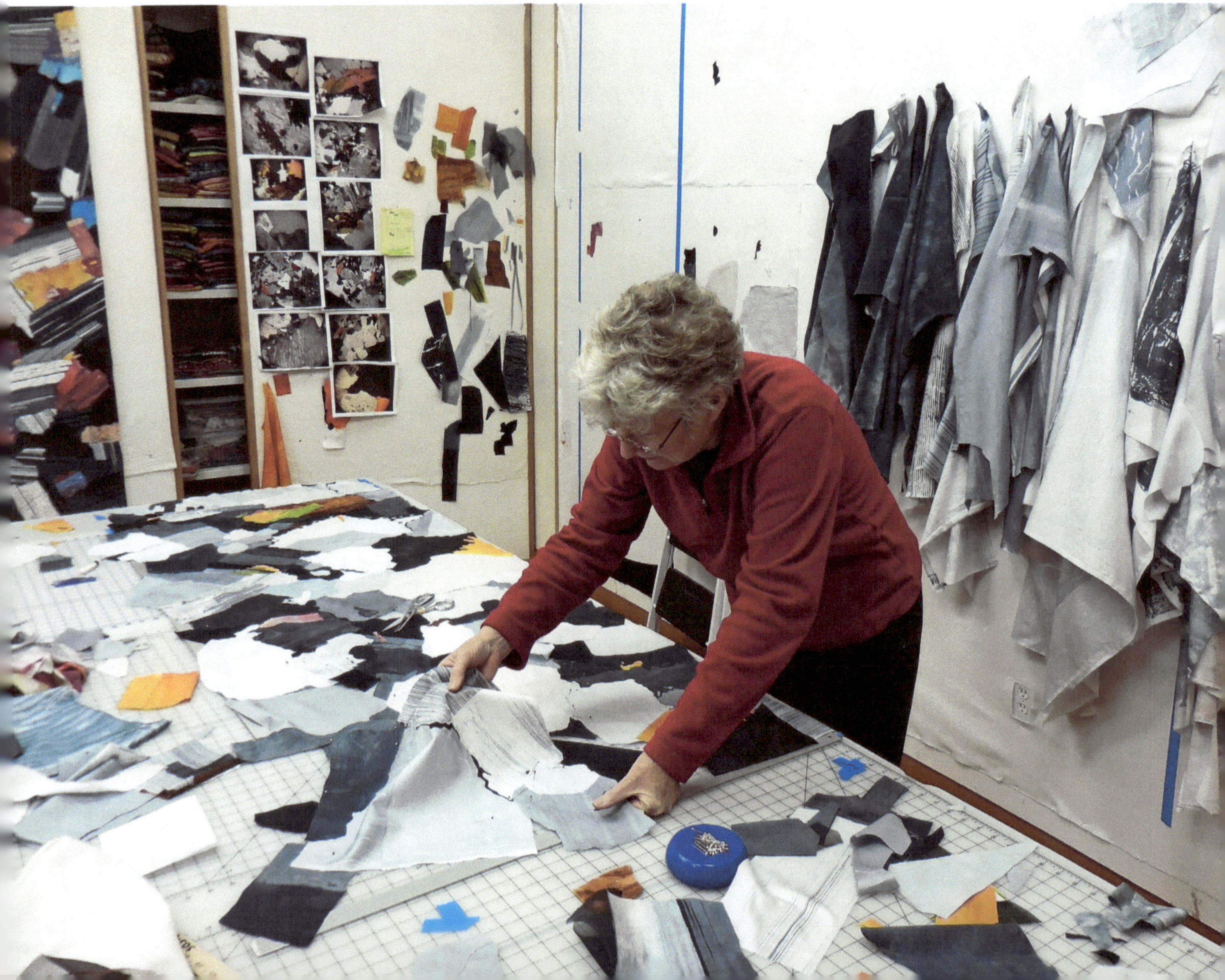

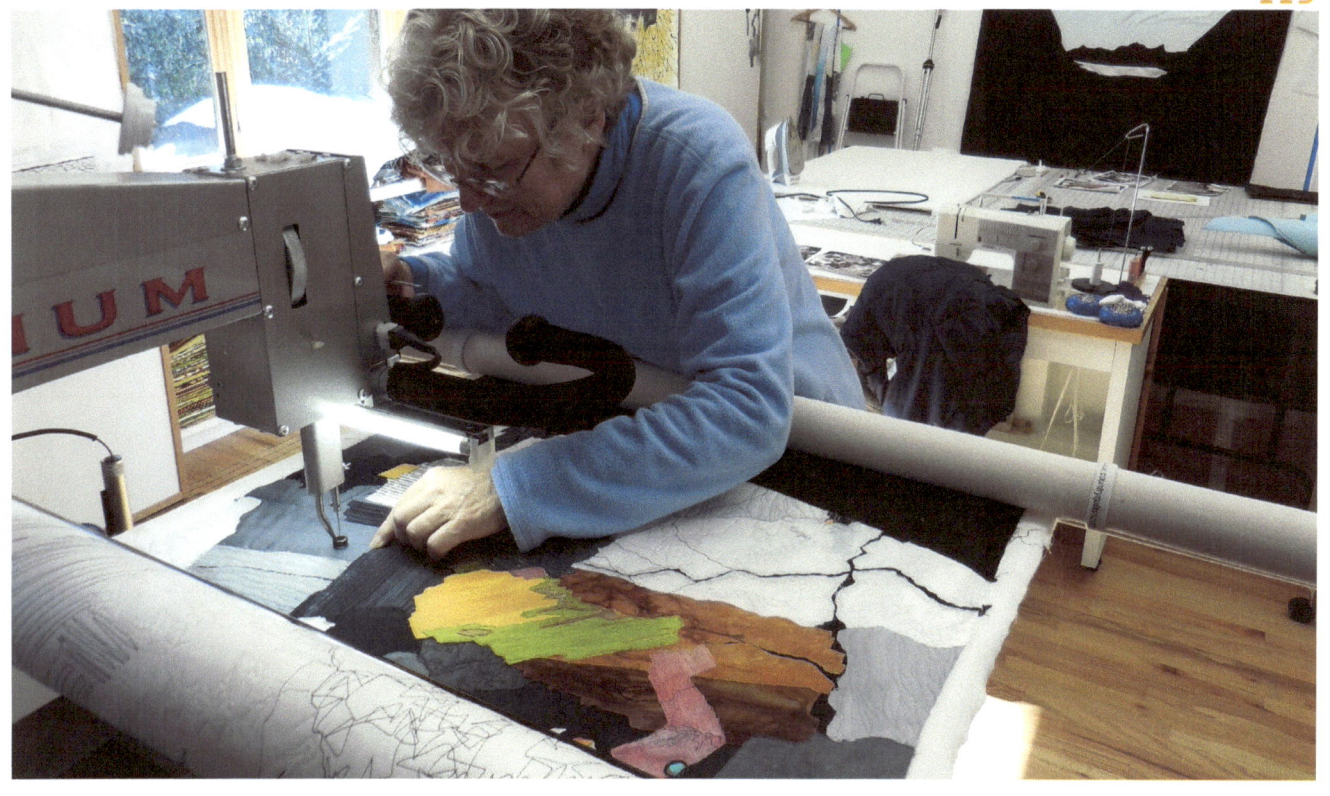

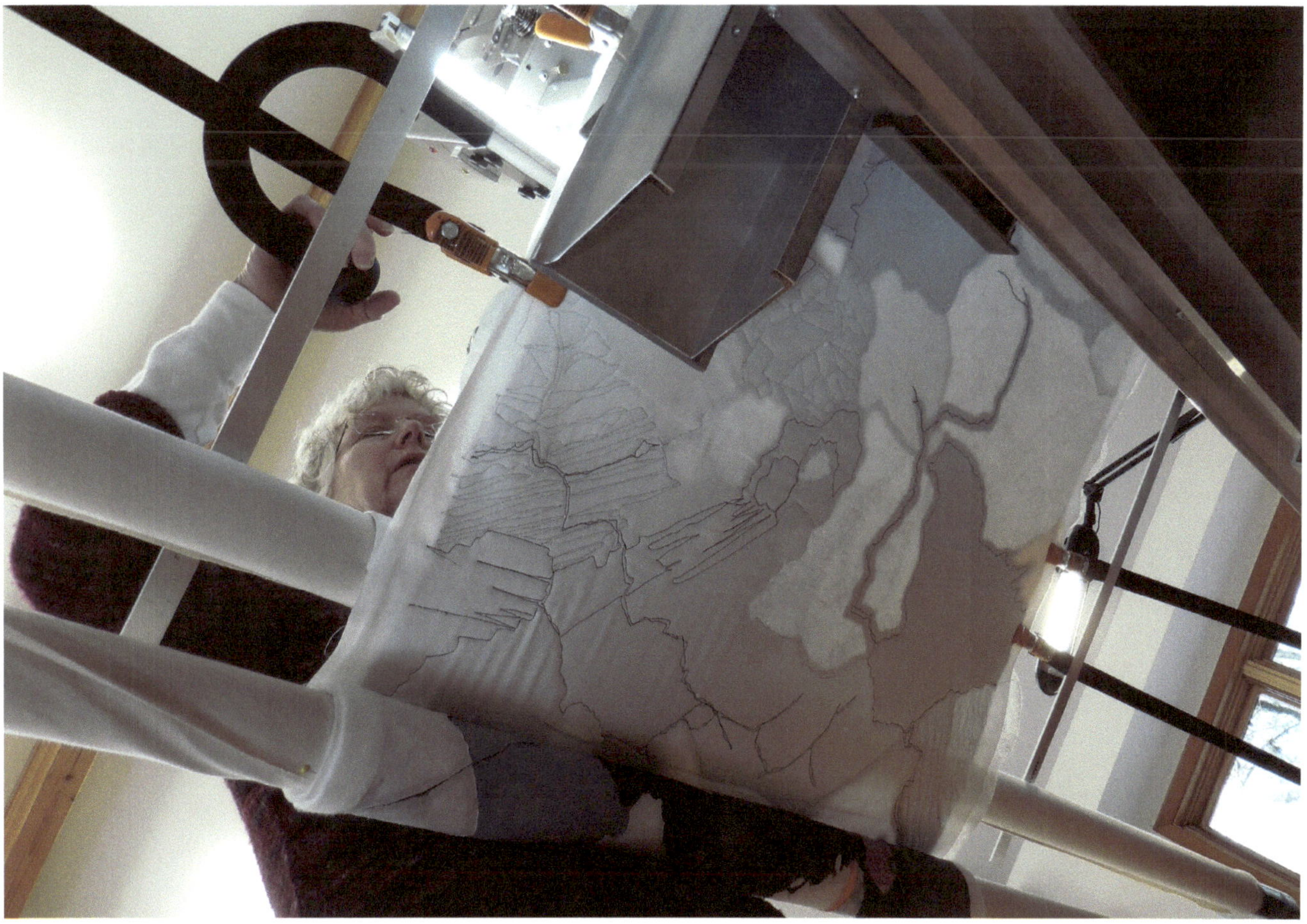

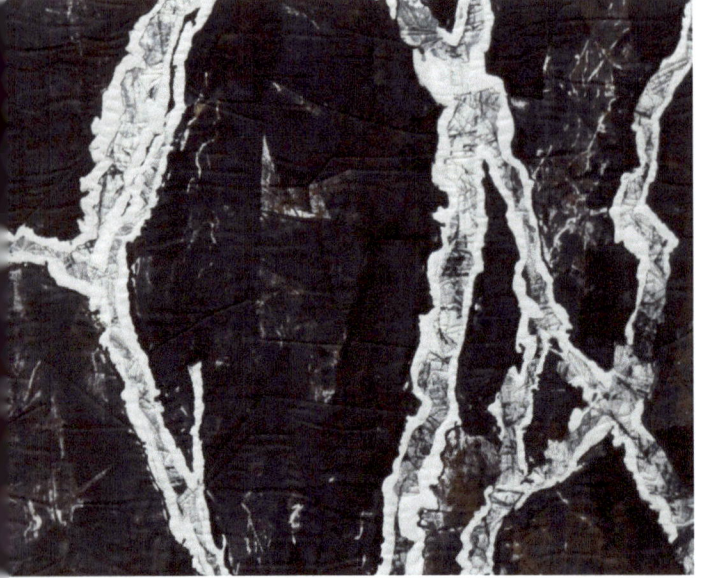

First, I dyed the fabric, below left, with rollers pressed over wrinkles to make scattered light and medium value gray marks. I used corn dextrin resist on white fabric, below right, then rolled thickened dye in large blocky shapes using dark rusts and grays over it. The resulting fabric was dark with bold white lines.

See quilt page 33.

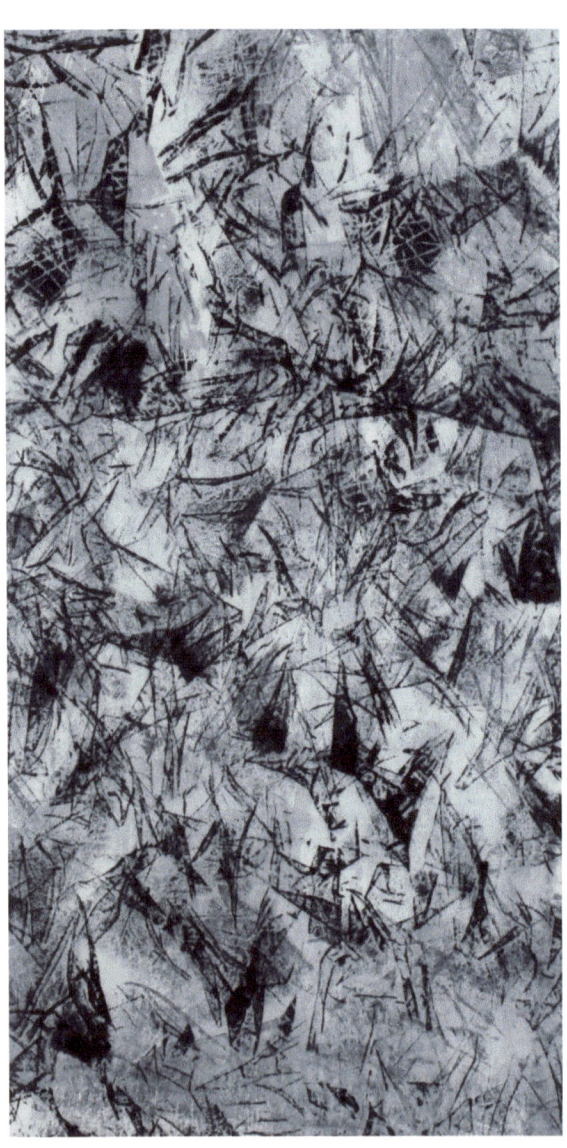

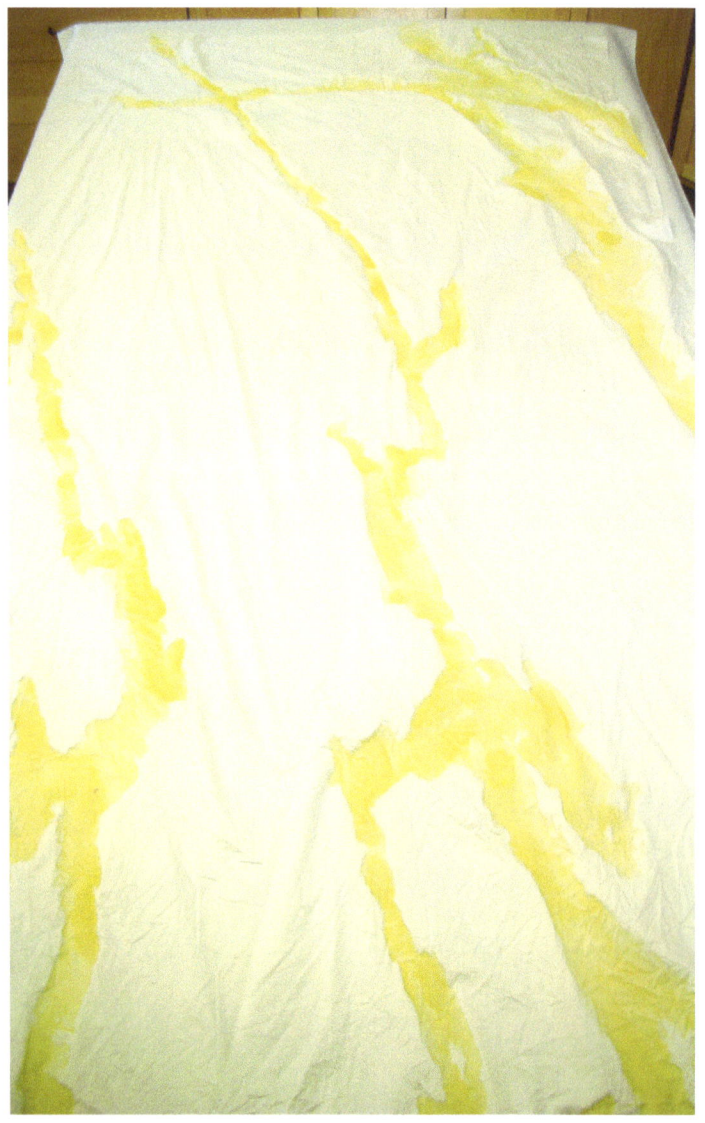

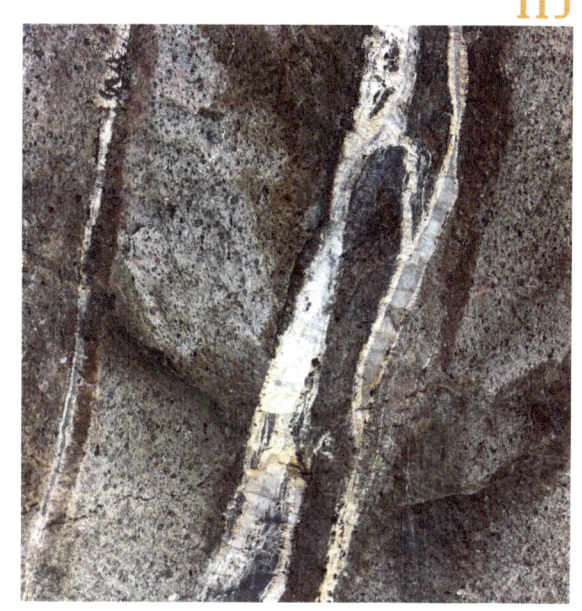

I placed the first piece under the second, sewing with matching threads and cutting away to reveal the inside of the veins. I used scraps of both the white and dark cloth to revise some of the lines and areas of color using raw-edge appliqué, detail below.

The dense yellow quilting lines in the veins create horizontal wrinkles in the surrounding areas, which I firmly steamed in order to retain them.

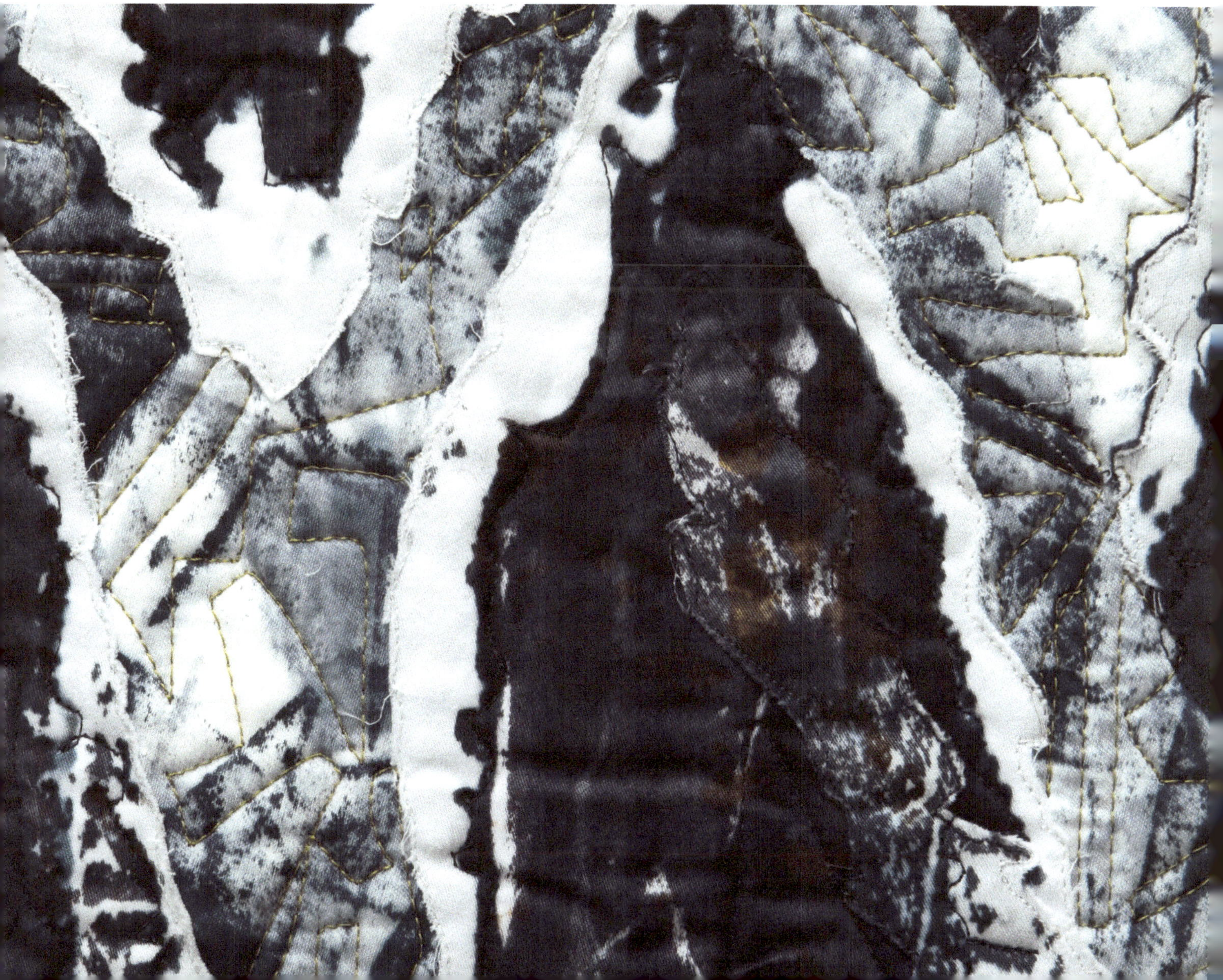

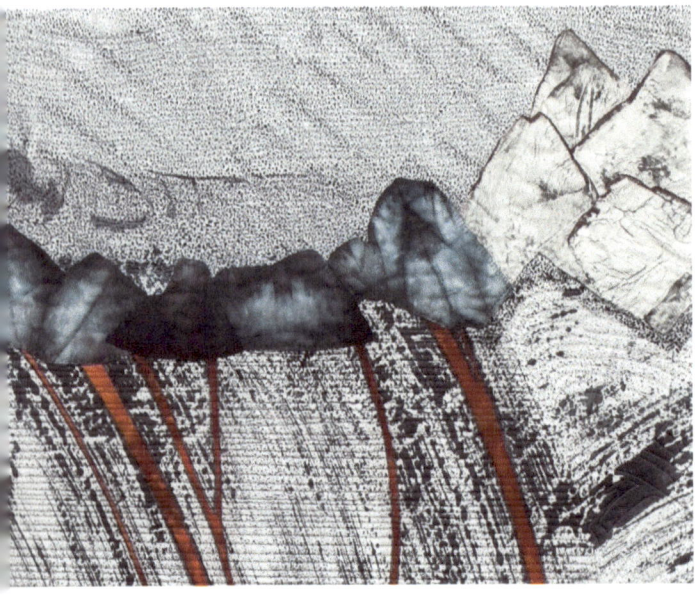

See quilt page 34.

Monoprinting several colors of gray, opposite, below, creates both the uniformity and variety I see in photos of granite, opposite, top. (See the back table in image on page 106.) I cut through it to reveal orange-red cloth. The dark mountain shapes are cut out from low-water immersion dyed fabric; the lighter Sierra shapes are selected from fabric made with potato dextrin resist.

I hand stitched over the raw edges in both black and red thread.

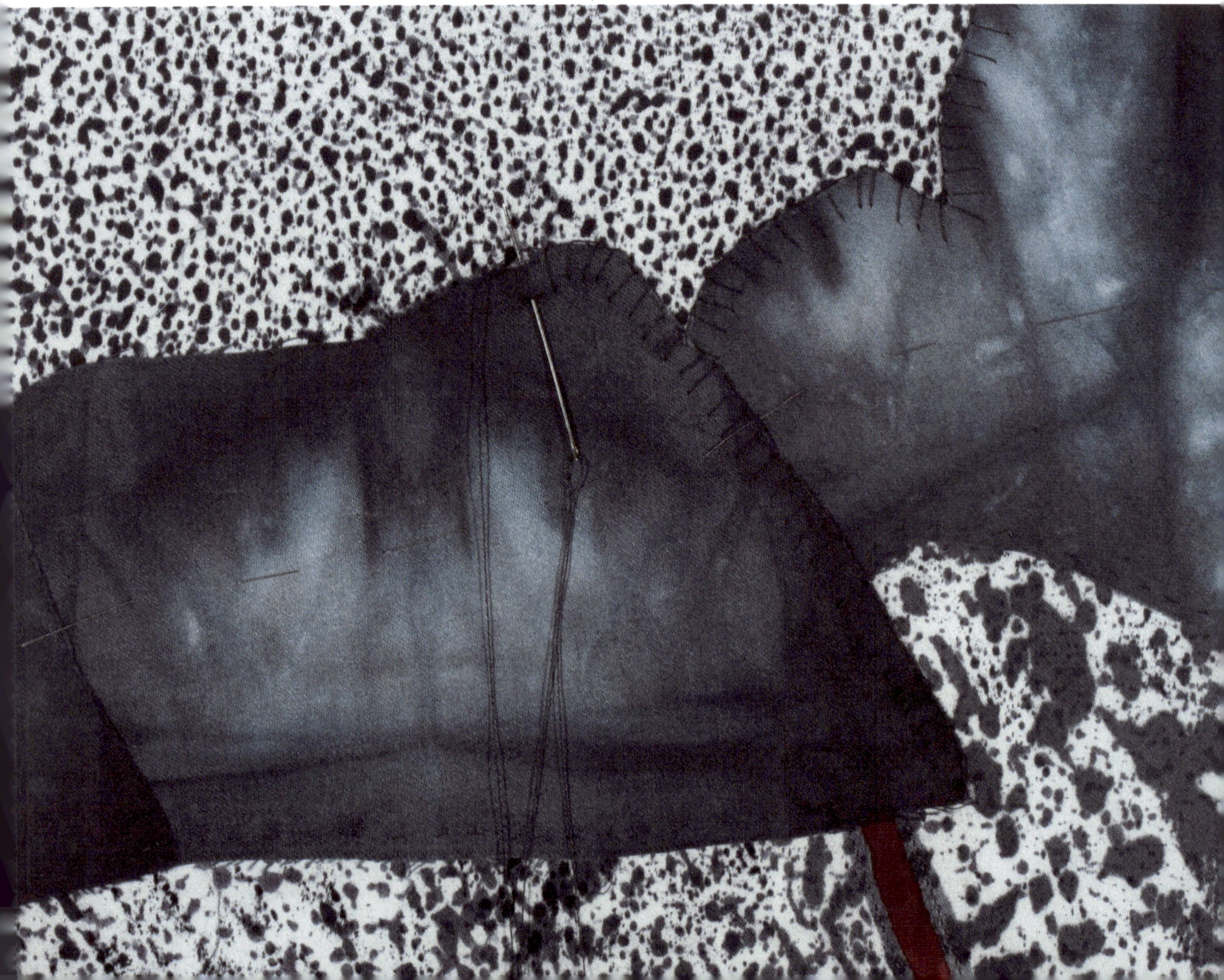

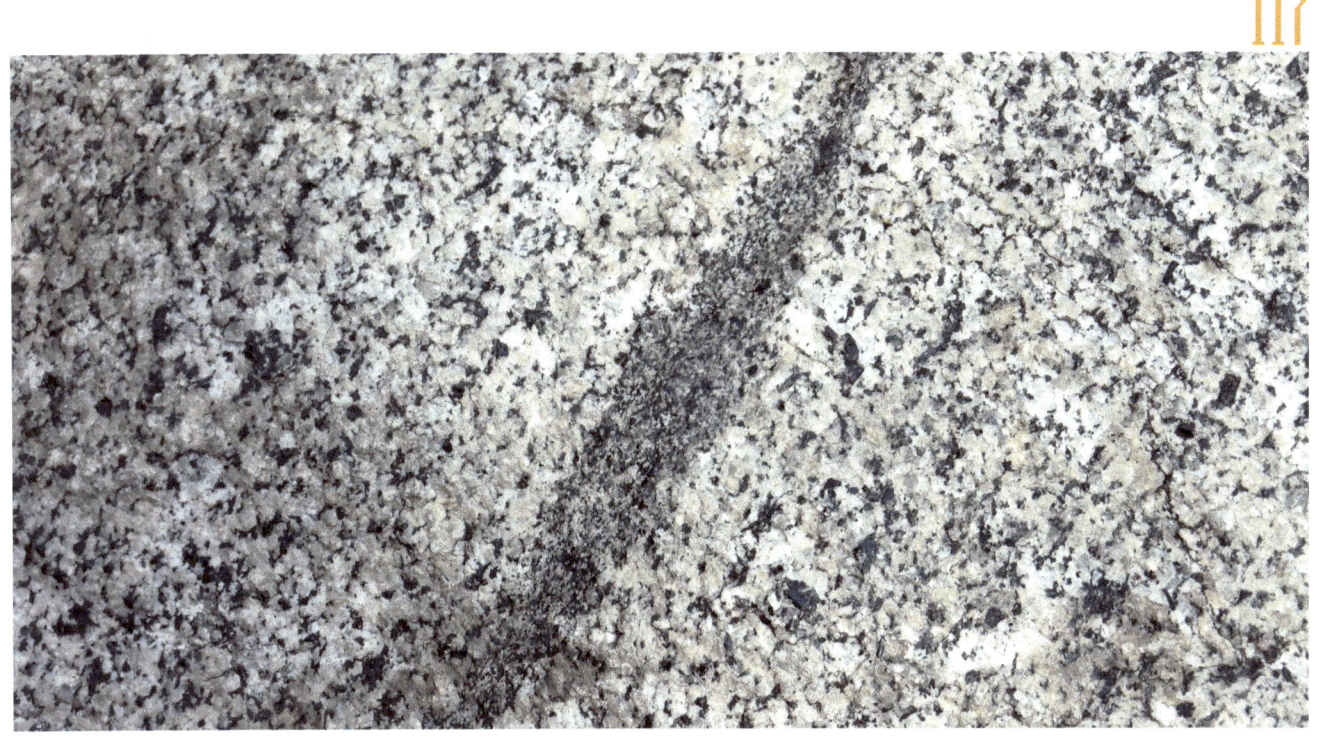

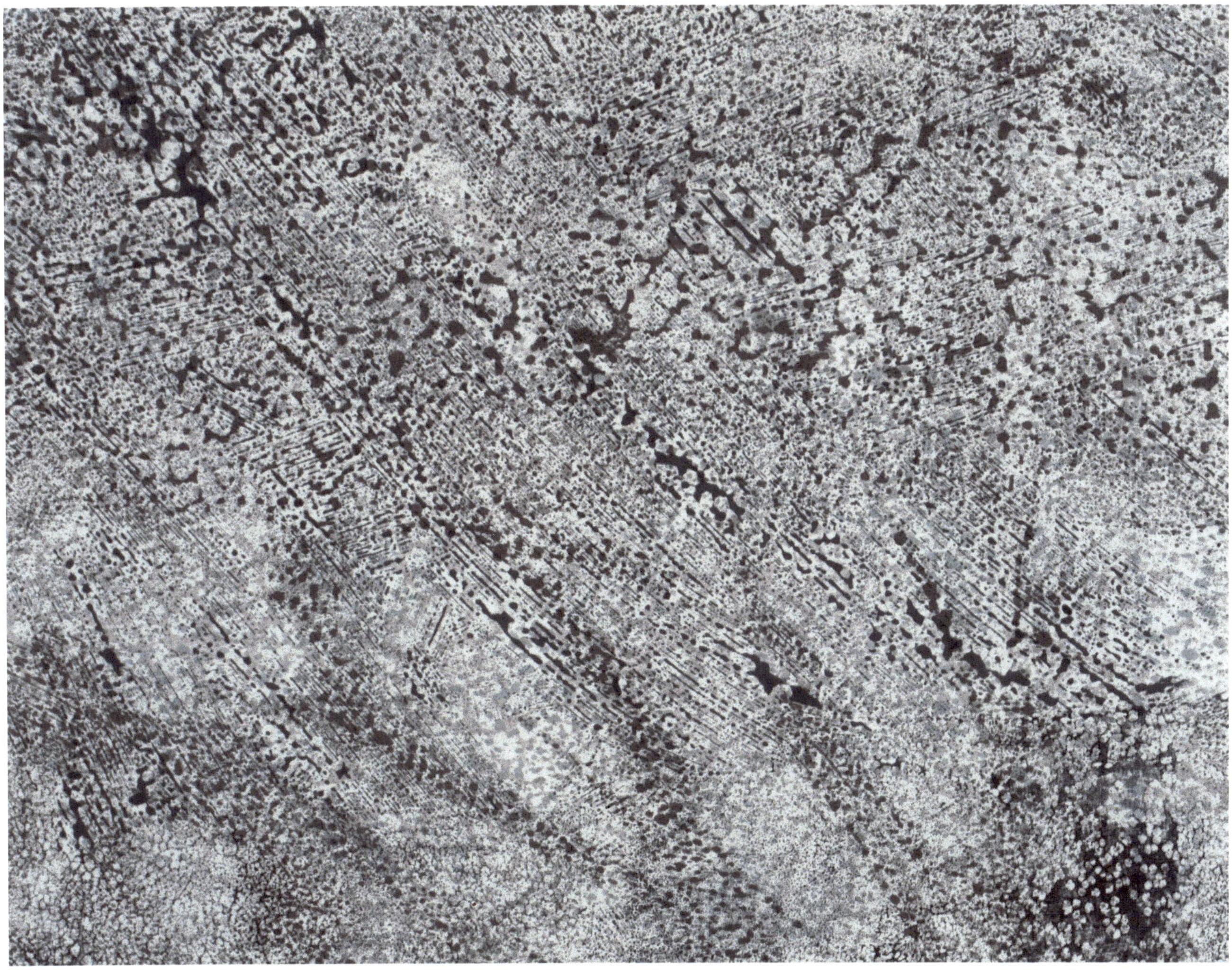

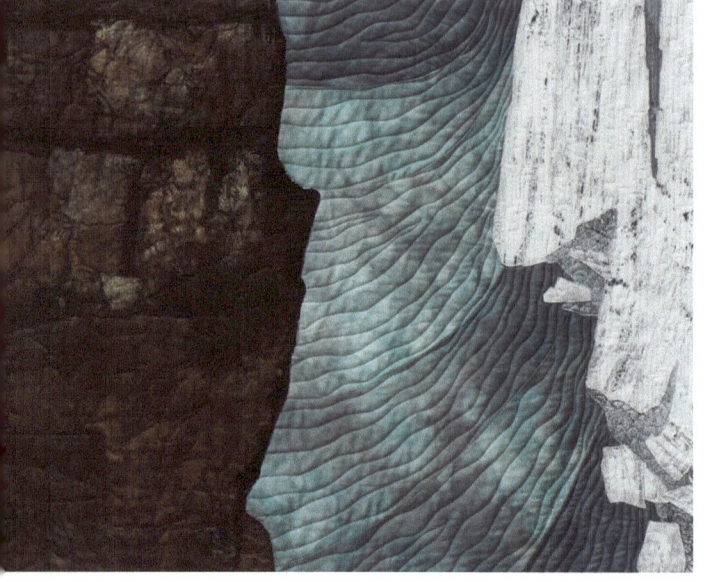

See quilt page 39.

I made the dark rock by first monoprinting speckles, then using blue tape as a resist, I added texture with a roller. I later painted dye over it all with rusts, greens, and some very dark lines for the shadows between the rocks.

I enlarged my sketch to actual size, and eventually cut the rock shapes individually, reassembling them with raw-edge appliqué. I made pattern pieces from the larger drawing to plan the U-shaped valley.

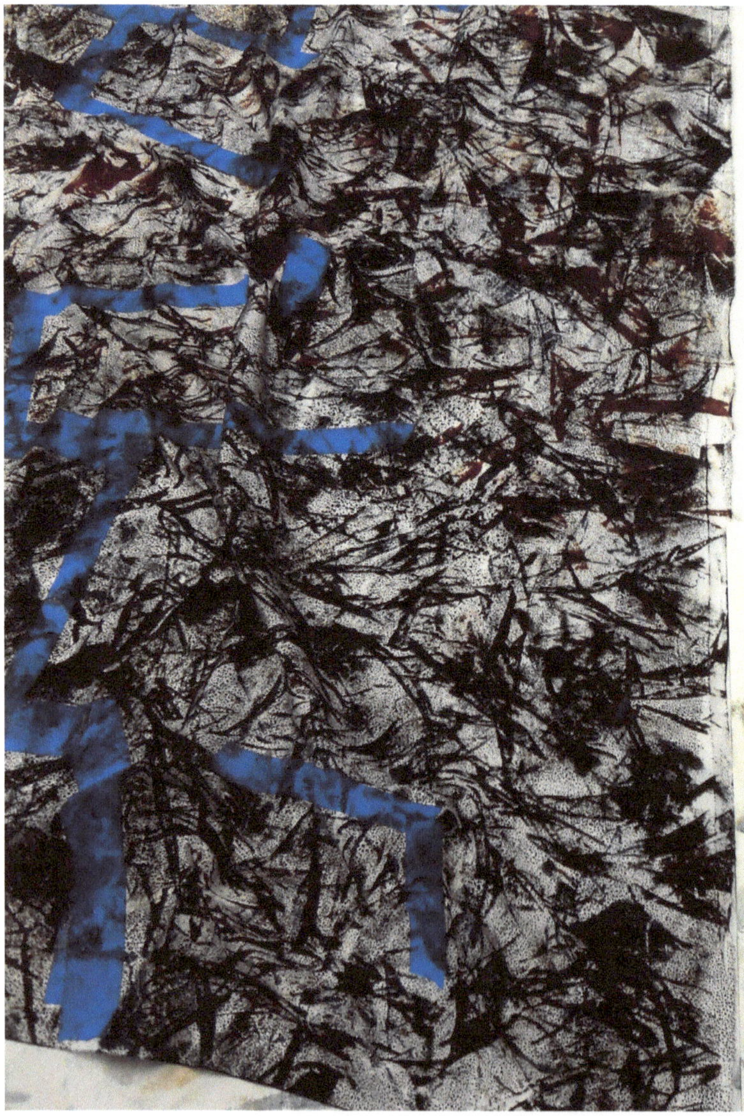

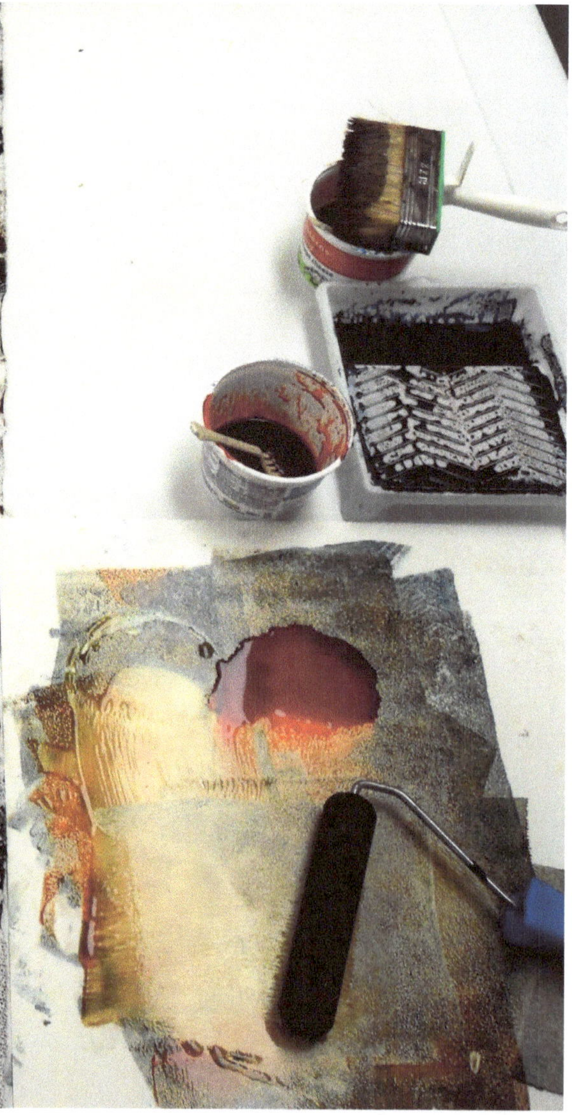

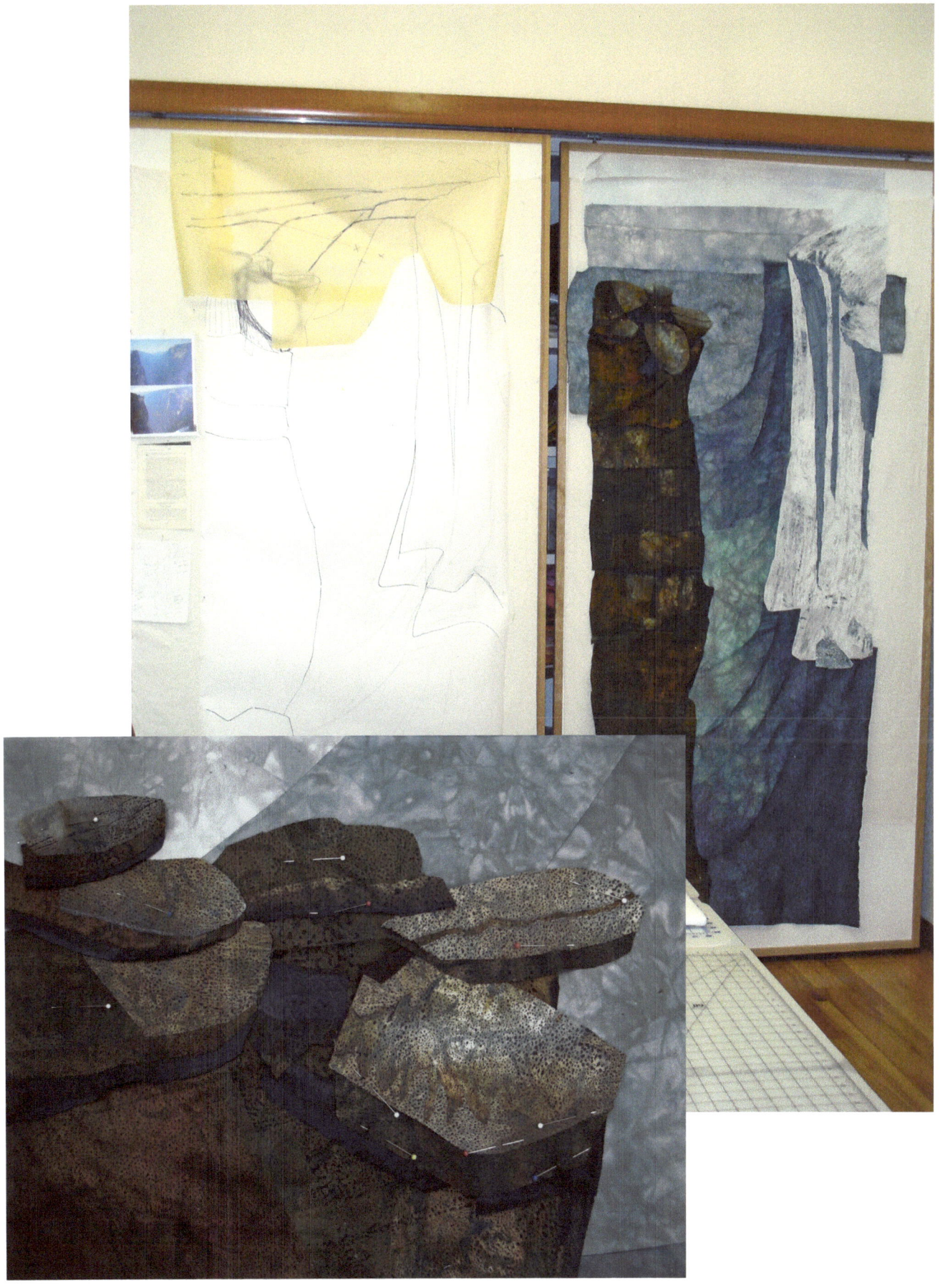

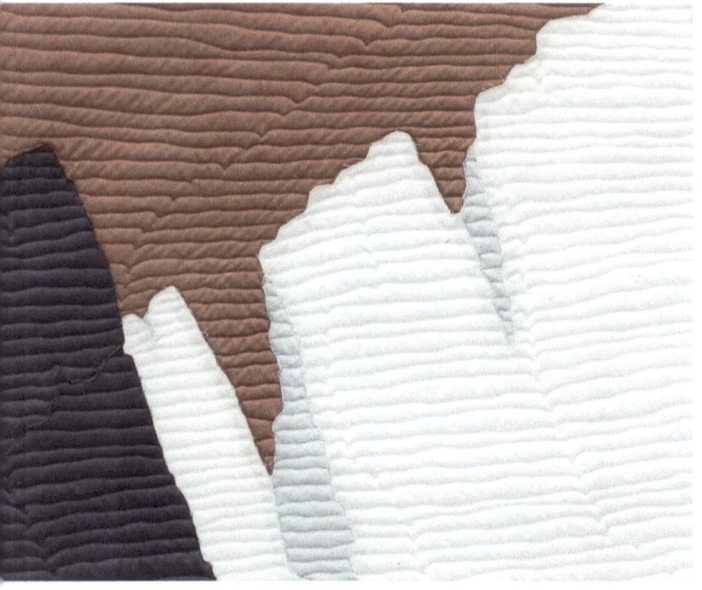

See quilt page 46.

I combined the shapes I saw in different images of the Very High Sierra for these quilts. The colors in the first were based on the real world in bright daylight. The second is based on exaggerated colors inspired by the light at the end of the day.

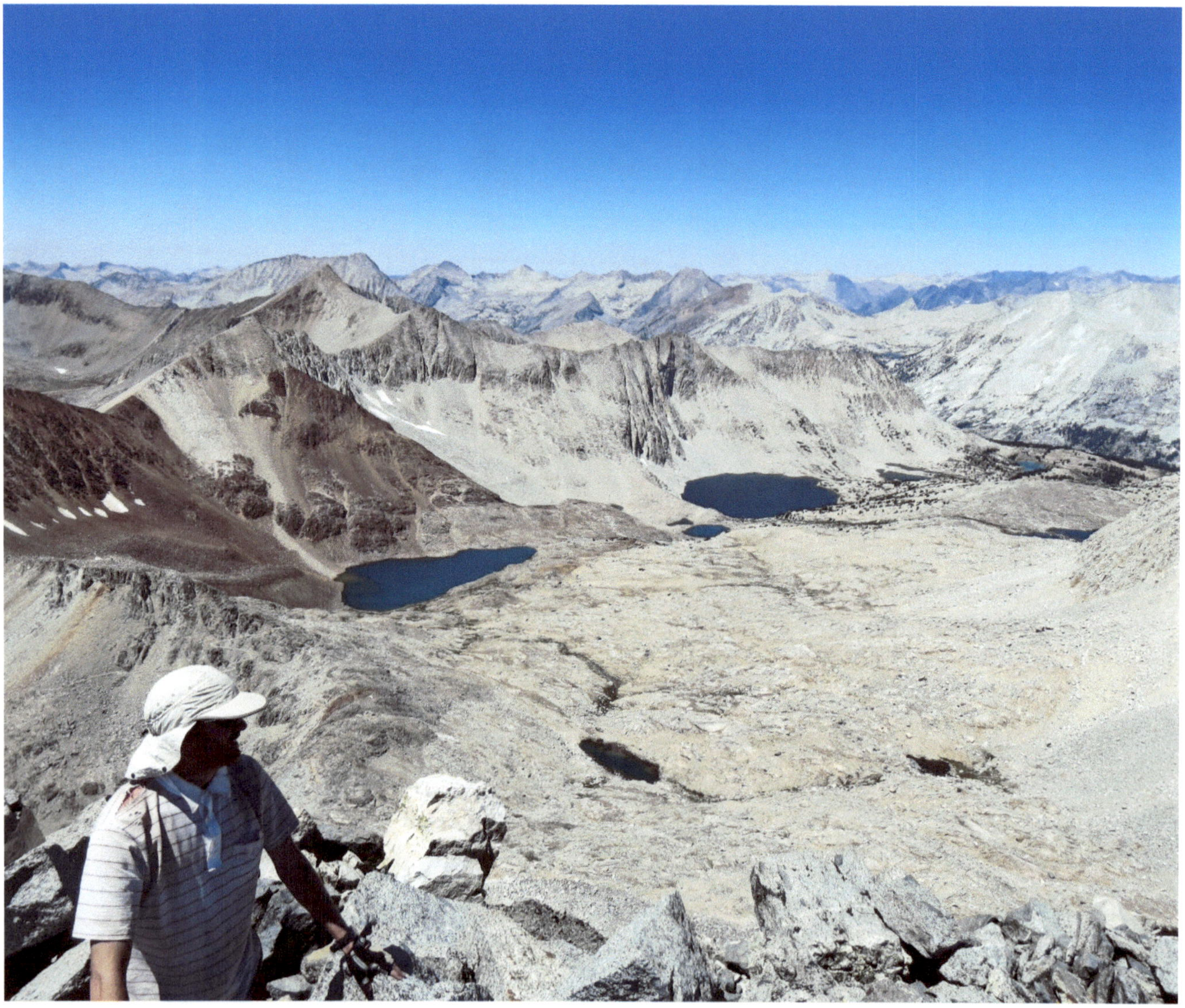

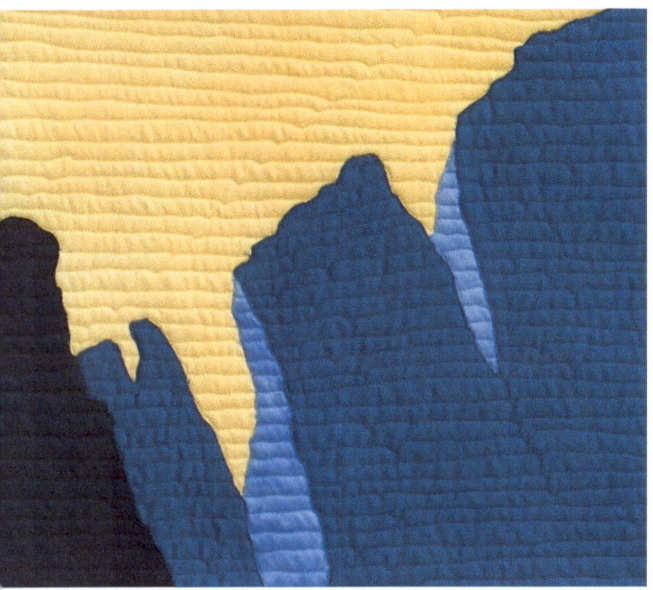

See quilt page 47.

My first sketch, next page, emphasizes the sharp edges with dramatic shadows from the image below. The second sketch, on the computer, adds the shape of the rust-colored country rock formation contacting the white granite, seen in the image opposite page.

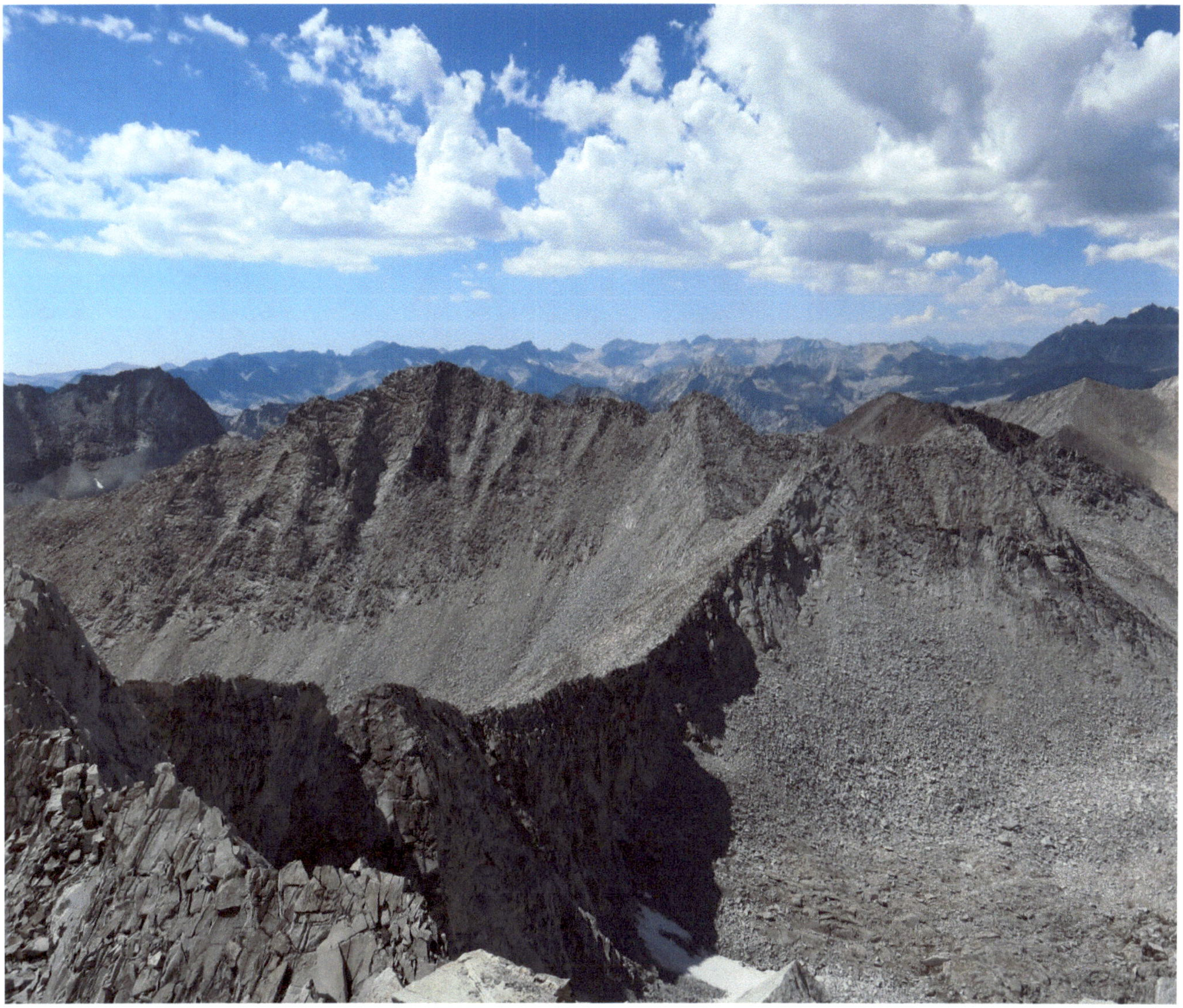

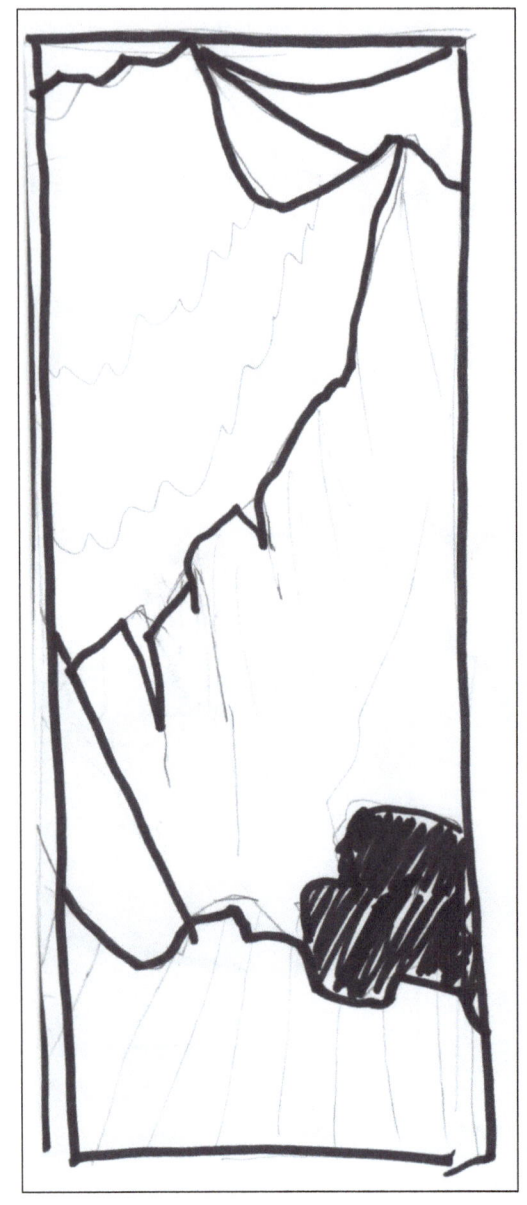

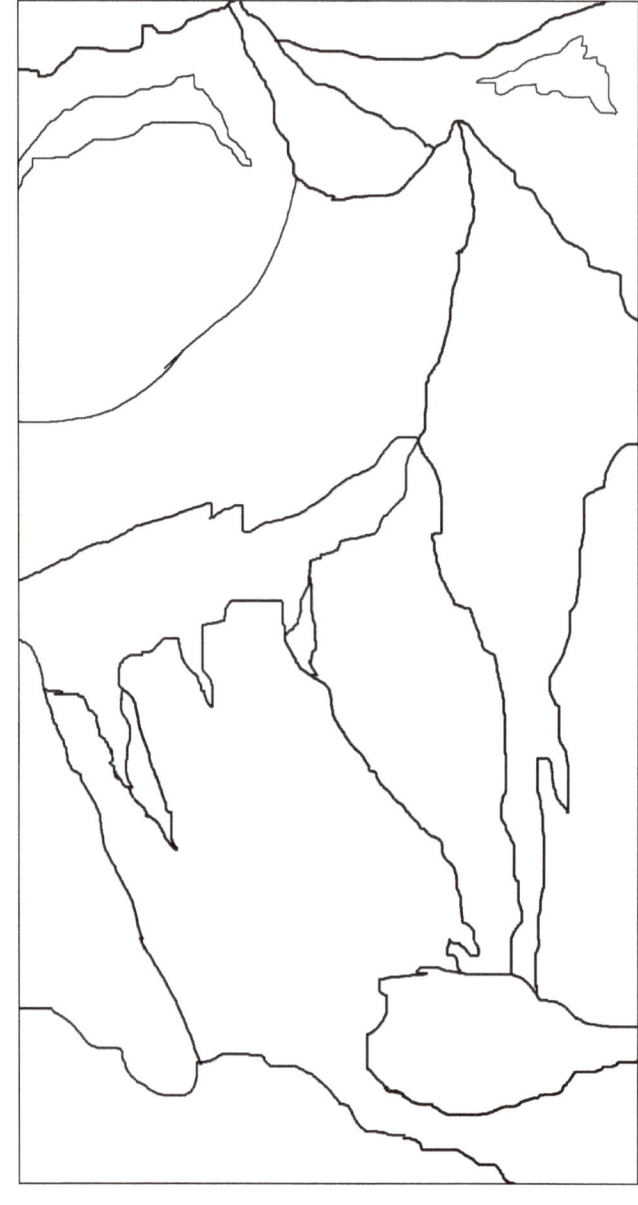

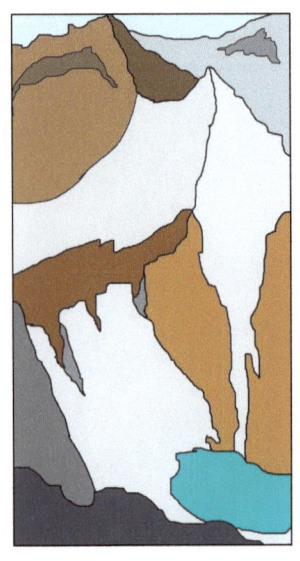

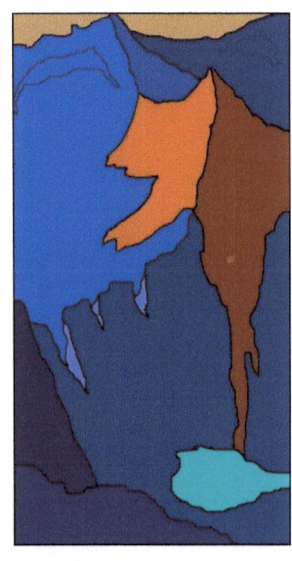

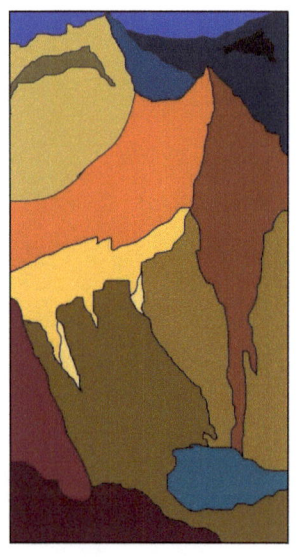

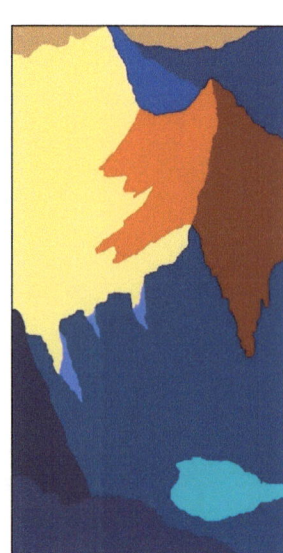

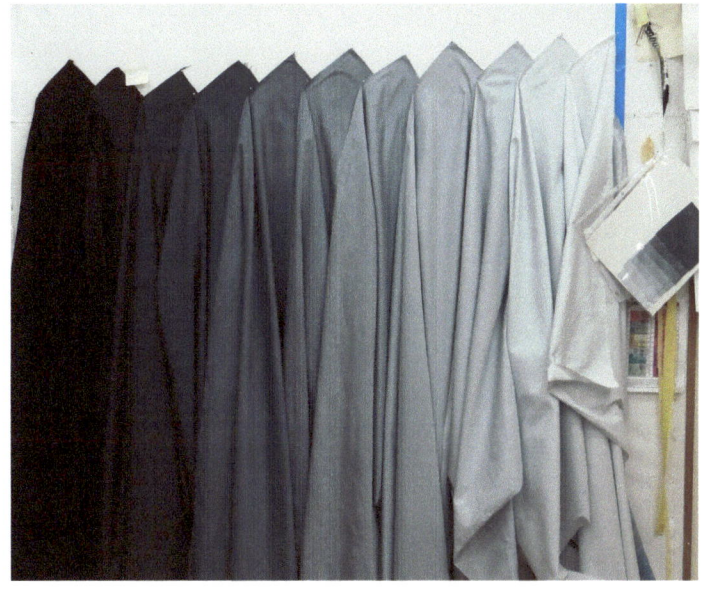

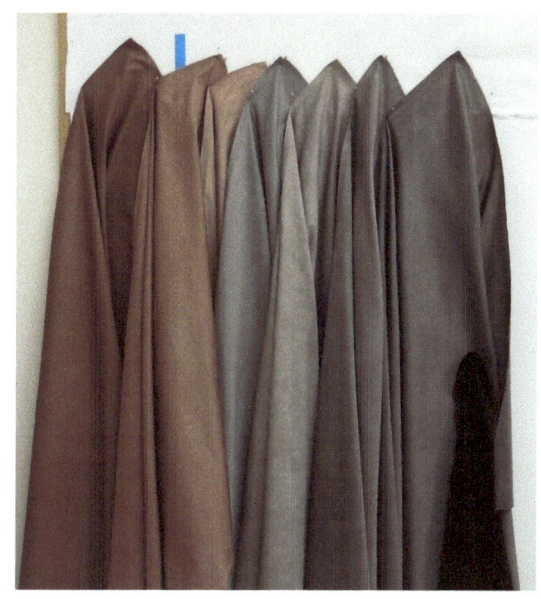

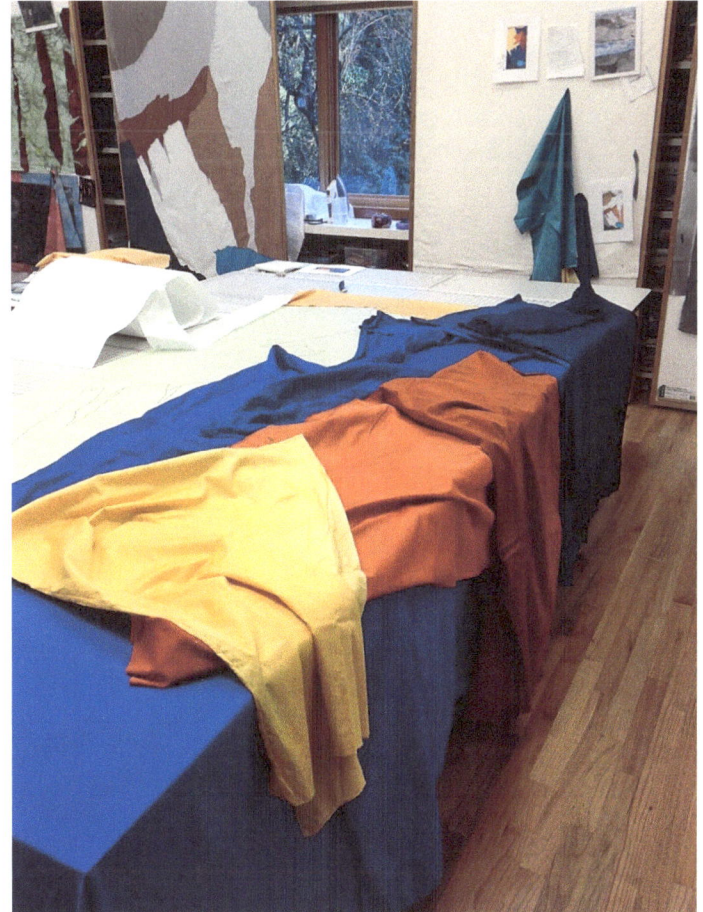

First I explored neutral colors using the computer sketch. Then I drew the design full size to see how much yardage of each color to dye. The pieces were assembled with raw-edge appliqué. When I moved on to the bright version, I slightly modified the shapes, referencing my drawings and images as in the fourth sketch, lower left. See pages 46 – 47.

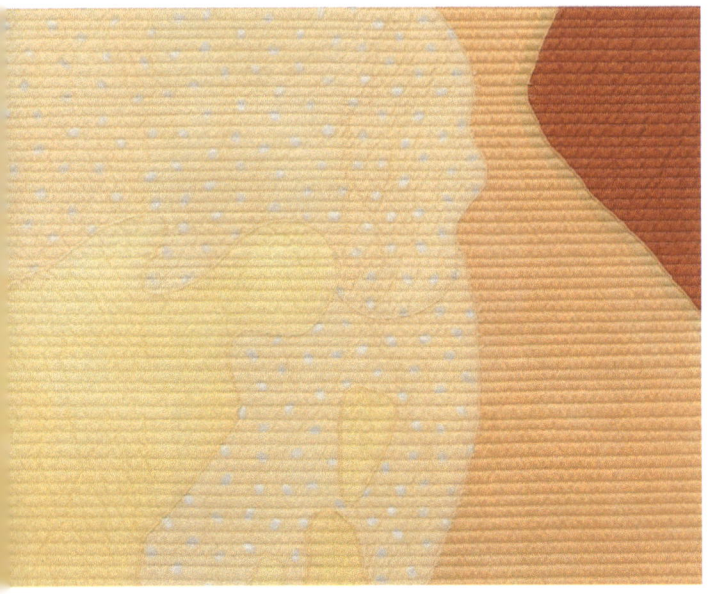

See quilt page 58.

I used a map of the regional bedrock geology as a guide, accurate even though I changed the colors. I dyed warm/light colors to represent the granites, and dark/cool colors for the metamorphic rocks that they pushed aside, to emphasize the contact between the formations. The lightest yellow with shiny squares of fabric paint indicates Cathedral Peak Granodiorite, an unusual rock with very large feldspar crystals.

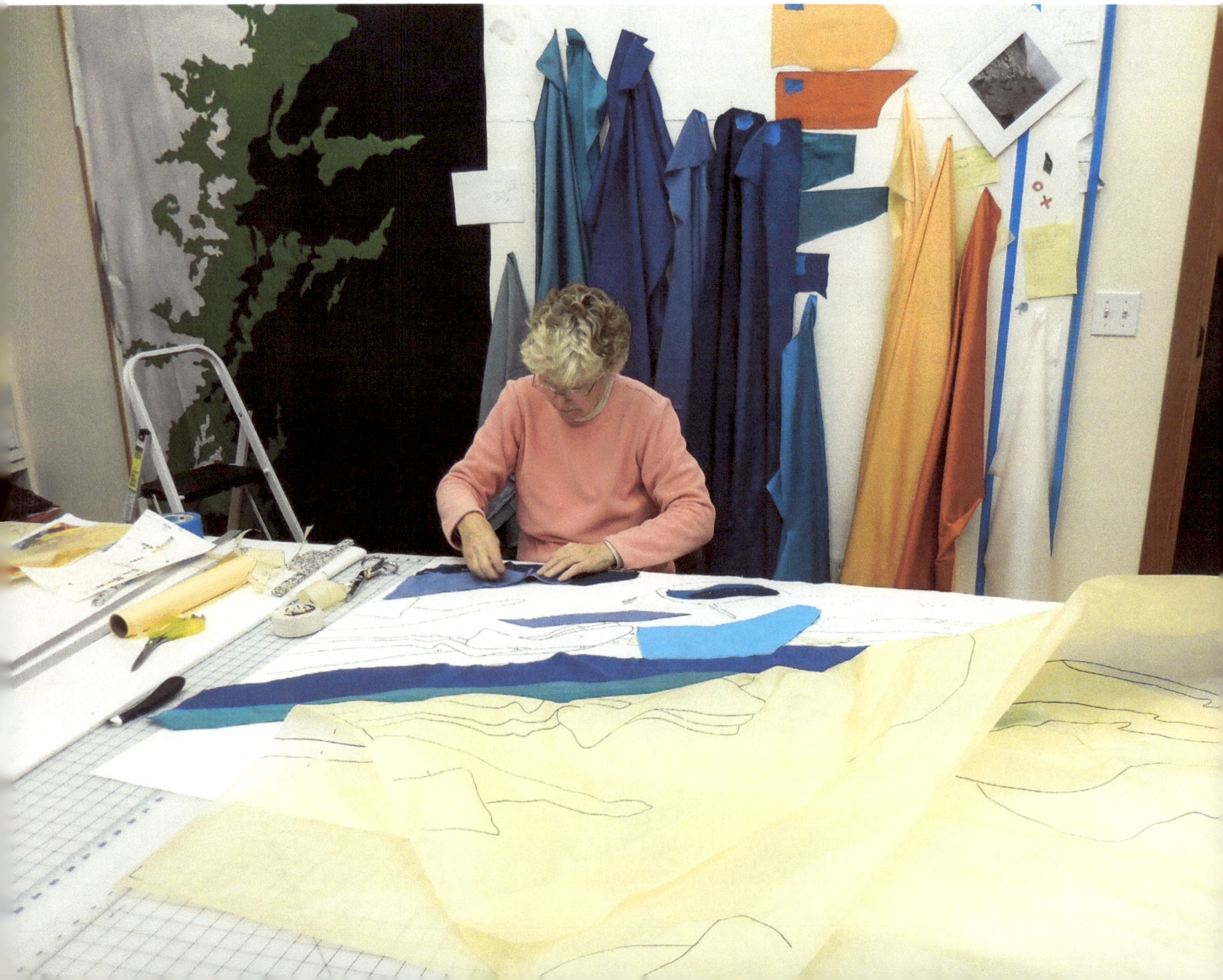

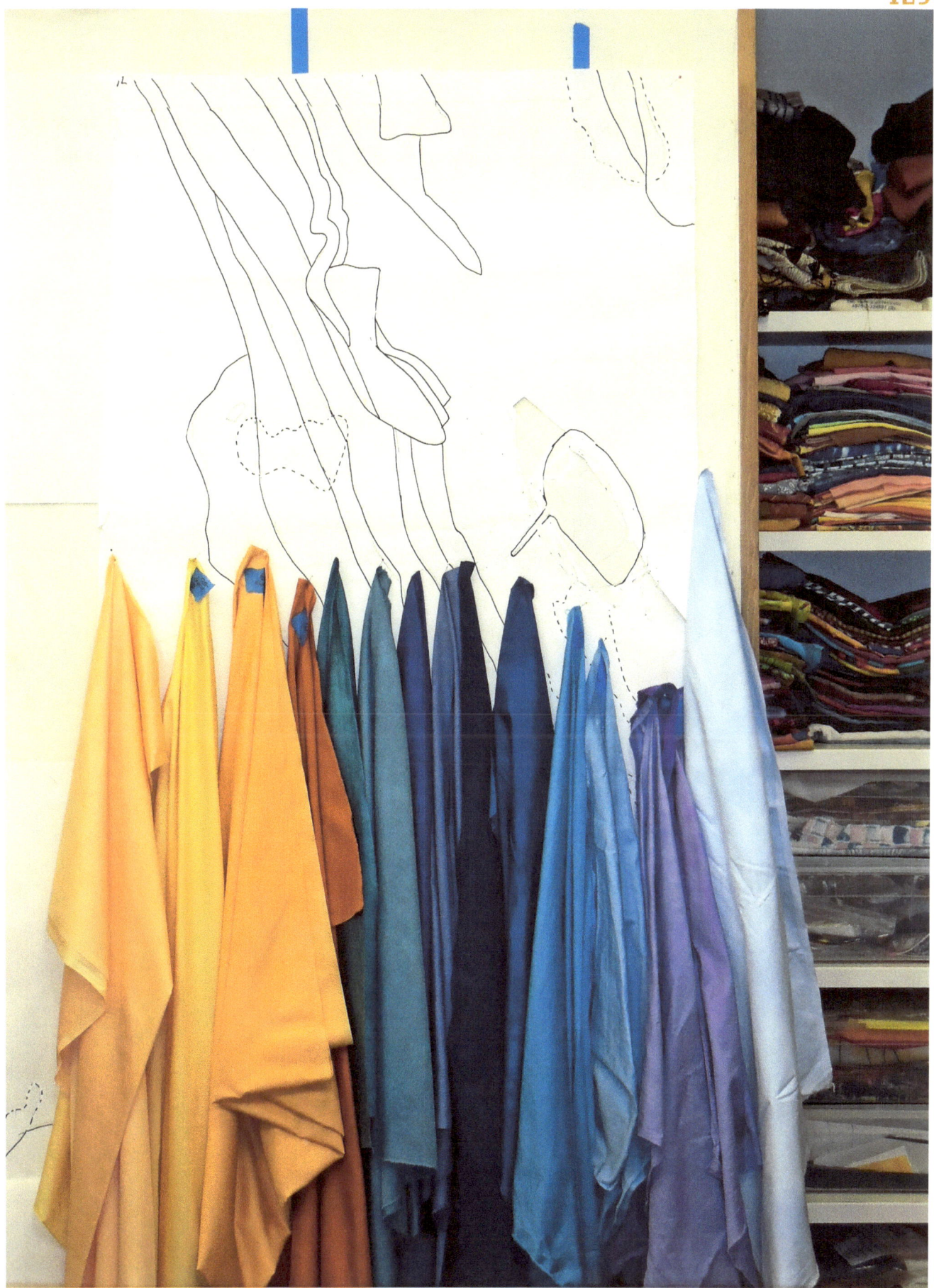

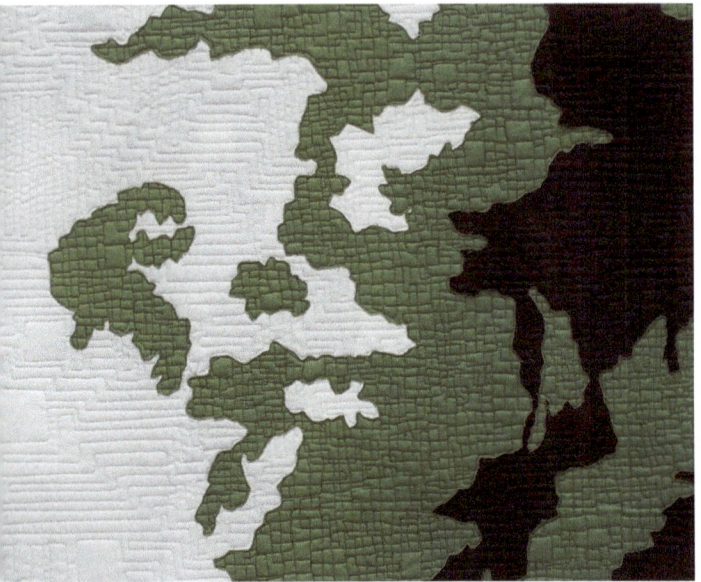

See quilt page 65.

This contact between light and dark formations is covered with spring vegetation, right; it can be seen more clearly from farther away on a day in late summer, below. I simplified to four shapes, distorted it vertically, and drew a full size pattern on white paper. Top right, the paper pattern is on the black fabric showing where I will sew the green onto the black. Below, the white paper is cut away showing where the white fabric will be sewn onto the green.

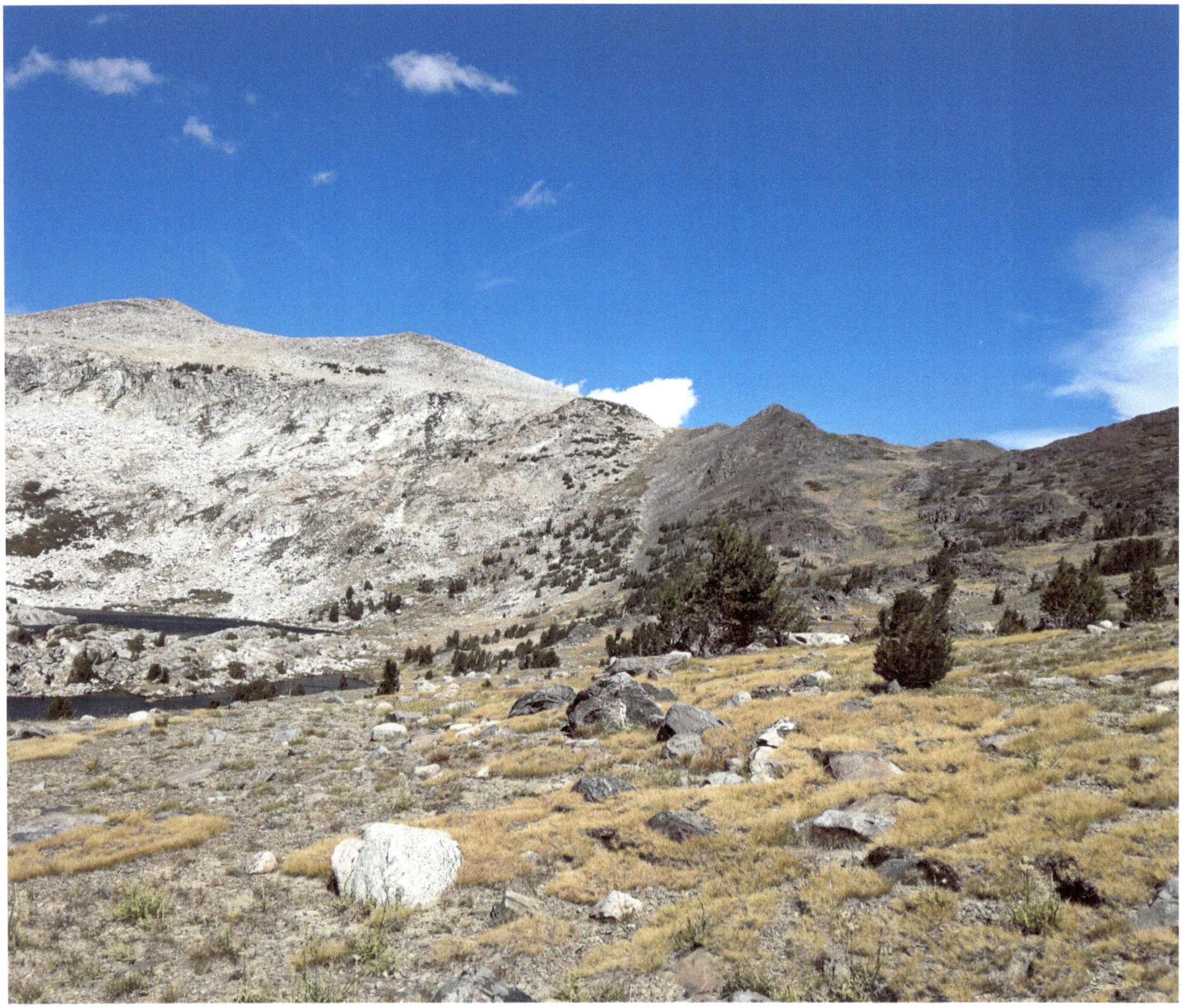

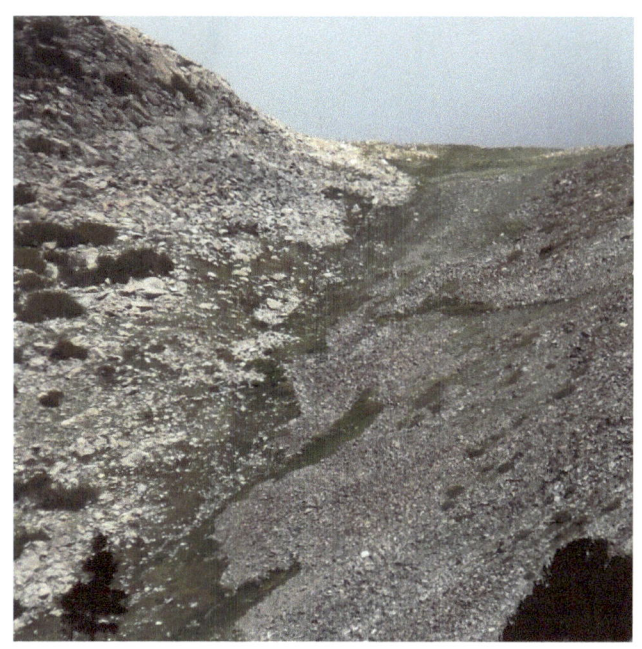

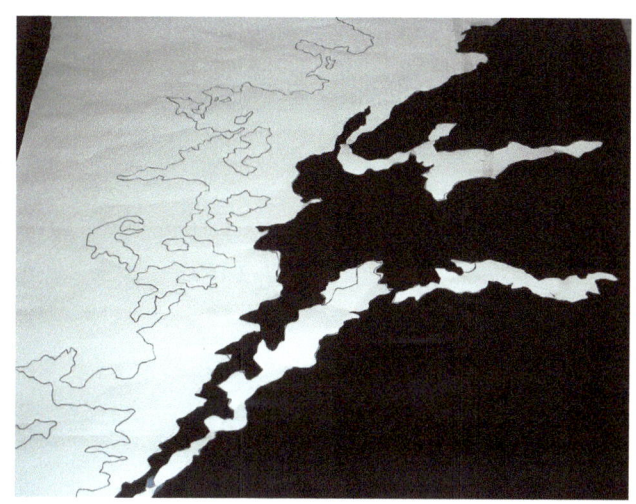

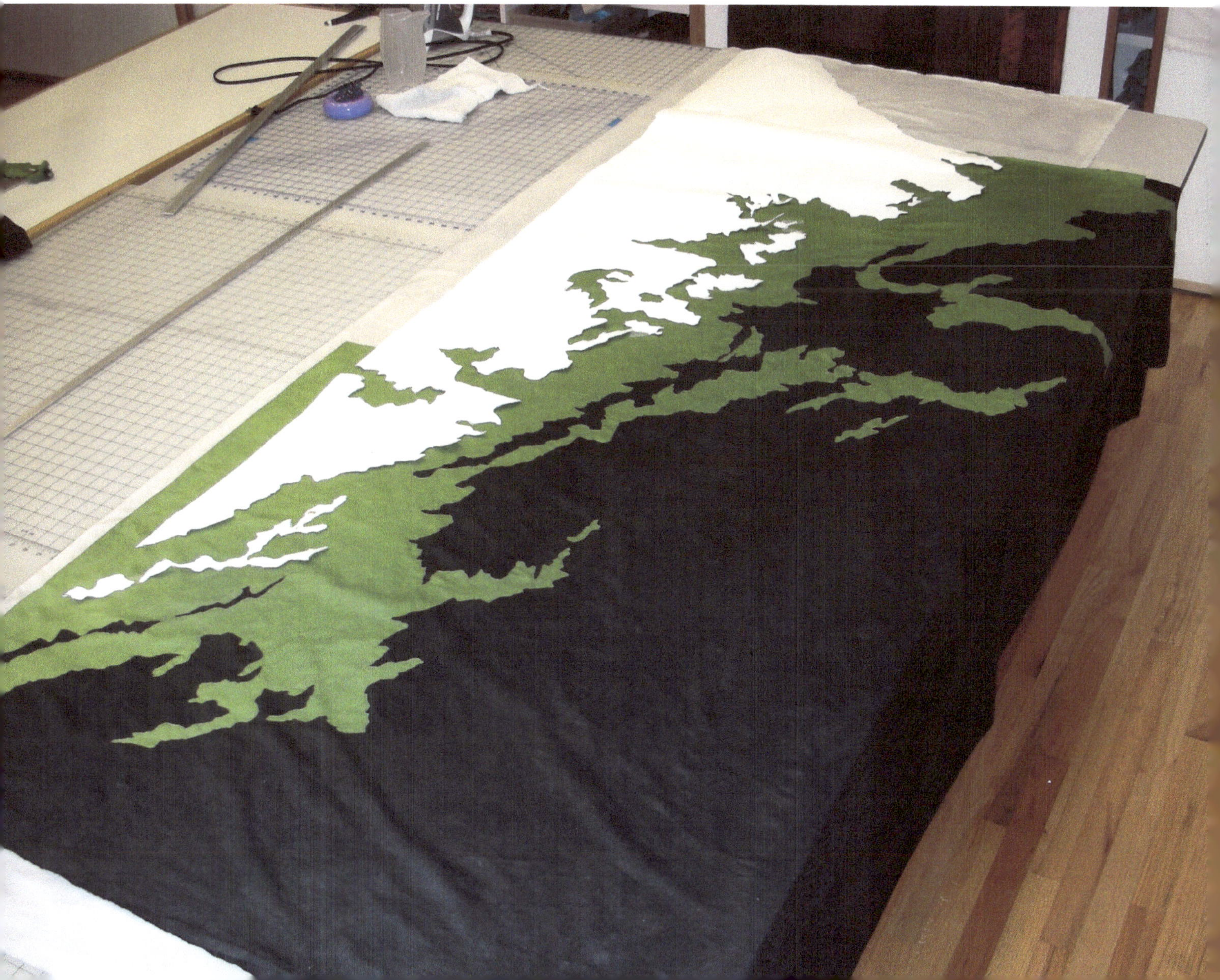

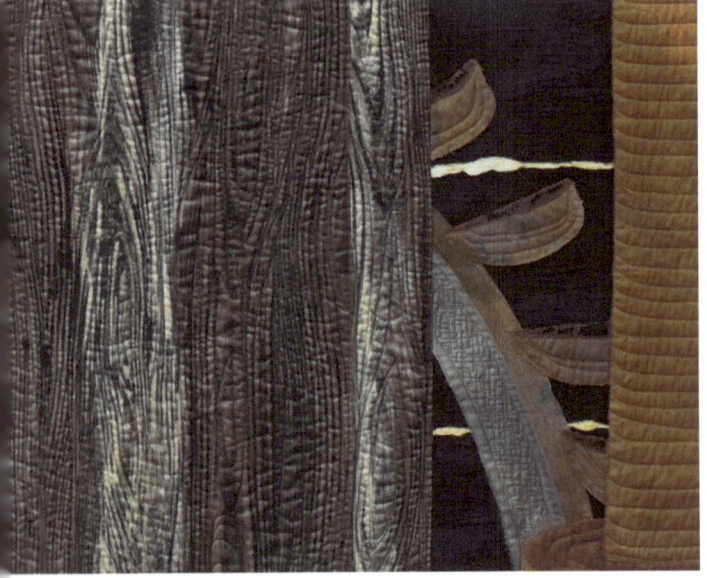

See quilt page 66.

I monoprinted this fabric in three sections, with three variations of wood grain textures. Then I blended thick and thin dye colors over the whole piece using different color combinations. Only the sections on the far left and lower part became the weathered beams. I assembled most of the parts and walls using raw-edge appliqué. The rust colors are low-water immersion dyed with some overlays of silk organza for shadows.

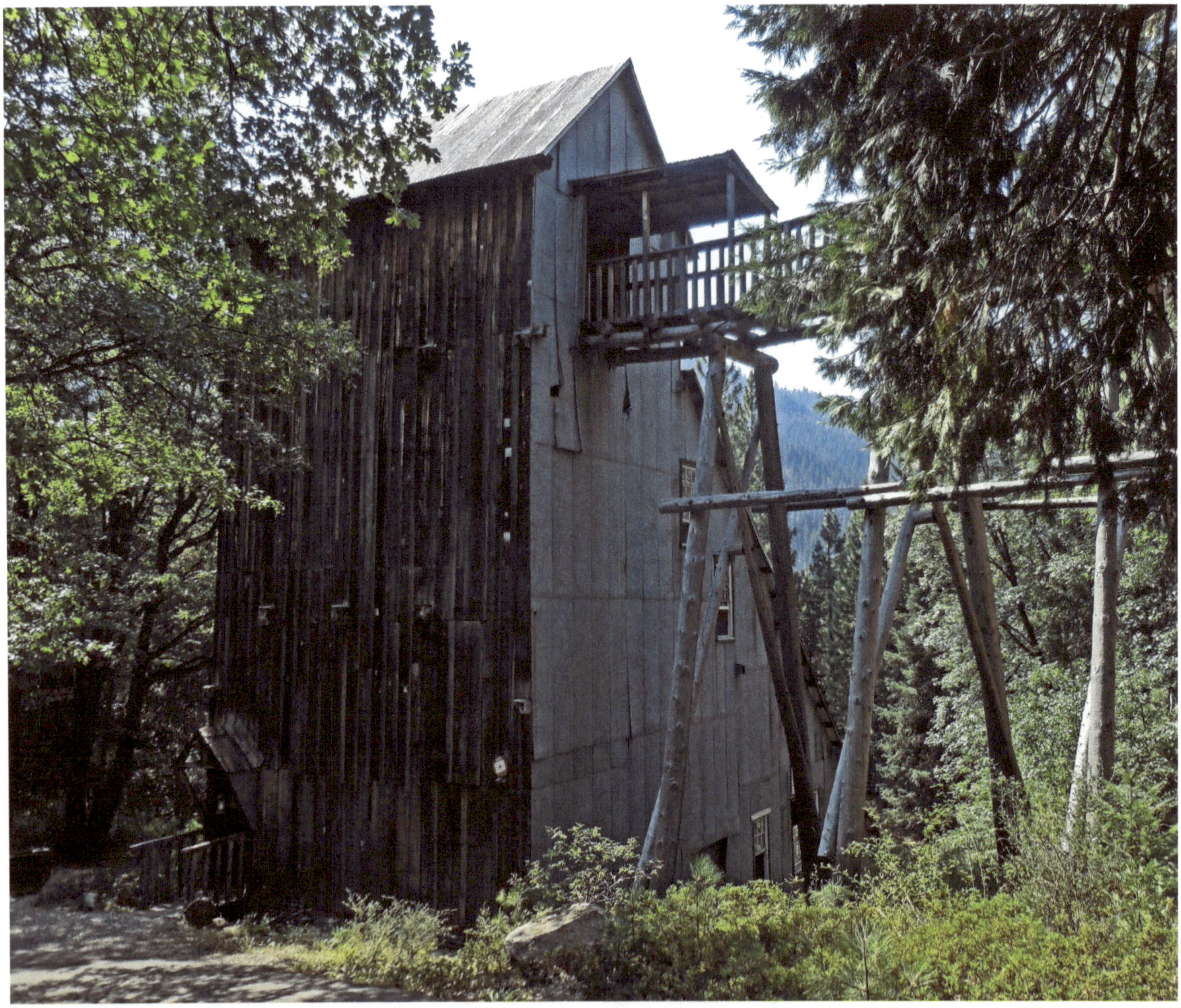

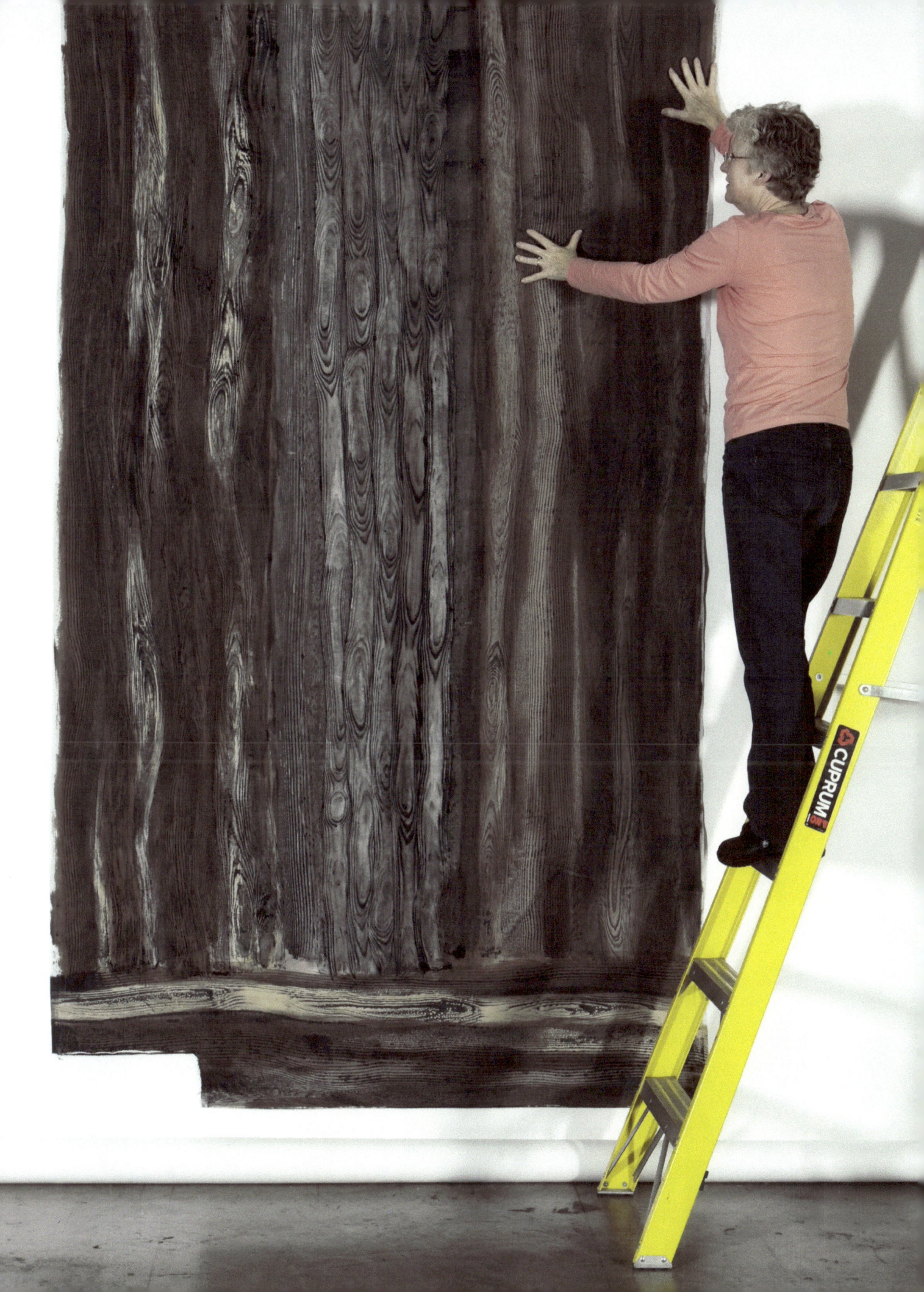

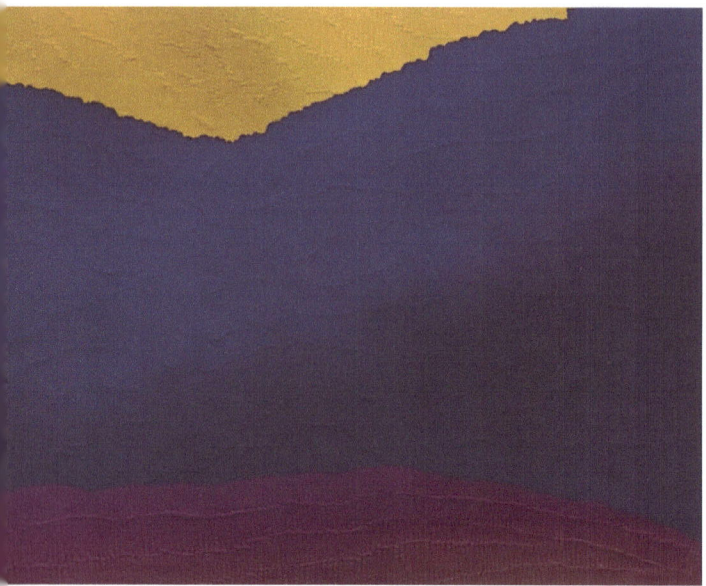

See quilt page 74.

This design resolved itself into five shapes, each with difficult color blends. I applied thin, liquid dyes to five separate pieces of fabric, each laid out flat on the table to make it easier to control the blending process. The challenge arises because some colors fix first so the later-reacting dyes can push the color in another direction from what I intend—requiring both overdyeing and doing over.

The spaces left between the vertical zig zag quilting create horizontal lines accentuating the shapes of the cliffs and pattern in the water.

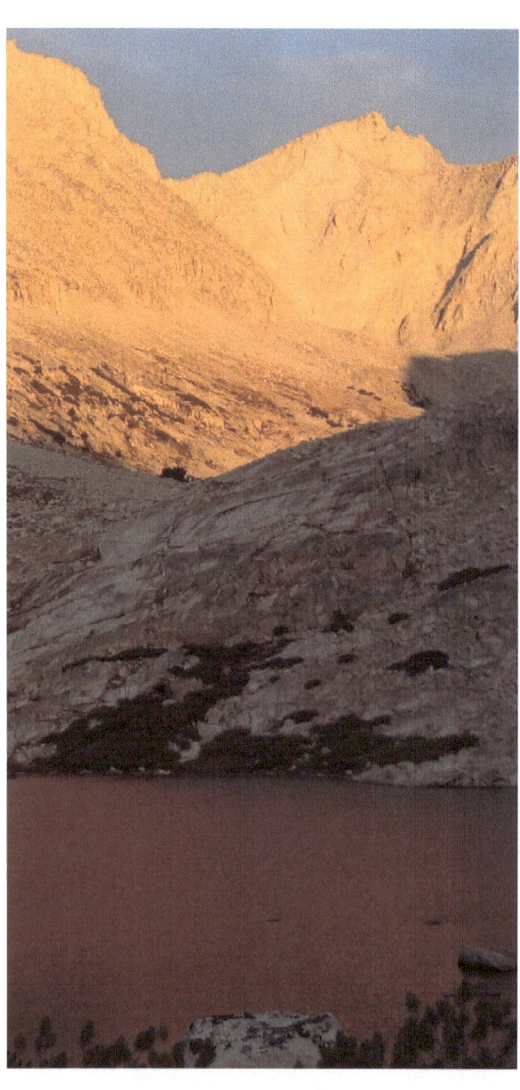

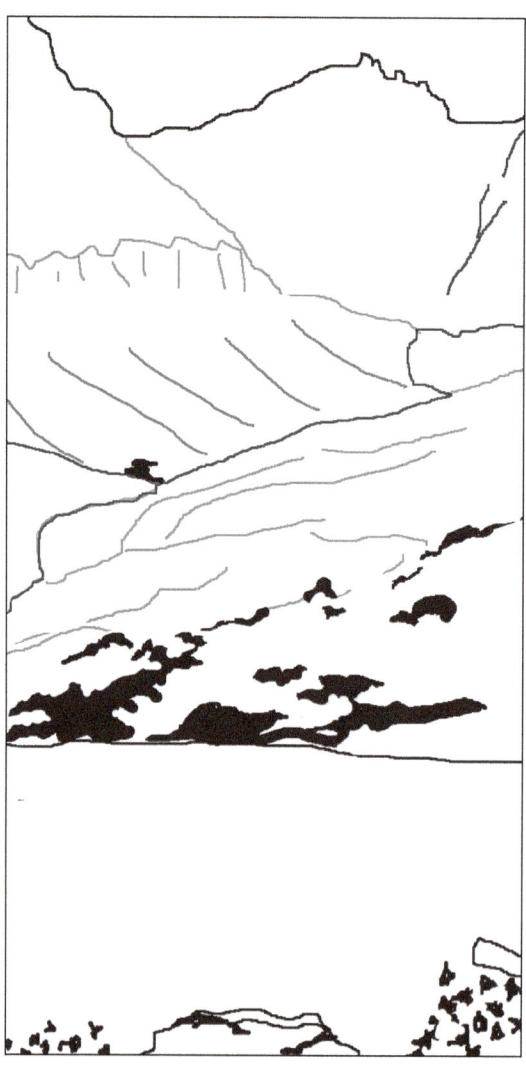

Back detail.

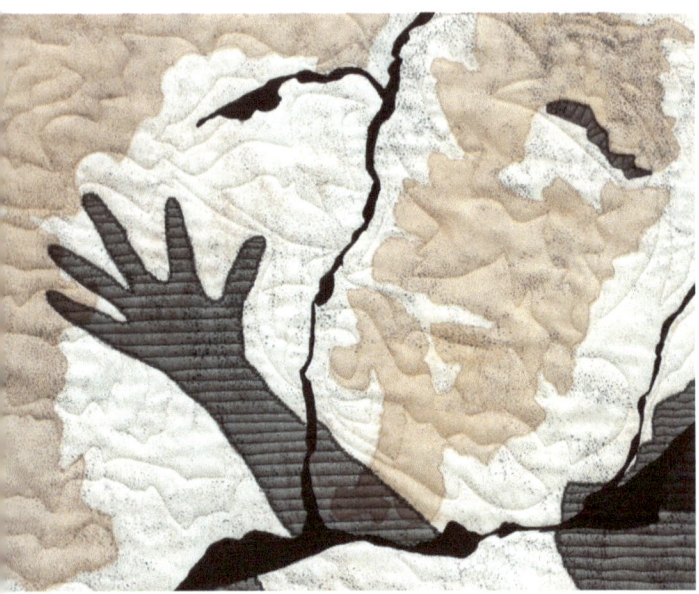

I planned to dye the fabric, then cut up and assemble the pieces, using the drawing on the right. Instead, after I monoprinted the granite texture on a very large piece, I continued to print and paint more, refining the shapes, resulting in a whole cloth that was close to my original plan. I recorded the order of steps—more or less—in the margin of my drawing.

See quilt page 78.

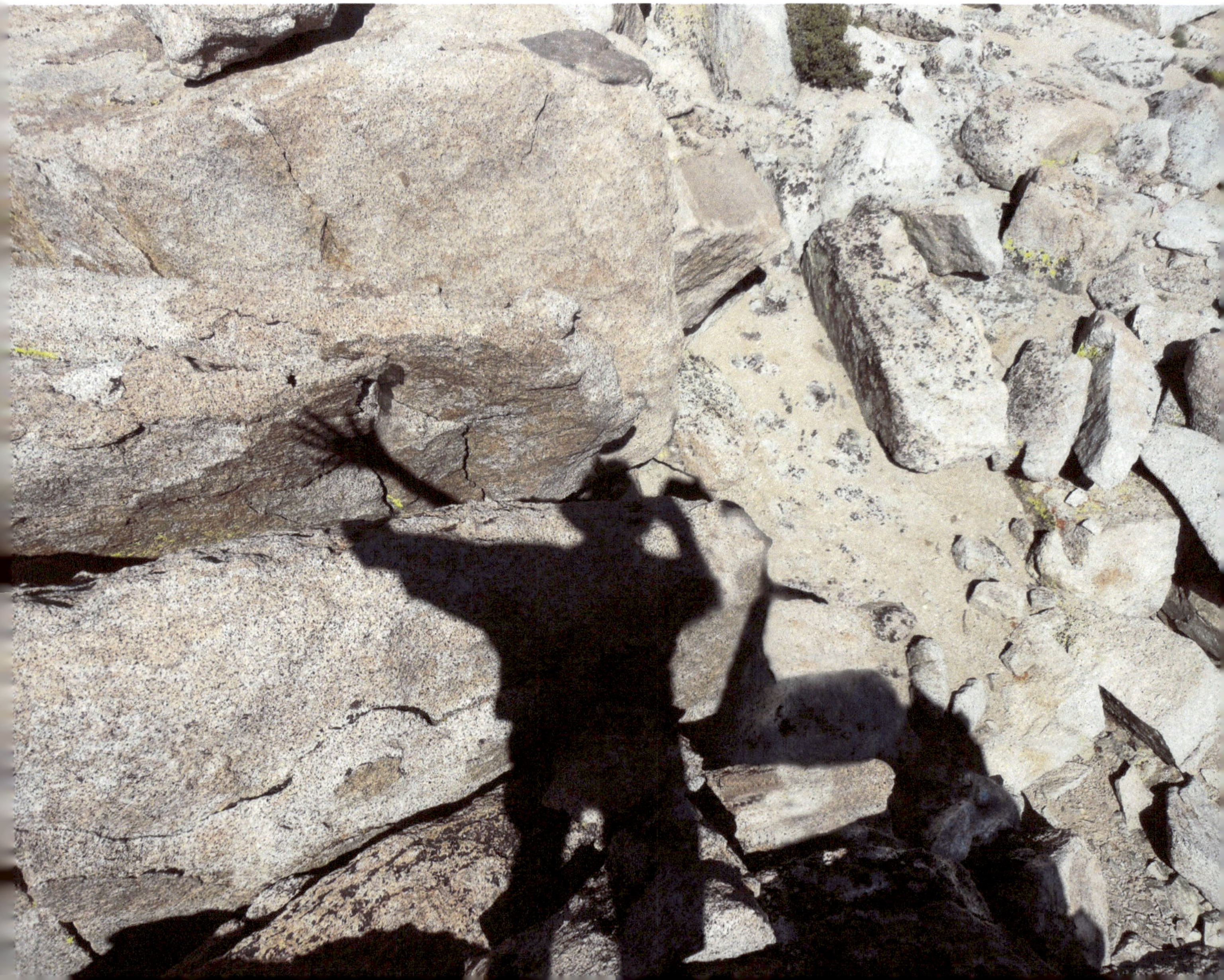

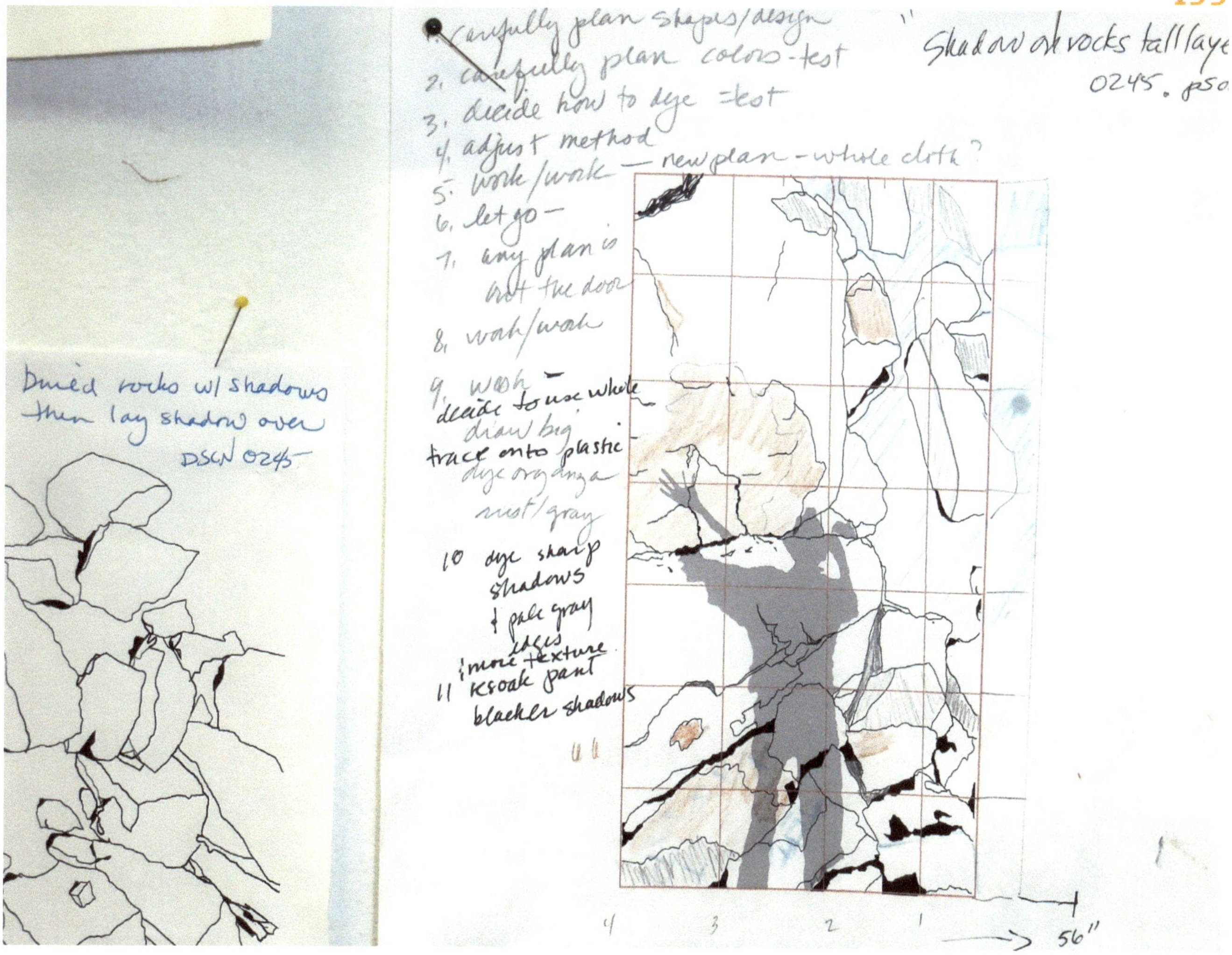

Dried rocks w/ shadows
then lay shadow over
DSCN 0245

1. carefully plan shapes/design
2. carefully plan colors - test
3. decide how to dye = test
4. adjust method
5. work/work — new plan — whole cloth?
6. let go —
7. any plan is not the door
8. wah/wah
9. wah —
decide to use white
draw big
trace onto plastic
dye organza
mist/gray
10 dye sharp shadows
+ pale gray edges
' more texture
11 Ksoak paint blacker shadows

Shadow on rocks tall layer
0245. p50

4   3   2   1   → 56"

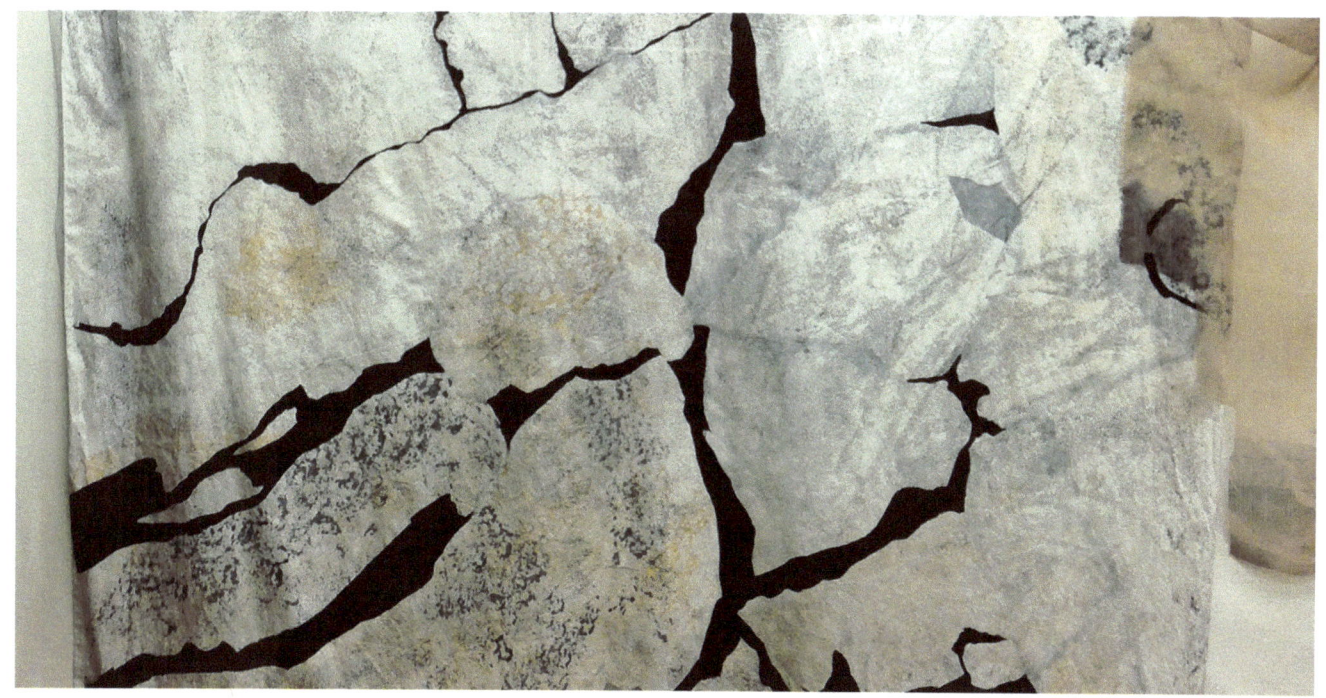

I basted long stitch marks to remind me where there was a subtle edge I might not see later for quilting, right.

I used transparent silk organza in several colors and values to stitch onto the surface, below.

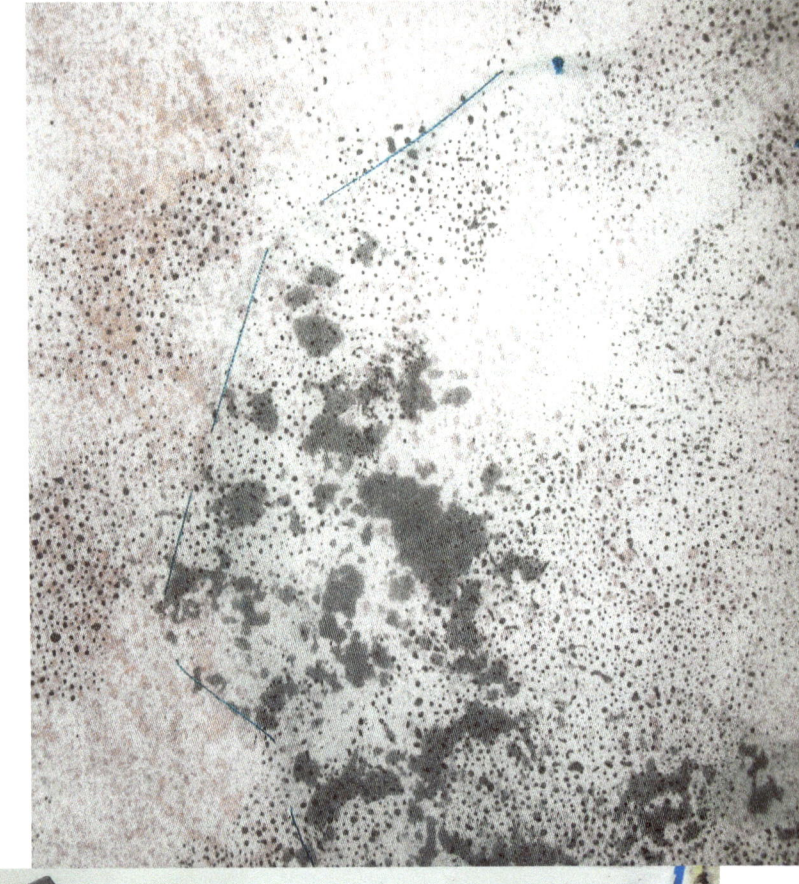

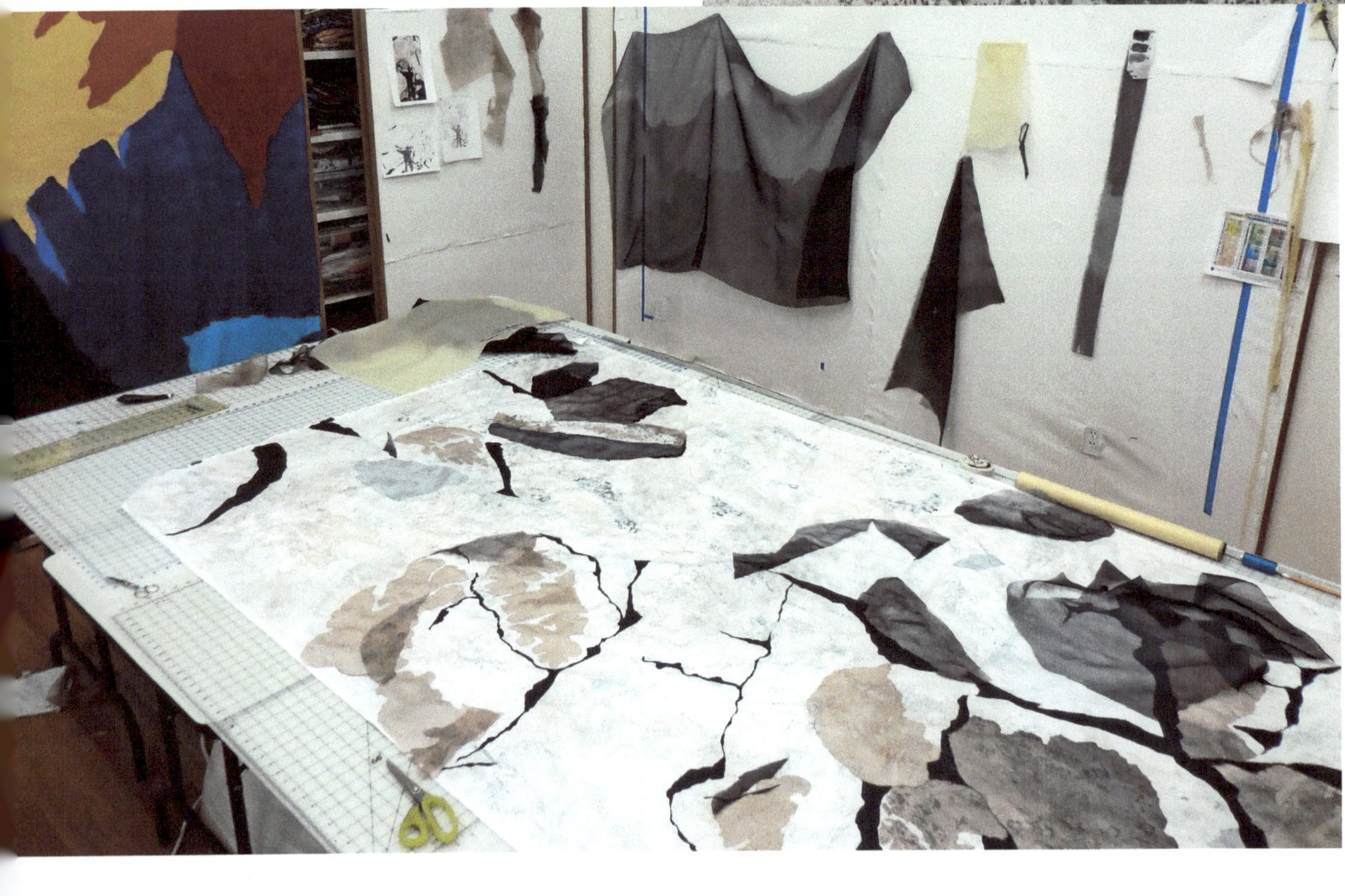

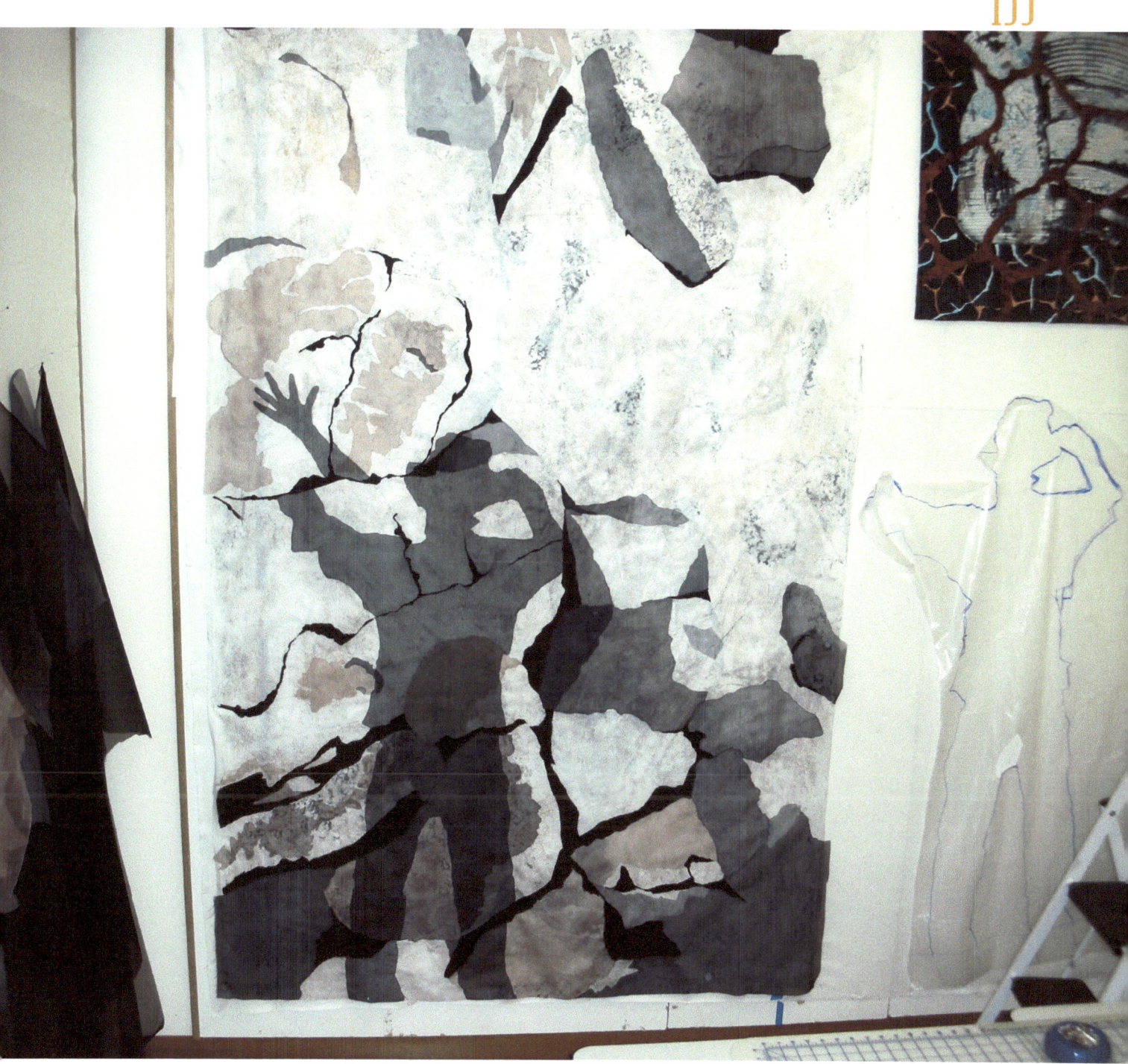

Unused organza hangs on the left. The whole quilt top ready to be quilted is next to the plastic pattern I used to help decide the placement of the human shadow.

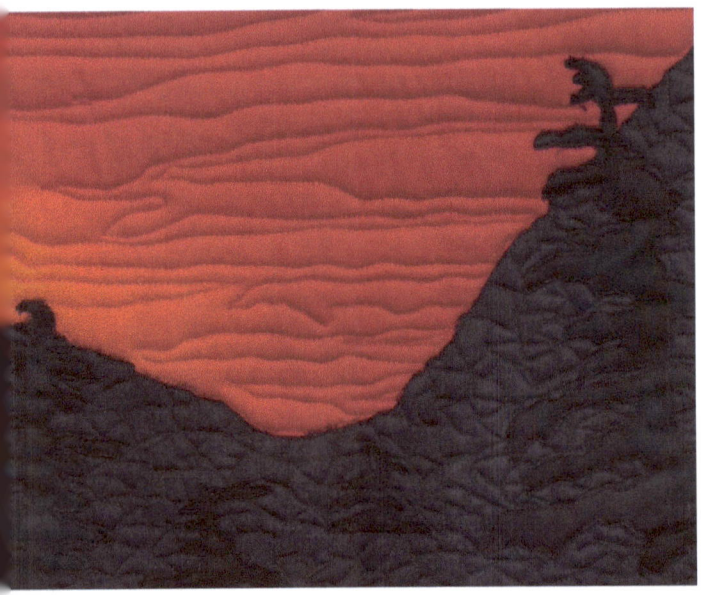

See quilt page 83.

I low-water immersion dyed a wide piece of fabric out flat on the table, then wrinkled it and added more dye. Later, I selected the portion of the piece that worked best. I dyed different values of dark for the trees and the wall of rock, grading in values, from far to near. Sewing involved overlapping them as the darker pieces came closer. I drew chalk marks on the pieces as I was ready for them, deciding with each where to sew and what to reveal.

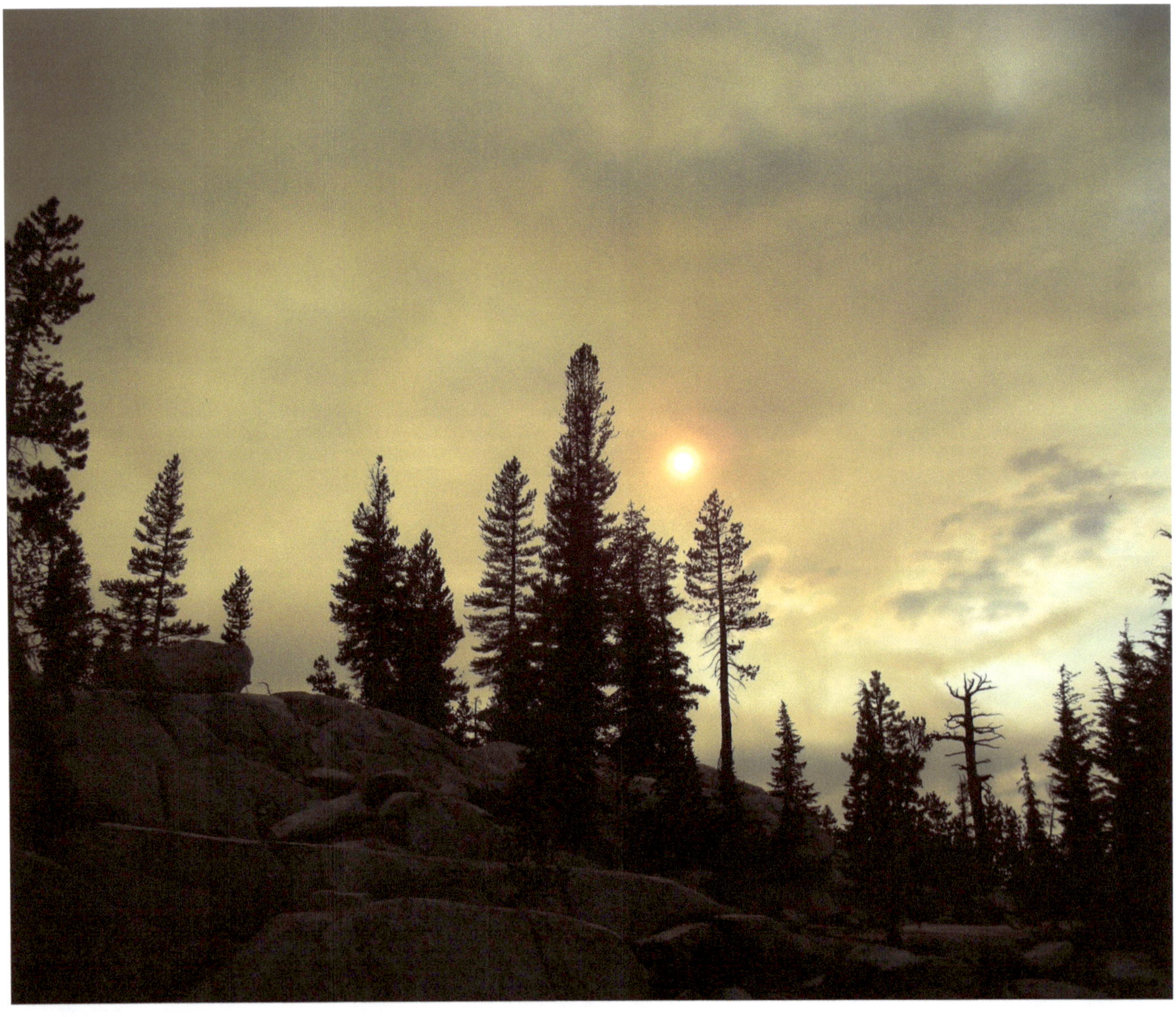

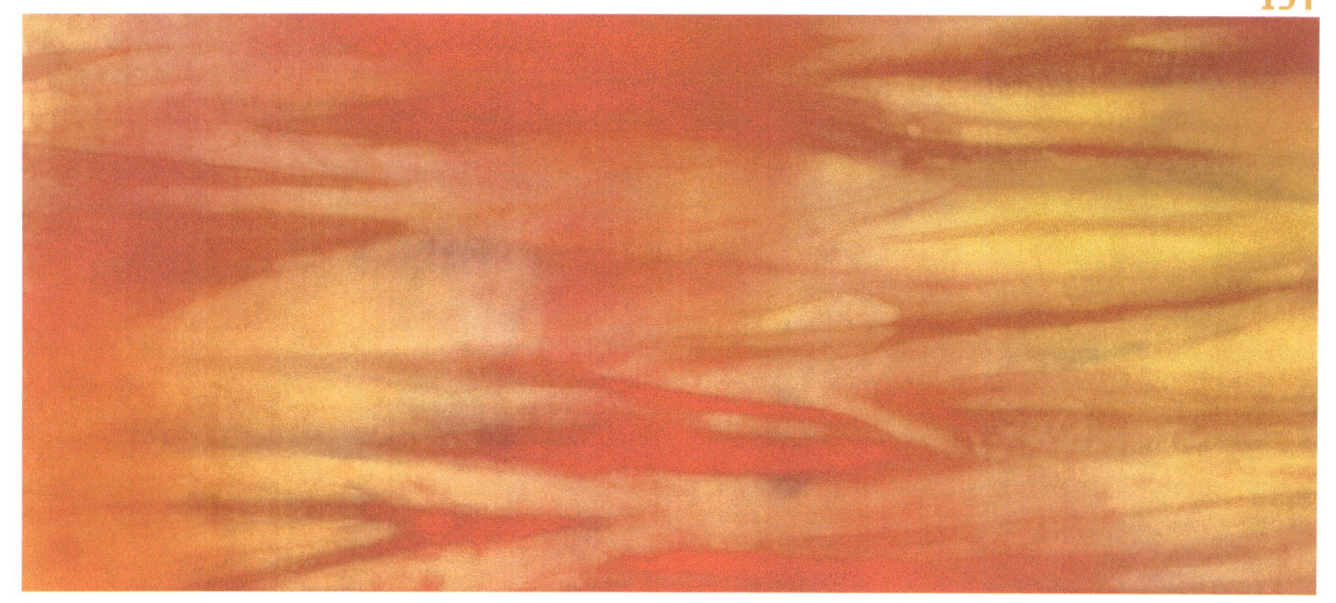

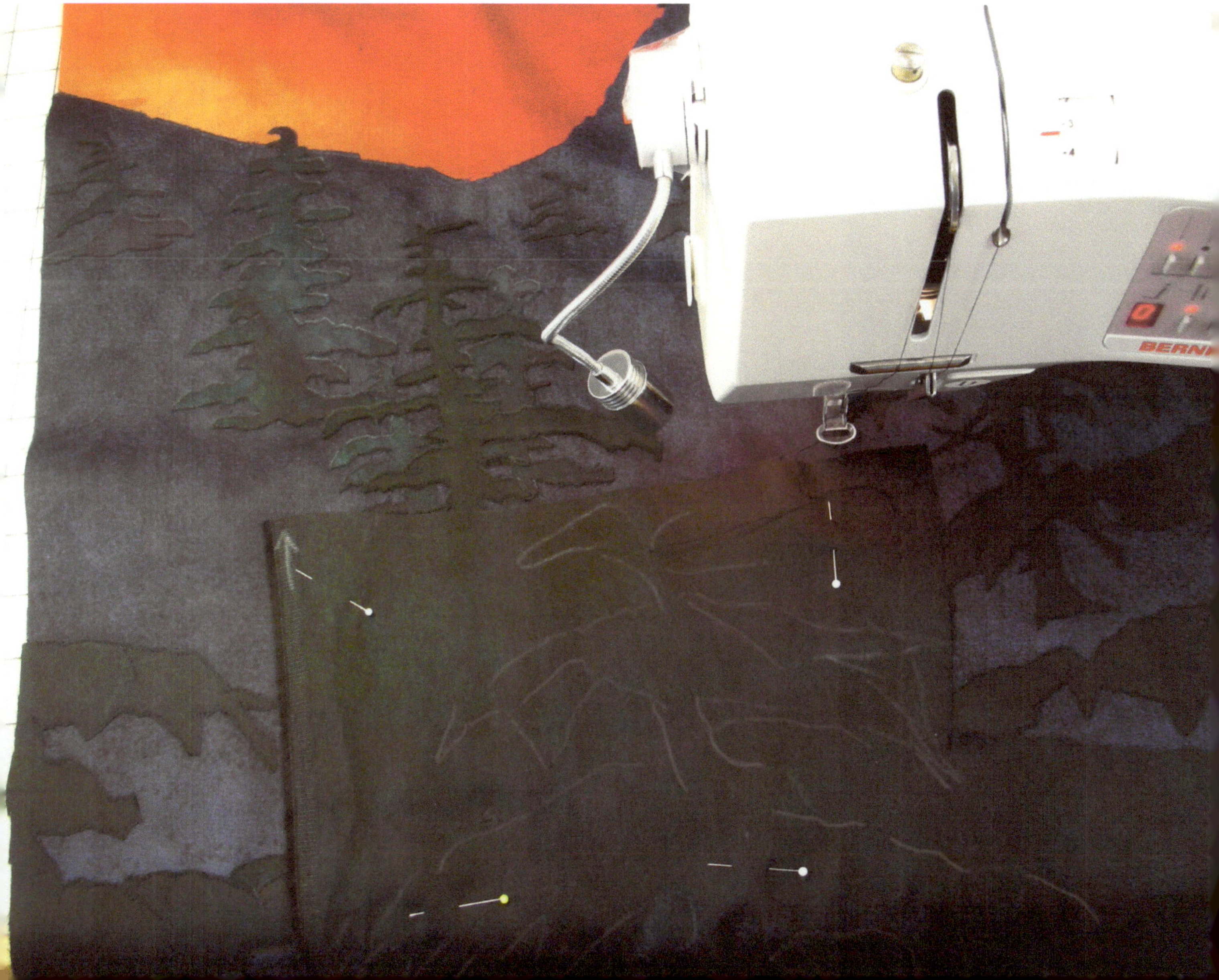

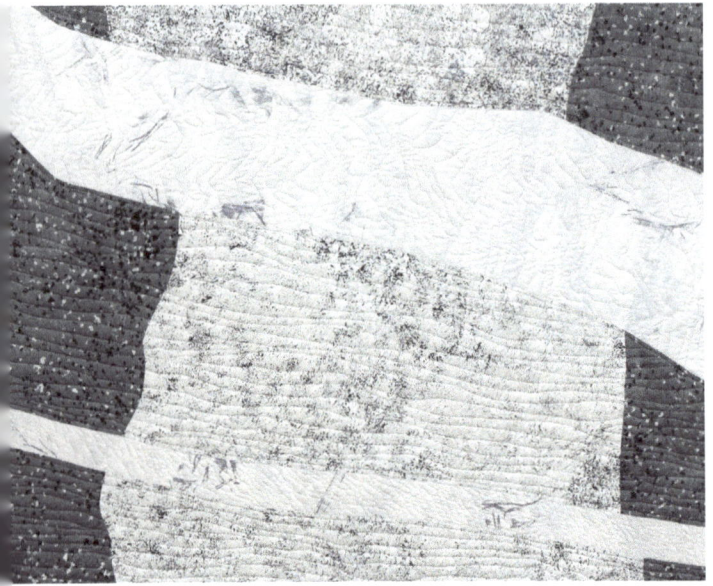

After making many small drawings, I used the blue paper for a full size pattern. I pieced the whole top, then found I wanted to change some of the shapes, so I cut into it and pieced those in to match.

I dyed the back of the quilt spreading liquid dyes with my hands, painting the silhouettes later with thickened dye.

I marked quilting lines on the front of the quilt to work with the design on the back. My friends at the Oswego Quilters helped me hand quilt it.

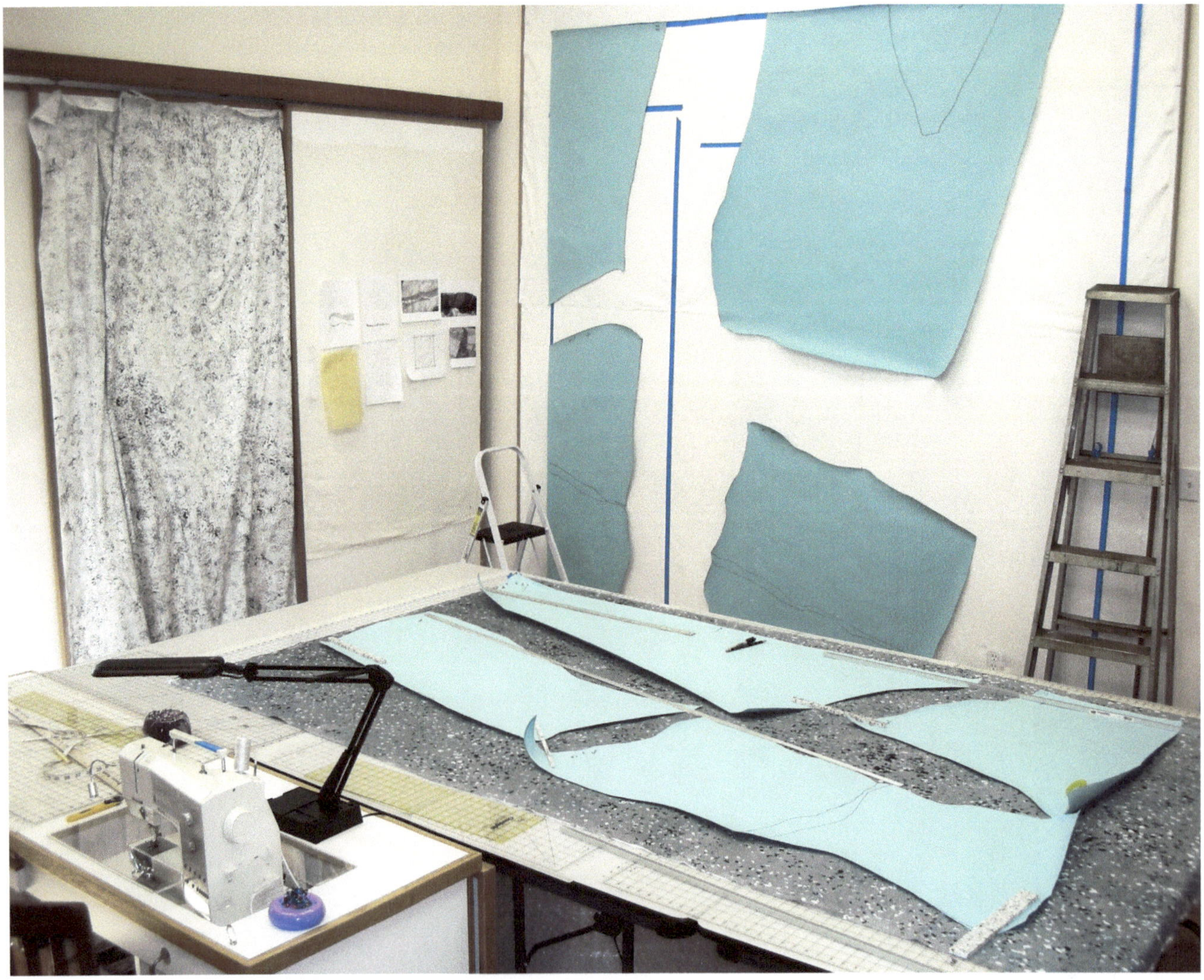

See quilt pages 86 and 87.

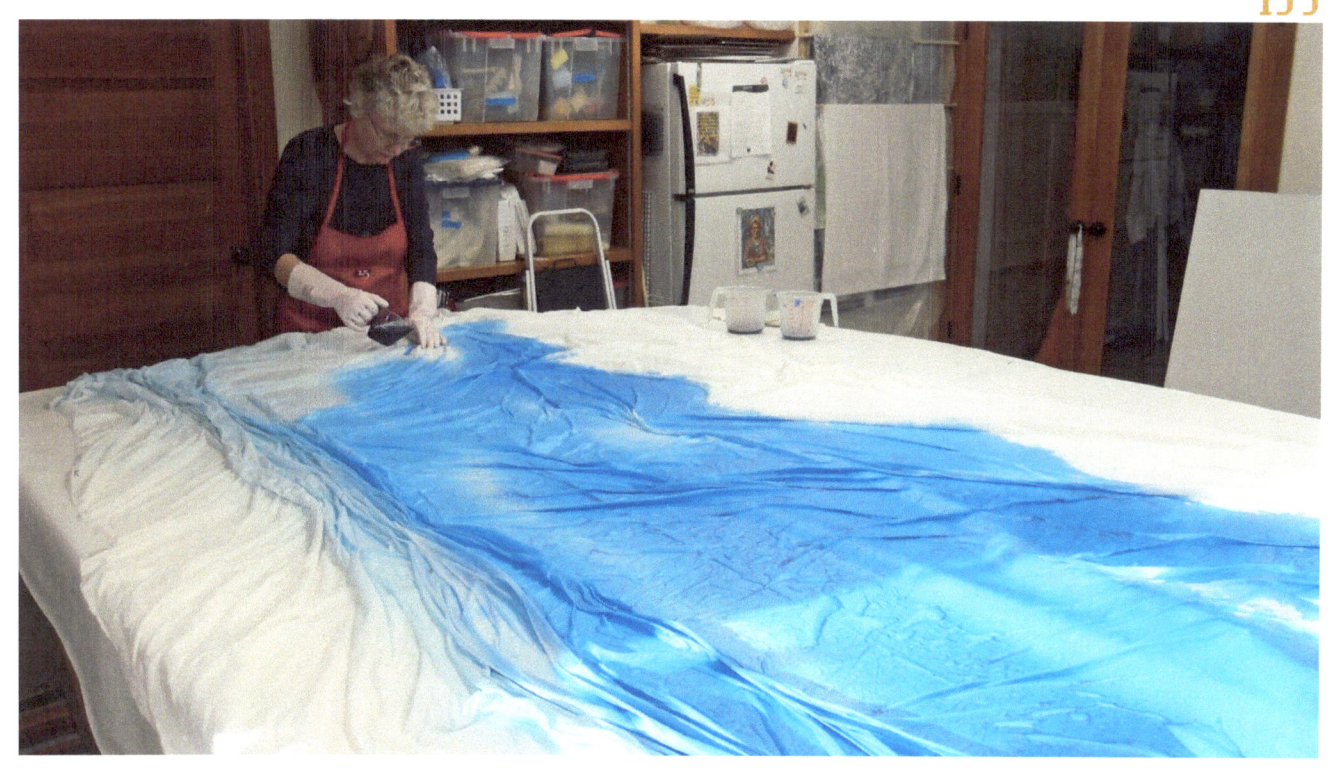

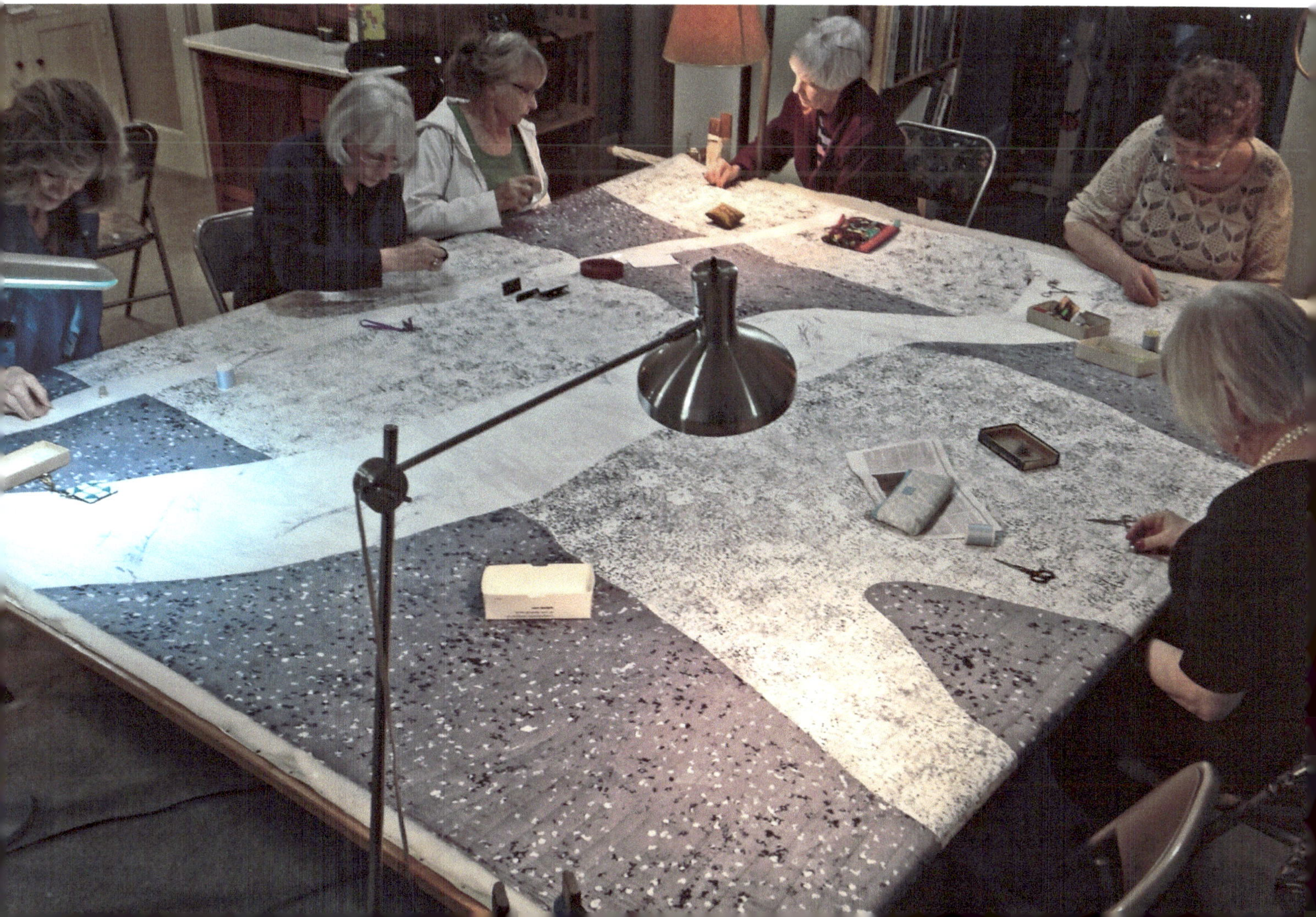

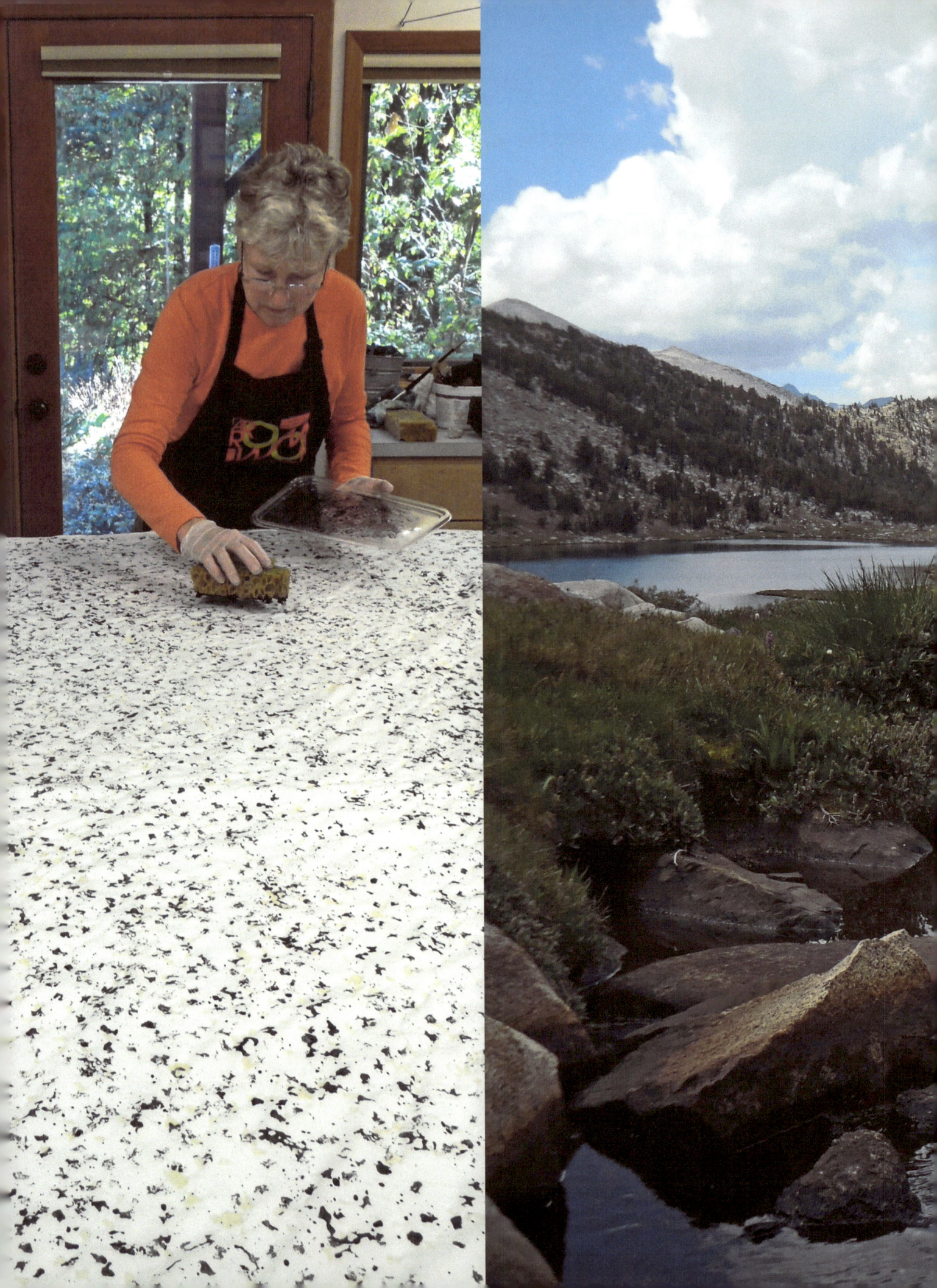

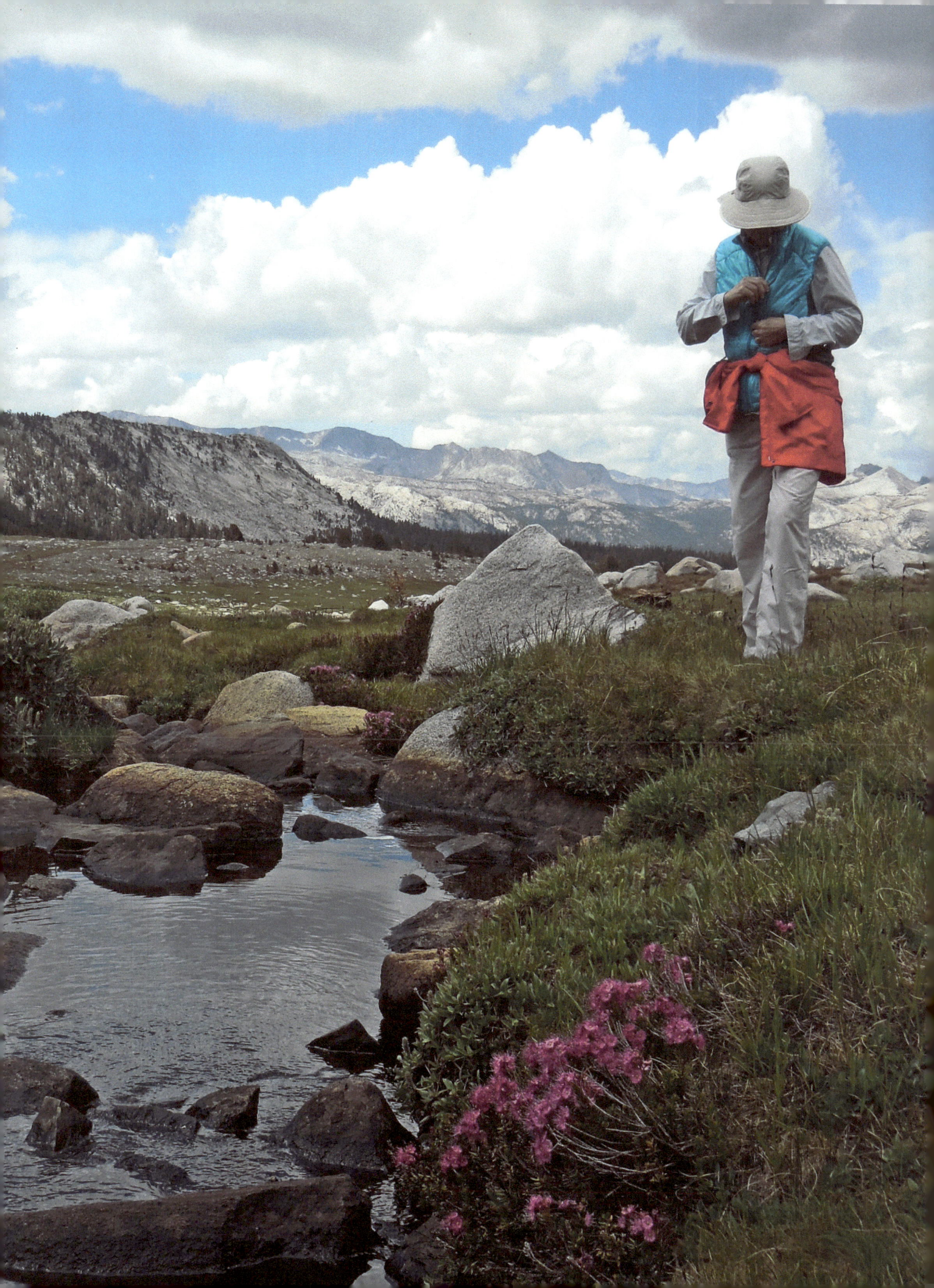

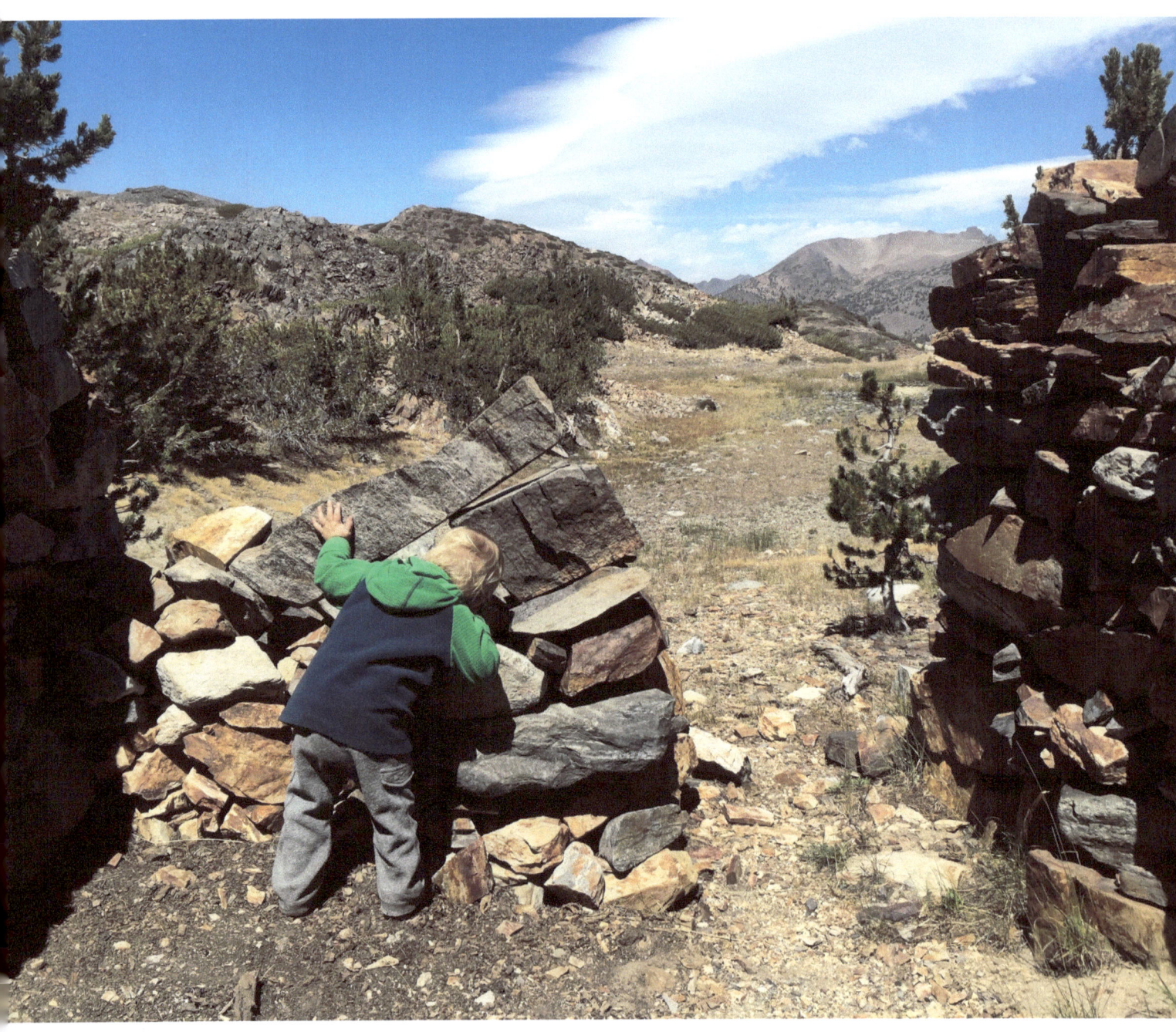

On the eastern edge of the Sierra Nevada, above 11,000 feet, looking north through the doorway in the remains of a cabin on our mining property.

Ann Johnston

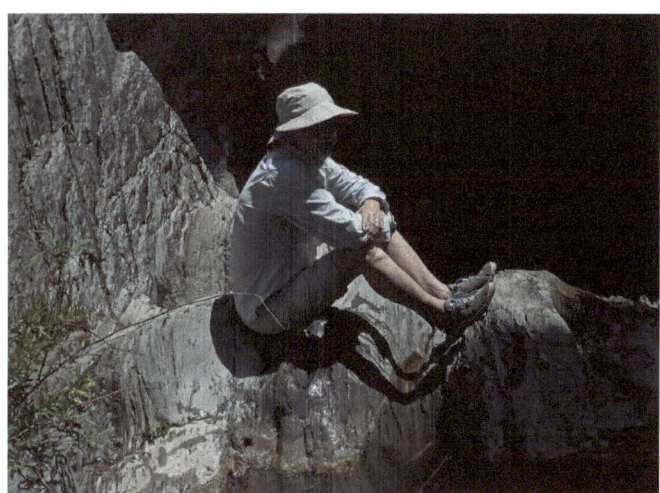

Since moving from Ireland to Jamestown, California, during the gold rush, Ann's family has either lived or vacationed in the Sierra Nevada for five—now six—generations.

Ann's father's mother taught her the family lore of early days in San Francisco, and her mother's mother taught her to sew a straight stitch. During the many family trips to the Sierra, Ann's mother taught her how to wait for a fish to bite, to mix watercolors, and to ride a rope tow up a ski hill; her father taught her how to read a topographic map, to light a fire, and to swim in a cold lake.

Ann earned a B.A. in literature from Stanford University where she met her husband Jim Johnston. Their wedding trip was a week in the Sierra, sleeping above the tree line and cooking on a fire. They went to Lima, Peru, with the Peace Corps and learned to live in another culture. An M.A. in geography from the University of Oregon led to more travels. Over the years and many more Sierra trips, Jim has taught Ann how to catch fish with her hands, to keep a light backpack, and to take small steps without stopping on the long passes.

A lifetime of making quilts, dyeing fabric, and exploring the Sierra Nevada of California has come together in Ann's most recent work, *The Contact*. Visit www.annjohnston.net to see a gallery of other work, publications, and a full resume.

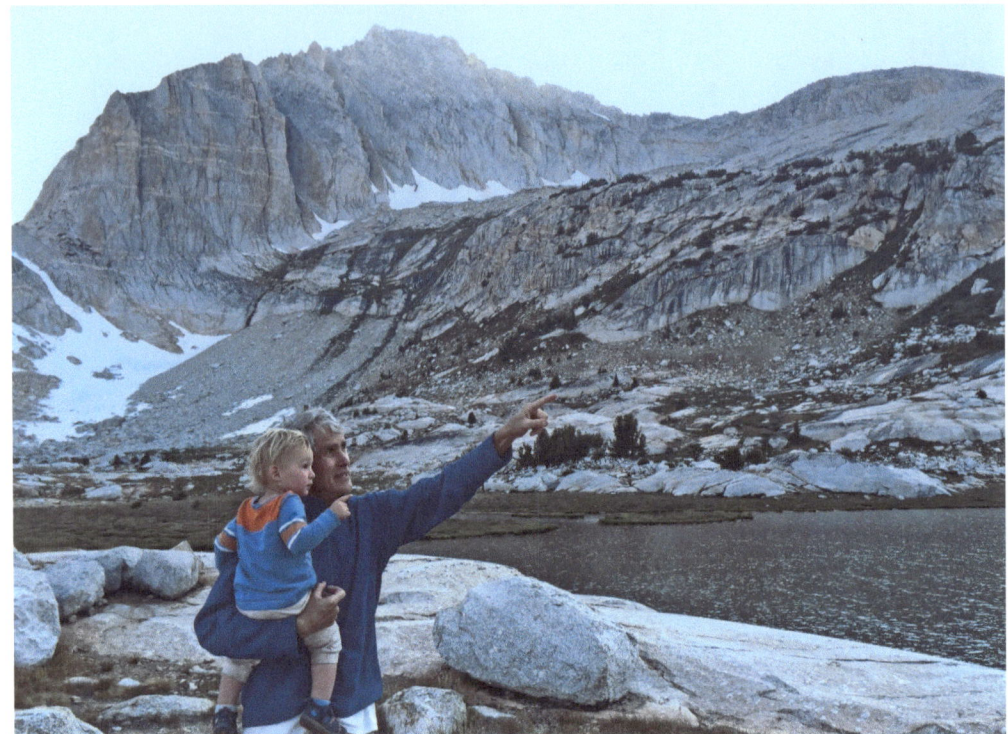

From the oldest to the youngest, my family has supported my fascination with the Sierra. We share what we see and love from our individual vantages, getting up there as often as we can, with as many of us as possible at a time. They tolerate just one more photo and just one more question about those rocks. Some of us focus on maps, others on climbing, or on fishing, or on sunsets, or on swimming, or on dinner, or on daydreaming, and for me, whether or not we need the rain fly on the tent tonight.

Exhibitions, left to right: University of California Merced; Stiges, Spain; Birmingham, England; Sainte-Marie-aux-Mines, France.

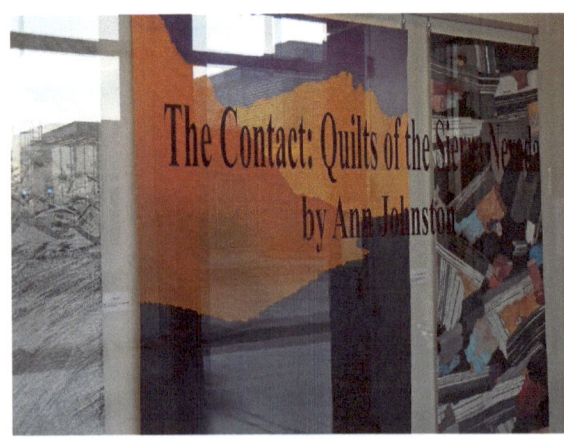

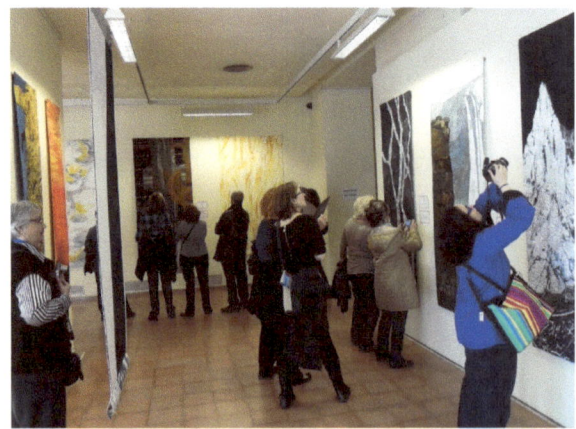

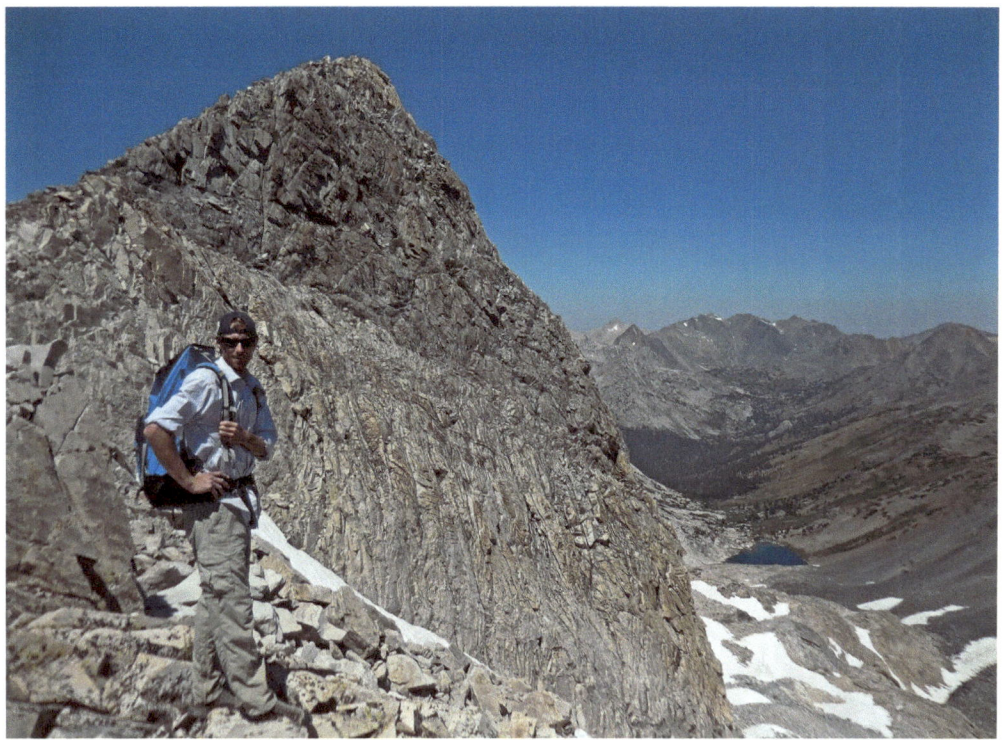

Our son Scott, a geologist, is my teacher. He has explained the inconceivable processes that have shaped our world, the specialized vocabulary that describes them and what is happening now, in our times, changing for ever. I ask questions that focus on details that a geologist would not particularly wonder about, but he is artist and dreamer enough to understand what I need to know. He stopped for this photo because he knew I would never climb up to see this contact at the top of the eastern slope of the Sierra, not far from our mine.

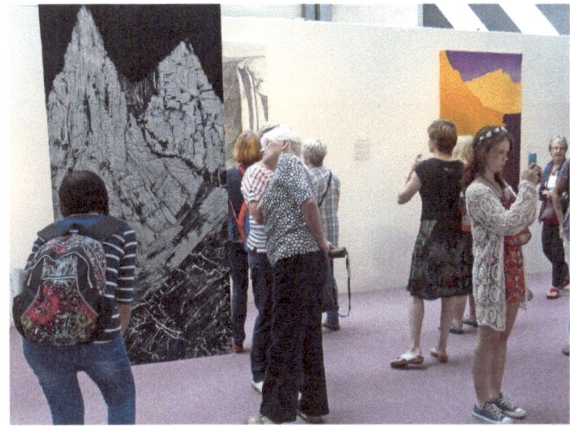

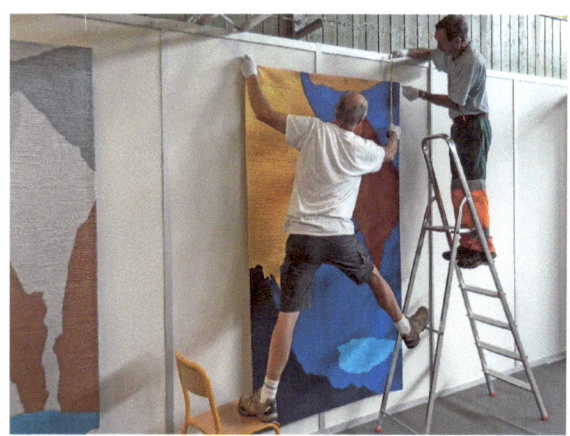

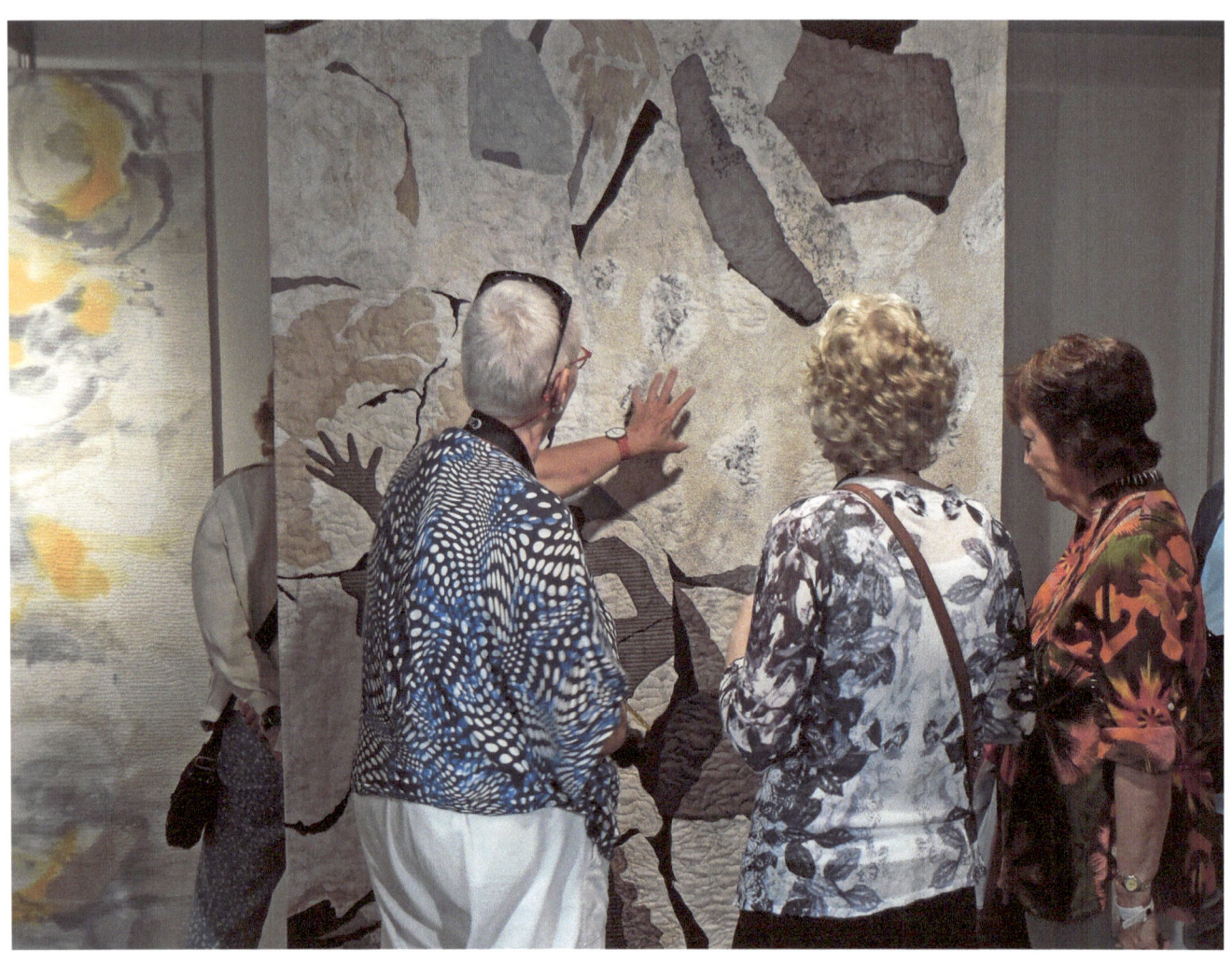

Other Publications by Ann Johnston:

Color by Accident: Exploring Low-Water Immersion Dyeing, DVD

Color by Design: Paint and Print with Dyes

The Quilter's Book of Design, Expanded Second Edition

For details about books, DVD, workshops, lectures, and to contact Ann, visit

www.annjohnston.net

www.ingramcontent.com/pod-product-compliance
Lightning Source LLC
Chambersburg PA
CBHW050848180526
45159CB00007B/2614